GAME SHOW CONFIDENTIAL

GAME SHOW CONFIDENTIAL

The Story of an American Obsession

BOZE HADLEIGH

LYONS
PRESS

Essex, Connecticut

An imprint of Globe Pequot, the trade division of The Rowman & Littlefield Publishing Group, Inc.
4501 Forbes Blvd., Ste. 200
Lanham, MD 20706
www.rowman.com

Distributed by NATIONAL BOOK NETWORK

British Library Cataloguing in Publication Information available

Library of Congress Cataloging-in-Publication Data
Names: Hadleigh, Boze, author.
Title: Game show confidential : the story of an American obsession / Boze
    Hadleigh.
Identifiers: LCCN 2022048494 (print) | LCCN 2022048495 (ebook) | ISBN
    9781493072583 (paperback) | ISBN 9781493072590 (ebook)
Subjects: LCSH: Game shows—United States. | Quiz shows—United States. |
    Radio programs—United States.
Classification: LCC PN1992.8.Q5 .H33 2023 (print) | LCC PN1992.8.Q5
    (ebook) | DDC 791.45/6—dc23/eng/20221129
LC record available at https://lccn.loc.gov/2022048494
LC ebook record available at https://lccn.loc.gov/2022048495

♾️™ The paper used in this publication meets the minimum requirements of American National Standard for Information Sciences—Permanence of Paper for Printed Library Materials, ANSI/NISO Z39.48-1992.

To Ronnie, and in loving memory of Judy Benes, who survived

Contents

CONTENTS

We play games at home, we play games at parties, we go to clubs and play games—Americans love games.
—BOB BARKER, HOST OF *THE PRICE IS RIGHT*

Game shows are uplifting, they lend people hope. . . . They can participate in a way they can't if they're watching a regular program or a film.
—DR. JOYCE BROTHERS, PSYCHOLOGIST, GAME SHOW
CHAMPION, AND FREQUENT GAME SHOW GUEST

My philosophy in a nutshell is: Life is a game show where people who have fun are the winners.
—ORSON BEAN, GAME SHOW PANELIST

In no special order, eight of the most popular game show catchphrases

"Come on down!" (*The Price Is Right*)

"I'd like to buy a vowel." (*Wheel of Fortune*)

"Will the real [John Doe] please stand up." (*To Tell the Truth*)

"Is that your final answer?" (*Who Wants to Be a Millionaire?*)

"Enter and sign in, please!" (*What's My Line?*)

"Say the secret word." (*You Bet Your Life*)

"I'll take door number (two)!" (*Let's Make a Deal*)

"You are the weakest link—goodbye!" (*The Weakest Link*)

ACKNOWLEDGMENTS

Heartfelt thanks to my ace editor Rick Rinehart and Alberta Aguilar, Sandy Babcock, Howard Bragman, Jim Brochu, Emily Cable, Duane Scott Cerny, Robert Clary, Charles Coffman, Grace Collins, Blase DiStefano, Linnda Durre, Rami Etessami, Ken Ferguson, Cris Franco, Bob Gerard, Gil Gibson, Mark Glubke, Myra Goldberg, Irene Griffin, A. Ashley Hoff, Kevin Imhof, Mark K. Johnson, Tomiyoshi Komiyama, Darrin Nogales, Chad Oberhausen, Max Reagan, Ray Richmond, Richard Rohrbacher, Sol Shapiro, Richard Simmons, Shelley K. Steward, Wendy Westgate, Betty White, and Hassan Zee.

INTRODUCTION

THE FIRST TV GAME SHOW I EVER SAW WASN'T REALLY A GAME SHOW and technically was a radio show. It was on an *I Love Lucy* rerun. In the episode, Lucy is way behind on her household bills. To win $1,000 she goes on a radio program titled *Females Are Fabulous*, a stunt show akin to *Truth or Consequences*. To earn the money, Lucy must introduce a strange man as her first husband to her current husband, Ricky Ricardo, that evening.

Ricky already knows about the stunt and arranges for yet another man to show up at their apartment and inform a bewildered Lucy that he's her ex. Of course, Lucy gets her money in the end.

Years before that, I viewed a few or several seconds of an actual game show, and not a rerun, called *Who Do You Trust?* I was too young to know the show's title or anything about the television set in our rented house or that the host was named Johnny Carson. We were living in Ann Arbor, Michigan, where my father taught at the university for one year (after we left Paris in July 1959). I was in kindergarten—again—because the previous kindergarten, one overseas, was bilingual and here it was in one language only—that makes sense? But I had no choice.

My mother picked me up from Burns Park Elementary School. When we got home, she turned on the television, and on the screen was the young adult male talking to someone or other. I wasn't paying atten-tion. I was staring at my mother staring at the small man in the machine box. Johnny Carson was the first person I was ever jealous of because I was in the room, regular size, and yet my mother kept looking at whoever that man was in the box instead of me—for a few minutes anyway.

My next memory of a game show was more developed. In Santa Barbara, California (my mother disliked cold weather) my younger sister and I sometimes watched the 1960s show *You Don't Say!* after school; it was hosted by Tom Kennedy. The only celebrity I recall from it was glamorous former movie star—there's quite a story there; see my book *Scandals, Secrets, and Swan Songs*—Lizabeth Scott. I still remember what the host said at the end of each episode: "It's not what you say that counts, it's what you don't say!"

It's been said game shows are TV's feel-good genre. They're especially popular during hard or stressful times, including during COVID. The all-game-show channels Buzzr and Game Show Network (GSN) are thriving, and more new network and cable shows and reboots of classic game shows have been aired and announced between 2020 and 2022 than ever before. Mostly it's not about money. The crash of the big-money shows that followed *Who Wants to Be a Millionaire?* in 1999 demonstrated audiences' preference for an interesting game played well rather than a contestant paid well.

More than any other type of program, game shows give viewers a chance to relate and participate—vicariously or in fact. Hasn't most everyone at some time or other considered the possibility of getting on a game show? If one lives in or near Los Angeles (and to a lesser extent Manhattan) or vacations there, it's quite possible, depending on the show. As this *Jeopardy!* contestant and winner found out, you have a better chance of being selected if you don't live in a media center. It took me more than a decade of trying to get on almost every year before I finally did. Afterward, when Alex Trebek stated, not asked, "Wasn't it worth the wait," I smiled without reply.

Psychologist Dr. Joyce Brothers, who won $64,000 twice when the average US family's annual income was $4,400, called game shows uplifting. They show people having fun. Betty White felt the salient characteristic of game shows was "fun," and frequent panelist Orson Bean's philosophy was that people who have fun are life's winners.

"There is speculation that people watch game shows because they get a sense of power or omniscience," theorized Kathryn Montgomery, professor of television at University of California, Los Angeles. "Often the show is structured so they know the answer before the contestant."

People watch game shows for different reasons. Programs vary widely. There are three basic kinds of game show: a quiz show, concerning knowledge via questions and answers; a show that poses physical challenges, including the stunts—fun or silly, humiliating or worse—that made long-running hits of *Truth or Consequences* and *Beat the Clock*; and the panel show involving celebrities and everyday people, sometimes trying to guess someone's secret or what their "line" is. Many shows combine aspects of two of these types. (Some in the physical category cross over into sports and aren't game shows because average individuals can't participate because of fitness requirements. For example, *American Gladiators* isn't in this book.)

Polls confirm that fans of game shows are also drawn by particular hosts (which now includes both genders). A major hosting change since the days of three commercial TV networks is that hosts are often chosen for name recognition rather than experience or connection to the material. Betty White pointed out, "Smart shows used to have smart hosts, like professors." Her husband, Allen Ludden of *Password*, was one of few hosts who held a master's degree.

Today's host is more likely to be a faded movie actor or sports figure, a comic, or a pretty face. Bob Stewart, producer-creator of the *Pyramid* game series, likened the trend to Broadway where, "today a familiar TV face may front a new show or revival in place of a seasoned and more talented Broadway performer."

TV critic David Sheehan noted, "The days of the [lifelong] professional host are over. There won't be any more careers like those of Alex and Allen and Gene and Wink and Bob and Bill." If charisma is now less of a qualification than a platform, at least there are plenty of interesting formats and shows coming and going. And when some start to pall, there's always GSN and Buzzr.

It's not common knowledge (the title of one game show) that the Federal Communications Commission tried to ban game shows with increasingly generous prizes after they became a small-screen staple. But in 1954, the Supreme Court upheld their validity—four years before the quiz show scandals erupted.

By ironic coincidence another *I Love Lucy* episode, "Lucy Gets Ricky on the Radio," concerns a quiz show contestant being given the answers before going on the air. Seems tricky Ricky overhears a quiz show before it airs and later rattles off the answers at home to impress. Convinced her husband is a genius, Lucy gets him booked on *Mr. and Mrs. Quiz* without his knowledge. When Ricky finds out, he demands Lucy get him the answers, so he won't be embarrassed on the show.

She gets the answers, he memorizes them, but on the show the questions are switched, so Ricky gets all three answers wrong. By an impossible but amusing fluke, he answers the big bonus question correctly and wins $500.

When that episode first aired during the sitcom's second season (*I Love Lucy* began in 1951), few would have thought it likely that a contestant could be given answers beforehand. The reason there were no laws governing the running of TV game shows was that the possibility of their being run dishonestly hadn't been taken seriously.

Then came *The $64,000 Question* in 1955 and *Twenty-One* in 1956, both consistently rigged, and each offering more prize money than ever before. *Twenty-One*, the show most implicated in the scandals (see director Robert Redford's 1994 film *Quiz Show*), was hosted by actor Hal March, who'd appeared in the *I Love Lucy* episodes "Lucy Fakes an Illness" (1952) and "Lucy Is a Matchmaker" (1953). March also appeared on *I Love Lucy*'s rival sitcoms *I Married Joan* (1952–1954) starring Joan Davis and *Life with Elizabeth* (1953) starring Betty White.

I Love Lucy was TV's most popular show until *The $64,000 Question* and *Twenty-One*. It may not have been a coincidence that 1956–1957 was *Lucy*'s final season. The big-money game shows that began in 1955 and 1999 were done in by their own greed, though the former at least resulted in laws governing the honesty of game shows (see chapter 8).

When the widespread deceptions became public knowledge, audiences were appalled and felt betrayed. Where was the integrity, good sportsmanship, and fun in cheating and favoritism? All game shows, including the honest ones, suffered a big ratings decline lasting into the 1960s. But before long, there were new and aboveboard shows like *Password, The Match Game, Jeopardy!, Let's Make a Deal, Hollywood Squares, The Dating Game,* and many more. What do those shows, all of which have had multiple reincarnations, have in common? They're *fun*!

Happy reading!

Boze (rhymes with *shows*) Hadleigh
Beverly Hills

1

Questions, We've Got Questions!

CROSSWORD PUZZLES, WHICH COMBINE ENTERTAINMENT AND KNOWL-edge, debuted in newspapers in 1913. They were a forerunner of game shows, although doing a crossword you didn't compete with anyone but yourself, and the prize was satisfaction at completing, more or less, the fun challenge and letting loved ones know how well you did.

Myriad game shows have been based on existing diversions like hangman, tic-tac-toe, crossword puzzles, and assorted card games. Mass entertainment took a huge leap forward in 1920 with the introduction of commercial radio broadcasting. Possibly the first game show—more aptly, quiz show—was the *Brooklyn Eagle Quiz on Current Events* on station WNYC in 1923. It was inspired by the newspaper's "current events bees" comprising questions for schoolkids, reprinted with answers in special editions that routinely sold better than the *Brooklyn Eagle's* regular editions.

Asking the questions by voice rather than in print added a new dimension and a slightly contest-like feel. The radio host, who simply recited the questions, was H. V. Kaltenborn. The show gave no prizes, and there were no visuals or carnival atmosphere, yet it lasted some 18 years. Again, the prize was satisfaction at answering correctly and being considered a brain.

One of the most popular 1940s radio quiz shows was *Doctor I.Q.*, which had two short-lived 1950s TV versions. The second, in 1958, was hosted by Tom Kennedy (born James Edward Narz and younger brother of host Jack Narz). Contestants were selected out of the audience and, if they answered correctly, earned 10 silver dollars. Kennedy, hosting his second network game show, had four female "assistants" (see chapter 19).

Game shows began with Q and A, initially for knowledge's sake but, even before television, soon became motivated by profit. A year after the *Brooklyn Eagle Quiz* program, *Time* magazine's circulation manager arranged free airtime on WJZ in New York for a radio quiz meant to boost sales. *The Pop Question* consisted of *Time* cofounder Briton Hadden reading questions taken from the magazine's latest issue. The program endured for three years.

In 1932, two Houstonites from station KTRH used airtime to ask a person on the street what they thought of the upcoming presidential election (it would be won by Franklin Roosevelt, the first of four consecutive wins). After the elections the two Texans continued roaming the streets with microphones but asked questions that were not political in nature. Their show was *Vox Pop*, from the Latin *vox populi*, the voice of the people.

The duo also started asking trivia questions. Many people, afraid of giving a wrong answer, declined to participate. To provide an incentive that overrode possible embarrassment, the men started bringing cash along with their mics and offered a few dollars for a correct answer. A new milestone was reached, and material rewards would become a game show requisite.

Vox Pop, however, wasn't primarily a game show. Public opinions and interviews predominated. The program lasted into 1948.

The quiz show went national in 1936 with CBS Radio's *Professor Quiz*. Its popularity resulted in some 300 similar local and national quiz shows within the next four years. The professor, no name please, asked contestants questions he devised. The question bee proceeded until there were only five contestants left to engage in a Battle of Wits round to determine a champion. Professor Quiz was his own fact-checker. Undeniably brilliant, he rarely erred, but he was human. When he announced that all porcine tails curl to the left, numerous farmers mailed in photos of their pigs' rear ends. The professor conceded that individual pig tails curl differently.

The professor's identity was a secret. There were no publicity photos. Only in-person radio audiences saw his face. But after his first, very popular year—the mystery probably boosted ratings—the smarty-pants was outed as Dr. Craig Earl. His past seemed fascinating: He was an orphan who earned a degree at Tufts University, traveled Europe as a magician and dancer, learned how to walk through fire in China, toured the vaudeville circuit with Harry Houdini, juggled with W. C. Fields, was a tightrope walker, practiced medicine, lectured on philosophy, and became a chess champion. The media ate it up.

In 1942, the nation learned that none of the professor's history was true. The truth surfaced because in 1935 the man had abandoned his wife, who'd since tried to track him down. His real name was Arthur Earl Baird, he'd dropped out of Tufts and earned no degree, and before *Professor Quiz*, he worked at a newspaper. His wife sued and received a then-hefty $25,000 settlement. Not only did the revelations not hurt the "professor," but his show also continued until 1949, referring to himself as Dr. Craig Earl.

Eight days after *Professor Quiz* bowed in 1936, the NBC Blue Network debuted *Uncle Jim's Question Bee*. The host was Jim McWilliams, contestants were eliminated via wrong answers, and the show lasted until 1941. By then McWilliams had left to host a new show, *Ask-It Basket*. Another host became the new "Uncle Jim." (NBC owned a Red and a Blue network. The latter aired from 1927 to 1945, but in 1942 for antitrust reasons, NBC had to divest itself of the Blue Network, which was owned by ABC from 1943 to 1945.)

These national quiz shows spawned successful box games for play at home. *Professor Quiz* produced two play-at-home games. *Uncle Jim's Question Bee*, though shorter-lived, yielded six home games and four books. Oh yes, program merchandising has a long history.

On July 1, 1941, television, previously experimental, went commercial via the Federal Communications Commission. TV would take longer to infiltrate the nation's homes than radio because it cost more to buy a television set than a radio. But quiz shows were there at the start. They were cheap to produce, popular, and more interesting than one hour's worth of a test pattern, which wasn't unusual. The first televised quiz or game show was *Uncle Jim's Question Bee*, though *Truth or Consequences*, which followed it on the same night, became more famous. Both shows were one-time specials aired on commercial TV's official birthday.

The first *continuing* TV game show was the simply titled *CBS Television Quiz*. It premiered July 2, 1941, and offered a mix of quizzes, stunts, and games. Broadcasting at night, it ran one season and was hosted by Gil Fates, who later produced *What's My Line?* for a quarter century.

Truth or Consequences, created and hosted by Ralph Edwards, bowed on radio in 1940 and ran 17 years. Outlandish, although some said humiliating, stunts meant to entertain audiences were added to the quiz element. For many years, the show did better on radio than television, though its stunts had to be described rather than viewed. Partly based on Forfeits, a children's game, the program's premise sounded wacky (originally spelled and pronounced "whacky"). Almost immediately after giving a contestant a question, often a trick question, a buzzer named Beulah went off, and Edwards giggled, "Since you didn't tell the truth, you must pay the consequences!"

Describing the stunt, he often cackled hysterically, "Aren't we devils!" A *Looney Tunes* cartoon from 1950 parodied *Truth or Consequences*, with Porky Pig as the unfortunate contestant on a sadistic radio quiz show titled *Truth or Aaaahhh!*, hosted by a manic Daffy Duck. That year the town of Hot Springs, New Mexico, voted to change its name to Truth or Consequences. One citizen explained, "There are 13 Hot Springs in the United States but only one Truth or Consequences."

On September 7, 1950, *Truth or Consequences* premiered on national TV via a coast-to-coast network of stations and not just one station as in 1941. It too was hosted by Ralph Edwards, eventually more famous for and more toned down as host and creator of the celebrity-themed *This Is Your Life*. In 1950, Edwards decided to film *Truth or Consequences* with multiple simultaneous cameras and 35-mm film. The pioneering move, copied in 1951 by the new sitcom *I Love Lucy*, eliminated dependence on fuzzy kinescopes and made reruns a feasible and profitable option.

Despite occasional controversy, and perhaps because of it, *Truth or Consequences* became a long-running hit. On the one-time-only show on July 1, 1941, the unfortunate contestant was instructed to crawl onto an audience member's lap and bawl like a baby while Edwards's assistants placed a diaper around the man. A reviewer wrote that the show "helped to begin television under commercial sponsorship on a pretty low level. . . . May destiny preserve this nation from . . . this kind of drunk-while-sober behavior."

Edwards enjoyed engineering surprises and reunions (best exemplified by *This Is Your Life*). One *Truth or Consequences* episode from September 1950 combined both and drew the wrath of several viewers. The host introduced two strangers, an older woman named Mrs. Cunningham and a soldier. He asked if the lady had ever seen a soldier. Indeed, she'd just learned her soldier son had been wounded while stationed in Korea. The soldier then retired behind a pup tent, from whose other side appeared Mrs. Cunningham's son, newly discharged from the army.

The following day, Jack Gould lamented in the *New York Times*, "Television reached a new low in taste last night . . . inexcusably exploit[ing] a mother's understandable shock when she unexpectedly saw her son, a Korean combat casualty. . . . The whole incident was a typical example of the warped sense of drama of Mr. Edwards, who by now is old enough to know better."

Perhaps Edwards was prompted by poor ratings. *Truth or Consequences* was viewed less in its time period than a detective series and got canceled after less than a year. It returned in 1954–1956 and was hosted by Jack Bailey, later better known for the taste-challenged *Queen for a Day* (see chapter 7). In 1956, *Truth or Consequences* moved from prime time to daytime with Bob Barker, theretofore a radio personality. He emceed the show for 19 years.

It returned in 1977 as the syndicated *The New Truth or Consequences*. Barker couldn't host, having signed to inherit *The Nighttime Price Is Right* from Dennis James. The 1977 show, hosted by Bob Hilton, lasted a year. A 1987 version, with actor Larry Anderson (who played Lucille Ball's son-in-law in her final sitcom, *Life with Lucy*), also ran one year. But by then *Truth or Consequences* had become TV's longest-running "comedy-stunt" game show, and the quiz shows of yore had long since evolved or devolved into less erudite entertainment.

However, the quiz show never died, though the general term "game show" superseded it, and many or most game shows incorporate some aspect of Q and A. The best-known example of the quiz show is *Jeopardy!*, which in 1998 begat a junior version titled *Jep!* for 10- to 12-year-old contestants. *Quiz Kids* was a radio show from 1940 to 1953 and a TV show from 1949 to 1956. "Quiz kid" became a national catchphrase and compliment. Audiences were fascinated by highly intelligent children, sometimes intimidated by them, and occasionally contemptuous (read: jealous).

Quiz Kids made comebacks in 1978 for 5 months in syndication and was hosted by Jim McKrell and again in 1981 for 14 months on CBS Cable and was hosted by progressive TV producer Norman Lear. Less successful was *The Quiz Kids Challenge* in 1990, pitting three kids ages 11 to 15 against three adults. Syndicated and hosted by Jonathan Prince, it lasted 3½ months.

Another national catchphrase derived from the title of a 1949–1955 quiz show, *Twenty Questions*. The prime-time show (also a radio show from 1946 to 1954) was based on the parlor game Animal, Vegetable, or Mineral with each member of a panel of five allowed to ask up to 20 questions to determine what a given object was. Real people and film characters in the 1940s and 1950s might respond to a persistent questioner with "What is this, *Twenty Questions?*"

2

Can't Stop the Music

"Since there's been music, people have enjoyed trying to guess the name of a given song or piece of music," said music director Harry Salter, who created the most famous musical game show, *Name That Tune*. "Studies indicate that people who like games are also fonder of music."

Most everyone's seen some old movie in which a family sitting at home is interrupted by a telephone call. The member who answers the phone excitedly informs the others that it's a quiz show calling to ask if somebody there can identify a particular song to win a prize.

The first popular TV music quiz show was *Stop the Music* in 1949, the year after it premiered on radio. Singer Bert Parks, later best known as Miss America's host, emceed both versions. The 60-minute show ran three seasons and often featured elaborate production numbers to showcase a song. At some point, announcer Kenny Williams interrupted the song to yell, "Stop the music!" A phone call was then made to a home viewer who got a chance to identify the song and win a merchandise prize, and if answered correctly, they had the opportunity of naming the more rewarding Mystery Melody. If the viewer was wrong, there was a sponsor's consolation prize.

One sponsor was Old Gold cigarettes, which explained (but didn't warrant) the show's dancing cigarette pack and matchbook. *Stop the Music* was off the air in 1953, returning in 1954 for two seasons as a 30-minute show. Again Parks hosted, and songs were performed by program regulars including Bert, who later starred on stage in *The Music*

Man after Eddie Albert (*Green Acres*) took over from original star Robert Preston. Parks played *The Music Man* for more than 300 performances.

Long before such shows as *America's Got Talent*, there was *Chance of a Lifetime* (1950), which aired on second-tier TV networks ABC and DuMont (the latter broadcast from 1942 to 1956). Hosted by John Reed King, *Chance of a Lifetime* comprised Q and A and stunts during its first two of seven seasons. When it returned with new host Dennis James (né Demie James Sposa), the format was a talent contest of amateur professional singers, musicians, dancers, and comedians judged by audience applause. The night's winner of two contestants then competed against the previous week's winner. Second-round winners won $1,000 and a week's booking at New York's Latin Quarter nightclub (owned by Lou Walters, Barbara Walters's father). Runners-up received an engagement at a lesser-known venue.

Very few *Chance of a Lifetime* winners achieved big-time success. The exceptions included singers Roger Williams, Diahann Carroll, and Dick Van Dyke, who later moved to Broadway, TV, and movies.

Name That Tune began on radio in 1952 and on television in 1953 and was hosted on both media by Red Benson. In 1954, it switched from NBC to CBS with Bill Cullen hosting; from 1955 to 1959, George DeWitt emceed. Players were distanced some 20 feet from two bells, one per player, that hung from the ceiling. The show's band performed a song, and the first contestant to recognize it ran to the bell and rang it. The running requirement could put an older or heavier player at an unfair disadvantage, but then, the 1950s was not the fairest decade.

Each game offered four songs. The first was valued at $5, second $10, third $20, and fourth $40. The contestant ending up with the most money won and moved on to the Golden Medley, with 30 seconds in which to guess seven songs. First correct answer was worth $25, each subsequent correct answer doubled in value, up to $1,600. The songs were chosen by a home viewer who actually earned the same amount of cash as the contestant. (Early radio and television frequently courted home listeners and viewers.)

If a contestant got all seven Golden Medley answers, the home viewer was flown to New York City and the pair played the Golden

Medley Marathon. If in 30 seconds they correctly named five songs, they won $5,000 and returned the following week. The marathon could run five weeks for a grand total of $25,000.

Producer Ralph Edwards revived *Name That Tune* in 1974. Its first two hosts were Dennis James and Tom Kennedy. The latter's musical "La La Girl" was brunette Kathie Lee Johnson, who later married Frank Gifford and cohosted *Live! With Regis and Kathie Lee* with Regis Philbin; after *Name That Tune*, she did the TV series *Hee Haw Honeys*. The new *Name That Tune* lasted seven years, partly on NBC and partly in syndication. The 1970s version switched cash for points, and the Golden Medley became the Melody Roulette. In 1976 the nighttime version was redubbed *The $100,000 Name That Tune*. In syndication *Name That Tune* continued through 1981.

A new syndicated *Name That Tune*, hosted by Jim Lange, formerly of *The Dating Game*, debuted in 1984–1985. In 2001, the VH1 network briefly presented Harry Salter's *Name That Video*, highlighting music videos and hosted by Karyn Bryant. *Name That Tune* finally resurfaced in 2021 via Fox TV, which was hosted by actress Jane Krakowski and filmed in Australia with American players.

Dough Re Mi, NBC's "answer" to *Name That Tune*, ran from February 1958 to December 1960 and was hosted by Gene Rayburn. One of its substitute hosts, actor and later TV producer Keefe Brasselle, said, "It was next to a copycat show. . . . I didn't find satisfaction or dignity in hosting. I changed tracks."

Kay Kayser was an affable, sometimes goofy big-band leader who also starred in film comedies from 1939 through the 1940s. They featured his band and musical protégés, including cornet player and comedian Ish Kabbible, who wore the same haircut as Moe of the Three Stooges. Kayser's first movie title was a game-show borrowing, *That's Right—You're Wrong*. On his popular radio musical quiz show, *Kay Kayser's Kollege of Musical Knowledge* (1938–1949), he wore a cap and gown and was called the Professor. (One of the show's writers, Bob Quigley, later teamed with Merrill Heatter to produce *The Hollywood Squares*.)

The show made it to TV in 1949–1950, was hosted by Kayser, and then returned briefly in 1954 as *The College of Musical Knowledge*, which was emceed by country singer Tennessee Ernie Ford. "It was simple," recalled Ford, "just folks tryin' to identify songs to get prizes. Maybe too simple—shows were gettin' more convoluted and prizes bigger 'n bigger." The 1954 show's announcer was future game show host Jack Narz.

Musical Chairs, a prime-time 1955 NBC summer game show hosted by Bill Leyden, had aired in Los Angeles since 1953. Its panel included its music director Bobby Troup, lyricist Johnny Mercer ("Moon River"), and cartoon voice artist Mel Blanc (Bugs Bunny, Porky Pig, and myriad others), plus a weekly guest. They answered musical questions submitted by viewers. A viewer's televised question yielded an RCA Victor radio and, if it stumped the panel, a giant 21-inch TV set.

A daytime *Musical Chairs* (1975) on CBS was the first network game show with an African American host, singer Adam Wade. Producer Don Kirshner was music supervisor for the 1960s pop-music sitcom *The Monkees* and, in the 1970s, produced and hosted *Rock Concert*. This *Musical Chairs*, unrelated to its 1950s namesake, had four contestants trying to supply missing lyrics, which was not so difficult when given three possible choices. Perhaps not "convoluted" enough, the show didn't last five months.

Another short-lived entry was NBC's nighttime *Hold That Note* in 1957, which was hosted by the imitable Bert Parks. The basic format had two players trying to identify songs performed by a studio orchestra. The first person to correctly name three songs in a row won money. The winner could retire at any time, but if said winner played a new opponent and lost, the new winner's winnings were subtracted from the previous champ's cash.

Basic game show formats are often revived, albeit with a twist. *Name That Tune*'s Harry Salter created NBC's 1958 nighttime summer replacement *Music Bingo*, which reemerged late in 1958 on ABC as a daytime show that ran 13 months. The twist was a game board that was five spaces high and five spaces wide and was based on bingo. As in tic-tac-toe, with one player's *x* and the other's *o*, each player used a symbol, a musical sharp or flat. The players tried to guess the song the band was playing. If correct, a player's sharp or flat filled any given board space, up, down, or diagonally. The first player to fill in five spaces in a row won.

Music Bingo was Johnny Gilbert's debut as a host. In the 1960s, he hosted *Fast Draw* and *Beat the Odds* but became better known as an announcer for several game shows, perhaps most notably *Jeopardy!* Gilbert, who sang on *Music Bingo*, had studied opera and been a big-band singer in his hometown of Newport News, Virginia.

Harry Salter struck again in 1961 with *Yours for a Song* (the expression meant something easily obtained), an ABC prime-time show its first year and a daytime show its second and final year. The announcer was Johnny Gilbert, and the host was Bert Parks. *Yours for a Song*, which featured lots of audience sing-alongs with Bert, popularized the concept of filling in missing lyrics that was employed after 2000 by shows like *The Singing Bee* and *Don't Forget the Lyrics!*

This was the third musical quiz show hosted by Parks and his last quiz show, period. His television hosting career began in 1946. ABC replaced *Yours for a Song* with its first "contemporary" soap opera, *General Hospital*.

What's This Song?, a 1964–1965 ABC show hosted by Wink Martindale, began as a 1930s radio show called *What's the Name of That Song?* Like *Password*, *What's This Song?* featured two teams, each pairing a star and contestant, both trying to identify songs. Part of the humor, intentional or otherwise, involved celebrity warbling via guests like *Bonanza*'s Lorne Greene and Michael Landon, Angie Dickinson, Ryan O'Neal, Phyllis Diller, and the inevitable Betty White.

What's This Song? was the host's first network game show; he was known at the time as Win Martindale. In 1959, the Tennessean, a friend of Elvis Presley, introduced the Top 10 song "Deck of Cards" on *The Ed Sullivan Show*.

What's This Song? was reincarnated in 1968–1969 as the syndicated *Win with the Stars*. Hosted by Allen Ludden following a six-year run with *Password* (both returned in the 1970s), its debut guest stars were fellow music lover Peter Marshall and singer Barbara McNair.

Martindale and announcer Johnny Gilbert returned in 1970 for *Words and Music*, an NBC daytime offering that didn't last five months. Perhaps it too was overly convoluted for a music show. Each of 16 game board squares held a clue connected to a word in a song (e.g., "right between the eyes" referenced the word "nose"). A player had to quickly and correctly identify that word after it was sung. An indication of the game's relative difficulty was that if a player won for three days in a row, the player got a new car.

By the end of the 1960s, game shows were falling out of favor. The year 1970 saw only two new game shows, *Words and Music* and the nonmusical *Can You Top This?*, both hosted by Martindale and both disappointments. Some insiders felt game shows, especially those with music and upbeat songs, were judged too trivial while there was a controversial war in Vietnam and national unrest.

Although game shows didn't go away, the decrease in music shows' popularity, said Betty White, was due also to "hummable, melodic songs giving way to more specialized music for the young. . . . A beautiful hit song used to be for all ages, and practically everyone knew the melody if not the lyrics."

Face the Music debuted in 1980, with an orchestra playing a song requiring identification and which person, place, or thing its title referred to. Besides music, it had faces—six sequential photos of a mystery celebrity, from infant and childhood to adulthood, which players had to identify. If a contestant guessed correctly after viewing just one photo, the prize was $10,000.

Oddly enough, the host was former TV Tarzan Ron Ely, who eventually replaced Bert Parks as host of Miss America. The syndicated program ran less than two years. By contrast, *Fandango* (1983–1989) was logically hosted by country singer Bill Anderson on the TNN cable network and found its limited but lengthy niche by focusing on a specific genre, country music. Its announcer was Edgar the Talking Jukebox (did "he" have an ak-say-ent?). The show originated in Opryland, Nashville. (Anderson had been a *Match Game* panelist.)

Major networks were taking fewer chances with music game shows, unlike syndicators. The one-season *You Write the Songs*, hosted by Ben Vereen, debuted in 1986. The novelty was each of three songwriters, amateur and pro, having a new song performed by one of the show's singers. The result was judged by a quintet: a record producer, a record company executive, a disc jockey and one of his listeners, and a singer. The winner competed on the next week's show against two new songs. After 12 weeks, the top five songs vied for $100,000.

Each *You Write the Songs* episode also offered a musical salute and a "chat" with a popular songwriter.

Turn It Up! (1990), its title acknowledging the youth market, focused on rock 'n' roll. Hosted by Jordan Brady, it was MTV's second game show, after *Remote Control* (1987–1990), whose college-age contestants, ensconced in leather recliners, used remote controls to signal responses to questions about music, TV, and pop culture. Tellingly, the totally musical *Turn It Up!* lasted little more than five months.

"The Great Pretender," a 1955 hit song, inspired the name of the 1999–2002 *Great Pretenders*, a Saturday morning youthfest on Fox Family that was hosted by the musical female trio Wild Orchid. It presented teens lip syncing and dancing competitively to popular songs for prizes, their performances judged by the studio audience.

The Singing Bee was a cross between karaoke and spelling bee, in which lyrics had to be sung correctly or else a player forewent a musical chair that was required for a possible win. The hybrid began on NBC in 2007, was hosted by singer Joey Fatone (NSYNC), and was derived from a UK program, *Sing It Back: Lyric Champion*. Off the air in 2008, *The Singing Bee* ran from 2009 to 2012 on country-themed CMT (owned by ViacomCBS), hosted by actress Melissa Peterman.

Its contestants were supposedly selected at random from the audience. In truth, they were preselected, and in shades of the game show scandals of the 1950s, home viewers could glimpse song lyrics scrolling down on a banner above the stage so that the contestants didn't make a premature error. The fact that the revealed lyrics weren't hidden from view seemed to make it okay. NBC aired 18 episodes of the show and CMT 48. In more recent decades, a TV season may commence and end at any chosen time and may consist of dozens or only 6, 8, 10, and so on episodes.

The Singing Bee had a 2008 spin-off, *The Singing Office*, that ran on TLC, a pay-TV outlet owned by Discovery, Inc. Hosted by Fatone and former Spice Girl Melanie Brown, the premise was singing groups formed in workplaces performing against each other during the program, and its winners chosen by a panel of judges. It didn't last long in the US but was licensed to some 20 nations for their own versions because group singing is more popular in many countries, especially low- or middle-income countries. Some American critics adjudged *The Singing Office* too close to an amateur night despite the groups' vocal coaching and choreography.

Once upon a time, it was about remembering a song's title, but now it's about remembering its lyrics. The task is harder, but the payoff is bigger. On *Don't Forget the Lyrics!*, players could earn up to a million dollars remembering words. Hosted by Wayne Brady, the show ran on Fox from 2007 to 2009 and then went syndicated in 2010–2011, hosted by singer Mark McGrath. Meat Loaf and his daughter Pearl appeared on the show in 2009 and won $500,000, which they donated to charity. Fox announced a revival of *Don't Forget the Lyrics!* in 2021 hosted by Niecy Nash.

A 2011 UK program, *Sing If You Can*, devolved into a less kind, less gentle US version, *Killer Karaoke*, in 2012. The former involved celebrities trying to sing in front of a studio audience despite various attempts to distract them. Proceeds went to the charity Teenage Cancer Trust. *Killer Karaoke* aired on TruTV. Its first season was hosted by Steve-O of *Jackass* fame who said he was fired because he protested the show's treatment of animals. The second and final season (each with eight episodes) was hosted by Mark McGrath.

Killer Karaoke's modus operandi was "No matter what happens, don't stop singing." Audience votes determined who won. It wasn't merely the quality of the singing, but it was also the singer's ability to keep warbling despite extreme distractions and turnoffs like going barefoot across a catwalk that included stepping into ice water, fish guts, maggots, ad nauseum or singing with a clear dog cone around one's neck while dirty socks, cow brains (right on, Steve-O!), and maggots spilled into the cone from on high. Imagine thinking up such garbage.

And then there was *Oh Sit!* that ran from 2012 to 2013, totaling 20 hour-long episodes on the CW, which replaced UPN and the WB—its new name via the first letters of CBS and Warner Bros. The corporate makeup of contemporary TV has an obvious goal of producing shows whose negative sensationalism can draw the most viewers and, thus, the most profits. *Oh Sit!* was described as "a high-octane musical chairs competition." It drew good ratings but soon plummeted yet was renewed for a second set, or "season," of 10 episodes.

Contestants raced through five obstacle courses to reach a musical chair, which game show impresario and nonfan Chuck Barris felt was "more of an excuse than a valid musical subject or theme.... On *The Gong Show* we made people laugh at bad musical acts but we didn't gross them out . . . or put anybody at risk."

Oh Sit! was hosted by actor Jamie Kennedy and Canadian TV personality Jessi Cruikshank and relied on eight writers to create its jokes, which were often not funny, including several for Cruikshank to indicate "what a slut she is," according to *Variety*. The *Pittsburgh Post-Gazette* found the show "a silly time-waster with terrible commentary" by its hosts. Perhaps to prove its musicality, each *Oh Sit!* episode featured a musical guest.

"It's not just that music has mostly gone non-melodic and noisy," stated Canadian actor and host Alan Thicke. "It's shows desperate for any crazy gimmick beyond the simple pleasure of music and recognition. . . . Since *Name That Tune* musical game shows have come a long way—down."

Music and its recognition remain the hallmarks of real musical game shows, for instance, the international franchise spawned by South Korea's *The King of Mask Singer* since 2015. *The Masked Singer* debuted in the US on Fox in 2019 and was hosted by Niecy Nash and later Nick Cannon. The premise is that a panel tries to identify celebrities singing in head-to-toe disguises from clues given by the performers themselves. The studio audience votes which is the best singer.

Each week's losing singer is unmasked, and the winner is announced at season's end; a year comprises two "seasons." In some countries where the show is live rather than pretaped, all viewers may vote. (A spin-off, *The Masked Dancer*, was introduced in 2020.) Celebrity contestants on *The Masked Singer* aren't paid and don't get to play for charity; publicity is the name of the game.

Commenting on *The Masked Singer*'s global popularity, reviewer Kim Hyungsuk enthused, "You can't stop the music!"

The Music Man

"The most natural quiz show format is answering questions or remembering songs," felt Oscar- and Grammy-winning singer-composer Peter Allen. "Not just in the States—music's the universal language."

The multitalented Australian (1944–1992) was known as Liza Minnelli's gay first husband (and first gay husband, the ceremony engineered by mom Judy Garland) and for his all-stops-out rendition of "I Go to Rio." A posthumous Broadway musical biography, *The Boy from Oz*, starred fellow Aussie Hugh Jackman.

A sometime actor, Peter starred on Broadway in 1988 as Prohibition-era gangster Jack "Legs" Diamond in *Legs Diamond*, music and lyrics by himself. The show's reviews were gratuitously vicious and also homophobic (the real-life hood was heterosexual). "That put paid to my future as a leading man." In 1989 Allen half-joked, "After acting dries up, one explores alternatives like . . . game show emcee."

In 1990, he hosted a pilot for a new version of *Name That Tune*. Producer Marty Pasetta noted, "As an international musician and performer, Peter knows that many popular songs are originally Italian, Spanish, or French before they're given English lyrics. . . . Peter is lively and likeable, very comfortable with audiences." However, the pilot didn't go to series.

Pasetta later picked Allen to host the pilot of what became a nighttime show called *The Hollywood Game*. Its two, 2-person teams of contestants answered movie and TV trivia questions. But before it bowed in summer 1992, Allen had become too ill to host it (Bob Goen was hired, but only four of six filmed episodes aired). Peter Allen died of AIDS at 48, the day before or, depending on the source, the very day *The Hollywood Game* premiered. It was CBS's last regularly scheduled prime-time game show until 1996 and *Big Deal*.

Hosts' Hits

A surprising number of game show hosts have delivered hit songs. Some weren't primarily hosts, like Bill Cosby with "Little Ole Man (Uptight—Everything's Alright)," which peaked at number 4 on Billboard's pop chart in 1967.

Others included:

- Jon Bauman—as a member of Sha Na Na—with "(Just Like) Romeo and Juliet" (number 55 in 1975).
- Bert Convy—as a member of The Cheers—with "Black Denim Trousers" (number 6 in 1955).
- Merv Griffin—with Freddy Martin and his orchestra—with "I've Got a Lovely Bunch of Coconuts" (number 8 in 1950).
- Buddy Hackett with "Chinese Rock and Egg Roll" (number 87 in 1956).
- Kay Kyser with "Jingle Jangle Jingle" (number 1 in 1942).
- Wink Martindale with "Deck of Cards" (number 7 in 1959).

3

Seeing Stars: Panel Shows

THE QUESTION "IS IT BIGGER THAN A BREADBOX?" ORIGINATED WITH Steve Allen in 1953 on *What's My Line?*, in which panelists tried to guess a contestant's profession. Or the product associated with that profession, ergo the question. (Before there was sliced bread in supermarkets, most households had a breadbox.)

Allen, who wrote some 14,000 songs and more than 50 books, was *The Tonight Show*'s first host and pioneered the TV talk show. "I get minimal acknowledgment for 'breadbox' though it's a staple question in real-life games, never mind game shows.

"But I don't think there's been, to date [1982], a television show more ongoingly successful than *What's My Line?* . . . Curiosity about what someone does for a living has been with us ever since people got the notion of going out to get a job."

For an amazing 17 years, *What's My Line?* aired invariably on Sunday nights at 10:30 p.m. on CBS. Through longtime national familiarity, its panelists became household names and TV stars, and the show eventually attracted movie stars and other top VIPs as "mystery" guests.

Three of TV's longest-running quiz shows debuted on prime time in 1950, 1952, and 1956, respectively, *What's My Line?*, *I've Got a Secret*, and *To Tell the Truth*. Each featured a panel of four celebrities interrogating unfamous but out-of-the-ordinary people. The first two shows weren't that dissimilar, whereas the third highlighted an extraordinary noncelebrity and two prevaricating imposters.

The huge success of the three shows, all via Mark Goodson-Bill Todman Productions and all on CBS, was key to establishing that pair of game show producers as the undisputed leaders in their field for decades to come and making CBS the longtime number one TV network. The popularity of *What's My Line?* paved the way for umpteen imitators, especially in the four-person panel format.

Where most shows before 1950 had required knowledge or asked contestants to tell something about themselves, *What's My Line?* wasn't scholarly, and the contestant didn't tell. Rather, the panel asked questions to ferret out the person's occupation.

What's My Line? had a prestige since unequaled in its genre. Game show staffer and writer Adam Nedeff called it "the classiest game show of all time" and felt that host John Charles Daly "gave the show an air of class unmatched on other shows." Born in South Africa and married to the daughter of Supreme Court Chief Justice Earl Warren, Daly anchored the ABC evening news from 1953 to 1960 and was vice president of ABC's news division. From 1951 to 1953, he hosted the news-oriented four-person panel game show *It's News to Me* (via Goodson-Todman), which returned as a summer replacement program hosted by Walter Cronkite.

Daly's Sylvania Television Award for Excellence as a Moderator or Master of Ceremonies officially noted, "[He] performs the difficult task of being dignified without being pompous. His voice is thoroughly agreeable, his speech is flawless, and [he] . . . is refreshingly literate and spontaneous." He was, however, prone to verbosity and a stickler who sometimes exasperated *What's My Line?* panelists.

(To many of this writer's generation, Daly was first observed in a cameo appearance as a newsman in the movie musical *Bye Bye Birdie*.)

The time slot for *What's My Line?* led to its comparison to the audience's welcome weekend nightcap before sleep and resumption of the work week's duties and cares. Whereas other shows' celebrities dressed up, this one's dress code was formal. The men wore tuxedoes, and the women evening gowns. "The lovely Arlene Francis," as she was often introduced, was an actress eventually best known as a game show fixture. She served on *What's My Line?* for a quarter century.

The other long-term female panelist was journalist and columnist Dorothy Kilgallen. Best known as the Voice of Broadway, she served until her mysterious 1965 death, which followed shortly after her announcement that she was going to reveal who killed President John F. Kennedy. Kilgallen played competitively and seriously. Reportedly, she once went backstage and cried because she hadn't guessed a contestant's profession in three weeks.

Steve Allen was a panelist in 1953 and 1954. Publisher Bennett Cerf was the male panelist with the longest tenure. Panelists asked a contestant questions that could be answered yes or no. After a no, the next panelist asked questions until the subsequent no. The contestant received a whopping $5 for each no; after 10 no's the contestant won.

The show's highlight was the Mystery Guest segment for which the four panelists donned chic blindfolds. As this segment featured the biggest stars in the biz, they disguised their voices (e.g., Barbra Streisand used an Italian accent, including Italian words and phrases). Sometimes the Mystery Guest was a duo (e.g., Lucille Ball and Desi Arnaz and, in 1956, Mark Goodson and Bill Todman).

In 1954, *What's My Line?* became the first panel show to be broadcast in color. The show's final network broadcast was in 1967. It was revived as a daytime syndicated show in 1968, airing five times weekly, and was hosted by newsman Wally Bruner. The sole returning panelist was Arlene Francis. The new edition tried to attract younger viewers. A regular panelist was comedian and kid-show host Soupy Sales, and contestants sometimes gave an end-of-segment demonstration of their occupation. For example, a woman who got sawed in half had her magician saw her in half. Former host John Daly was aghast at what he termed "this show business stuff."

The original *What's My Line?* set was plain or "classic." The new one was more colorful and festive. "Hunk" actors like Bert Convy and Alejandro Rey of *The Flying Nun* sometimes sat on the panel, and whereas Ms. Francis's husband, actor Martin Gabel, had sometimes joined her on the panel, she was sometimes joined by son Peter Gabel on the new version. Bruner left the show in 1972, with actor Larry Blyden emceeing until the show's demise in 1975.

Over the decades, several planned revivals of *What's My Line?* failed to occur. But one-hour live versions were staged in Los Angeles from 2004 to 2006 and New York in 2008.

Allan Sherman, comedy writer and TV producer, gained a public identity with the novelty song "Hello Muddah, Hello Faddah (A Letter from Camp)." In a pitch meeting with Mark Goodson, he referenced the enviable success of *What's My Line?* by suggesting Goodson plagiarize his own show. "If you don't, some other producer will."

Goodson took Sherman's advice to heart (or pocketbook). The company eventually released so many panel shows that insiders joked that every time Goodson and Todman eyed a table and four chairs, they started concocting a new program. Their most successful "rip-off" was the one Sherman pitched, *I've Got a Secret.* Rather than guess a contestant's profession, its panel tried determining their secret. Host Garry Moore's favorite was that of a 2-year-old with a 10-year-old brother. The elder announced, "I collected 40 bugs for a school project." His kid brother revealed, "I ate them all."

A highlight from 1962 involved a Mr. and Mrs. Armstrong who disclosed that their son had just been chosen to become an astronaut. Moore half-joked how it would be quite something if son Neil someday became the first man to walk on the Moon. Less than seven years later, he did.

Moore had been straight man to rasp-voiced, big-nosed comic star Jimmy Durante in the 1940s. He debuted on radio in 1939 as Thomas Garrison Morfit before offering $50 to the listener who would gift him with a suitable new name. A woman won by doing away with his first name, adapting the middle one, and chopping the surname in half and spelling it differently. Moore hosted *The Garry Moore Show*, a popular variety show that aired off and on between 1950 and 1967. It helped launch Carol Burnett, Don Knotts, Lily Tomlin, Alan King, George Gobel, Don Adams, and Jonathan Winters, among others. Until his death in 1993 from throat cancer and emphysema, which was caused by smoking cigarettes, the chipper host with the crew cut and bow tie was one of TV's most popular personalities.

Two things distinguished *I've Got a Secret* from *What's My Line?* The latter was talk-oriented; early on, the former went in for demonstrations.

Sometimes a contestant or guest secretly brought something along (e.g., a snake in their pocket, a wallet a pickpocket stole from an audience member, or sometimes it was their identity). The panel was stumped by Harpo Marx because he was really Chico Marx convincingly dressed up as the silent Harpo.

Additionally, panelist Henry Morgan, a sarcastic, easily bored humorist, didn't take the show seriously. Its panel started out copying the sedate and urbane *What's My Line?* quartet, but Morgan grew impatient. Fellow panelist Bill Cullen had an infectious sense of fun, as did host Garry Moore. The two male panelists remained on the show for its entire network run. The most durable female panelists were Bess Myerson, the first Jewish Miss America, and actress Betsy Palmer.

Each panelist had 30 seconds to question a contestant and then guess the secret. Contestants got $20 each time a panelist guessed wrong and $80 for stumping all four.

It was said that viewers "kept a date" with *What's My Line?* but tuned in to *I've Got a Secret* for the curiosity or fun of it. Sample secrets were: "I've been struck by lightning eight times." "I dived into an empty pool." "I went on a date with Marilyn Monroe and she paid for dinner." One guest was a six-year-old billiards expert, another was Pete Best, who two years previously had been fired from the Beatles and replaced by Ringo Starr. The panel was stumped by the secret achievement of Philo Farnsworth, who invented electronic television in 1922. He departed with $80 cash, a carton of cigarettes (Winston sponsored the show), and the host's thanks: "We'd all be out of work if it weren't for you."

Other guests' secrets were "I saw John Wilkes Booth shoot Abraham Lincoln" (1956), "I was Elvis Presley's platoon sergeant" (1959), and "Our grandfather was a soldier in the American Revolutionary War" (1961). In 1964, Harland Sanders disclosed, "I started Kentucky Fried Chicken with my Social Security check of $150.50."

Where *What's My Line?* had a stellar mystery guest whose identity had to be guessed, *I've Got a Secret* had a weekly celebrity who either had a secret—the original Frankenstein's monster, Boris Karloff, confessed he was afraid of mice—or did something. Former game show emcee and *Tonight Show* host Johnny Carson shot an arrow into an apple atop Garry

Moore's head. Silent-movie comedy icon Buster Keaton judged the panel in a pie-eating contest, Liberace gave them quickie piano lessons, and Paul Newman's secret was he'd sold Henry Morgan a hot dog earlier that day while disguised as a vendor.

The show stayed fresh partly because it was open to innovation. Gil Fates, a producer on *What's My Line?* and *I've Got a Secret*, recalled that when anything new had been proposed to John Daly he'd threatened, "Get yourself a new boy." Fates termed the *What's My Line?* situation a "hardening of the creative arteries." (Yet it did outlast *I've Got a Secret*.)

In 1960, Garry Moore boasted, "The success of *Secret* lies in its basic format, which allows us to do anything. It changes every week, with something new to see and talk about. We always have one guest with an unusual secret that he has with him."

Moore left the show in 1964 to sail around the world and was replaced by Steve Allen. *I've Got a Secret* and *What's My Line?* were both canceled in 1967. The former returned in syndication for one season in 1972, hosted by Allen, and on CBS prime time in summer 1976 with host Bill Cullen.

In 2000, Oxygen, the female-targeted cable channel, revived *I've Got a Secret* and was hosted by radio personality Stephanie Miller (who later came out as gay). It lasted a season. So did a 2006 Game Show Network version hosted by heterosexual Bill Dwyer; the four panelists' not-exactly-a-secret was they were all gay.

Bob Stewart (born Isidore Steinberg) worked for Mark Goodson-Bill Todman Productions and proposed a game show called *Cross Examination*. To wit, three people claiming to be the same person were cross-examined by a panel who then voted on which one was the real McCoy. Goodson deemed it a lousy idea, partly because he thought nonactors wouldn't be convincing lying about themselves (what planet did he come from?).

Positive the idea was viable, Stewart requested Goodson to round up four celebrities for a trial run at TV personality Gene Rayburn's house. Stewart rounded up a friend and two imposters. He described the truth-teller's background to the four celebs and the Goodson-Todman staff. Then everybody grilled the trio for 20 minutes. After which, Bob asked the assemblage, "If you're positive that you know who the real person is, and by that I mean you'd be willing to bet money on this, raise your hand."

No one raised their hand. Goodson was convinced, and the company contacted CBS. Mike Wallace (later of *60 Minutes*) hosted the pilot, but by the time the show was broadcast-ready, opted to focus on journalism. Walter Cronkite was willing, but CBS News felt it would detract from his news credibility. Actor Ralph Bellamy was short-listed but unavailable. Likewise Vincent Price and Don Ameche. Final choice Bud Collyer, already hosting *Beat the Clock*, was hired.

The show had been retitled *Nothing But the Truth* and was listed that way in *TV Guide*. A copyright issue provoked a final change to *To Tell the Truth*. It debuted in 1956 and lasted on CBS for 12 years.

Each show began with "Number 1, what is your name, please?" They would state the name that the next two individuals would also give. Before the trio walked to their seats, they stood motionless while the host read a sworn affidavit explaining what the real person had done of note. The imposters had already become acquainted with the facts and been coached on how to sound convincing and what to say or do if they drew a blank, and so on. The segment ended with the polite order, "Will the real [John Doe] please stand up?"

In 1956 guests earned $250 for each wrong vote by a panelist. If guests received no wrong votes, they split $150. *To Tell the Truth*'s first "central" guests were West Virginia governor Cecil Underwood and sportswriter Jeane Hoffman (it was that rare then for a woman to write about sports). In 1957 Kitty Carlisle joined the panel and stayed through 1991 (like Arlene Francis she'd dabbled in acting; her one significant film credit was the Marx Brothers' *A Night at the Opera*). Once when the guest was a pro bowler, Kitty stopped the show by innocently asking, "How much do men's balls weigh?"

Frequent panelists included sometime actress Peggy Cass (Agnes Gooch in *Auntie Mame*), Bill Cullen, Gene Rayburn, Johnny Carson, Ralph Bellamy, and comic actor Tom Poston. The show highlighted many people who'd become well-known but not famous or not instantly recognizable as famous. Audiences enjoyed putting a face to a familiar name, for instance children's author Dr. Seuss, cosmetics maven Mary

Kay Ash, H&R Block cofounder Richard Block, Motown founder Berry Gordy, *Dick Tracy* artist Chester Gould, Robert Moog of the Moog synthesizer, David Prowse, who wore the Darth Vader costume in *Star Wars*, and John Scopes of the Scopes Trial of the 1920s.

Imposters who made appearances before they found fame included Lauren Hutton and Cicely Tyson and baseball's Jerry Coleman and Ralph Houk.

When *To Tell the Truth* switched to syndication in 1969, former *I've Got a Secret* host Garry Moore became emcee for eight seasons. When he retired, he was succeeded by Bill Cullen and baseballer Joe Garagiola until cancellation in 1978. In 1980, Canadian actor Robin Ward hosted a syndicated season whose panelists included Peggy Cass and Soupy Sales. *To Tell the Truth* went network again in 1990 on NBC and was hosted by, in turn, reporter Gordon Elliott, former football player Lynn Swann, and Alex Trebek (who was also hosting *Classic Concentration*). It lasted one season.

A syndicated *To Tell the Truth* aired from 2000 to 2002 and was hosted by actor John O'Hurley and, more successfully, ABC's version, which began in 2016 and continues, hosted by Anthony Anderson (from the sitcom *Black-ish*). During the height of COVID, to maintain social distancing, the panel was reduced from four to three. (In 2002, a video slot machine game based on the show was released by Bally Gaming Systems.)

Mark Goodson, a less retiring personality than Bill Todman, played host twice in his career, both times on *To Tell the Truth*, filling in for Bud Collyer in 1967 and Alex Trebek in 1991.

Bob Stewart came up with more ideas for Goodson-Todman, including one called *Auction Aire* (retitled *The Price Is Right*, 1956), whose host was to be Dick Van Dyke. Unfortunately, the two bosses didn't much like the young comic, and he didn't like the show's concept. After hosting several practice games for Goodson and Todman, Van Dyke told his wife, "This is the dumbest idea. People are just trying to guess how much things cost. That's a show?" Bill Cullen was hired to host.

Bob Stewart's contributions to Goodson-Todman were monetarily undervalued. He was also displeased by Goodson's habit of publicly taking credit for concepts and shows he hadn't originated. Goodson didn't want to lose Stewart's valuable services and finally offered him an ownership stake in the company. Stewart asked if his name could be added to that of the company. Goodson said it couldn't. Stewart left and formed his own company in 1964.

Stewart's game shows included the *Pyramid* series, *Chain Reaction*, *Jackpot!*, *Three on a Match*, *Pass the Buck*, *Winning Streak*, and *Shoot for the Stars* and its revival *Double Talk*. "It's really a shame Goodson and Stewart couldn't find a way to [coexist]," said Goodson-Todman staffer Mike Gargiulo. "If those two could have got along, the company would have grown to the size of Warner Bros."

4

This Has Been a Mark Goodson-Bill Todman Production

"This has been a Mark Goodson-Bill Todman Production." For several decades that spoken tag was heard at the end of thousands and thousands of game show episodes. The Goodson-Todman company produced so many programs that part of the public assumed any given game show was a Goodson-Todman production. Mark Goodson stated he saw no advantage in denying the misconception that their company produced "all the hits."

Game show emcee Bert Convy explained, "Mr. Goodson once told me, and I'm not sure he wasn't joshing, 'We do not produce all the shows. . . . We produce most of the hits.' I felt like saying, 'How nice for you.' But didn't." Convy's most successful hosting gig was Goodson-Todman's *Tattletales*.

The more aggressive partner, and eventually the only one, Mark Goodson was a UC Berkeley economics major who moved into radio soap opera announcing. Ironically it was Bill Todman, a Johns Hopkins Medical School student turned advertising copywriter, who would oversee the financial side of their company. The two met in 1941 while employed by a New York City radio quiz show. Their company devised game shows, including *Winner Take All*, which aired on CBS and then NBC from 1948 to 1953. The Q and A show, which began on radio in

1946 with host Bill Cullen, popularized the concepts of buzzing in and the returning champion.

Goodson was more adept than Todman at devising programming ideas, but their company soon benefited from the services of a large creative staff. However, if a staff member created a winning game show concept that went to network or into syndication and perhaps also yielded foreign editions, they couldn't expect to receive royalties. "They were a closed circle of two," offered producer Allan Sherman. "They were the corulers, they sat on the thrones. Everyone else was part of their court."

Game show insider Adam Nedeff noted that Goodson took "far more credit than he really deserved for creating the shows done under his banner . . . as far as any research can determine, the Goodson-Todman radio shows were really the only ones plucked from his own brain." Employees admitted that the detail-oriented Goodson was expert at improving a concept, eliminating flaws, and patiently shepherding a future show until it was ready for mass consumption.

The company proved less successful with programs that were not game shows. "Goodson-Todman wanted the prestige of drama shows, award-winning fare. . . . it didn't work," said *Let's Make a Deal* host Monty Hall. "They were tops in their field, and that is the field they belonged in." Dramatic anthology shows were esteemed on early TV and in 1950 Goodson-Todman produced *The Web*; in 1963 another anthology series, *The Richard Boone Show*. Their westerns included *Jefferson Drum* (1958), *The Rebel* (1961) starring Nick Adams, and *Branded* (1965) starring Chuck Connors. They also tried their hand at a sitcom, *One Happy Family* (1961) costarring Dick Sargent before his stint on *Bewitched*.

"Mark was more disappointed than Bill at their 'outside' results, at being solely identified with game shows," said Hugh Downs, host of *Concentration* for 10 years. "Bill was more about the size and [cash] inflow-outflow of the company. . . . Mark is the corporate public face."

Helping fund the numerous Goodson-Todman pilots and programs were company-owned newspapers, radio stations, and real estate, thanks to wise investing by Bill Todman. Goodson-Todman saved most of its shows' original tapes, rather than erasing them to tape newer shows, which made reruns a profitable possibility. (The industry practice of "wiping" was mostly discontinued by the 1980s.)

Wealthy, they were; generous, they were not. Allan Sherman, who devised a show called *I Know a Secret*—it became *I've Got a Secret*—wasn't paid for his contribution. Rather, he was hired as the show's producer in 1952. But who can be hired can be fired. One 1958 episode was to feature movie star Tony Curtis teaching the *Secret* panel childhood games. On air it soon became apparent Curtis wasn't familiar with them, and the props Sherman provided either failed to work or worked too slowly. Curtis was forced to extemporize. He mentioned the impending birth of his child (Jamie Lee Curtis, by movie star wife Janet Leigh). Mark Goodson was furious and embarrassed at how "boring" the segment was. He fired Sherman.

Rose Marie, a Hollywood Square for 14 years, said in 2006, "I'm glad I worked for Merrill Heatter and Bob Quigley," the producers of *Hollywood Squares*. "They were all right fellas, I mean compared to some . . . . I heard about this guy who the one time he met Mark Goodson and said 'game show' found out the hard way Mr. Goodman didn't appreciate that term."

Goodson felt the term was too general because shows like his *Match Game*, *I've Got a Secret*, and *The Price Is Right* have little in common. But "game shows" long ago replaced "quiz shows" (likewise Boris Karloff felt his pictures weren't horrible and preferred "terror movies," but the universal term became "horror movies"). *Match Game* panelist Debralee Scott of *Mary Hartman, Mary Hartman* mused in an unpublished interview for *Us* magazine, "I'd be real curious about Mark Goodson how, you know, outside his professional life how many or if any game shows on his own time he watches?"

Goodson-Todman sometimes attempted their own versions of popular game shows, for example *Beat the Clock* after *Truth or Consequences* and *Two for the Money* after *You Bet Your Life*. But they became upset, not to mention litigious, when they thought someone else was copying one of their popular shows. Game show producer and host Jan Murray (*Treasure Hunt, Chain Letter, Dollar a Second*) remarked, "As businessmen I won't say they're hypocritical . . . I'm sure someone else already said it."

Goodson didn't want Monty Hall to sue them over a pitch of his that Goodson-Todman rejected, which was similar to their subsequent *Match Game*. Hall, then hosting *Video Village* on CBS, was persuaded by a network executive and Goodson not to go to court by the sharp implication that CBS, which aired several successful Goodson-Todman shows, might not care to do business with him in future if he sued.

But when the two men felt the 1963 game show *You Don't Say!* was too similar to their *Password*, they sued. Both shows comprised two teams, each a celebrity and a contestant, and had to do with words. The partners lost. But the judge did order that *You Don't Say!* host Tom Kennedy not be positioned (like Allen Ludden) between the two teams. Instead, he had to stand at one end of the set.

Goodson-Todman sometimes threw their weight around if they wanted a particular time slot from a particular network. Doing so helped cause cancellation of the popular *Press Your Luck*, which was hosted by Peter Tomarken (see chapter 23). Dennis James, who hosted the prime-time version of *The Price Is Right* when it revived in 1972 (Bob Barker hosted in daytime), disliked the two men but like most in the business didn't dare say much about or against them.

His widow Marjorie, known as Micki, confessed, "He found them sort of pompous, especially Mark Goodson. He was a bit of a show-off. The best clothes, the best cars. . . . Dennis resented their attitude that hosts were quite replaceable. . . . For Goodson and Todman, money and ratings came first, not relationships."

Despite the company's success and wealth, at times Goodson-Todman cut corners. "They watch their pennies, I can tell you," said *Match Game* host Gene Rayburn, whose hosting talent and ratings were inadequately compensated according to several insiders. "When they do spend a bundle, it's anticipating a sure thing that'll bring them in a larger bundle."

In 1973 *Match Game*, a daytime hit, added nighttime syndication to its schedule. To save money, Goodson-Todman stacked the tapings: After shooting five shows in a row, they held over the host and celebrity panel to tape *Match Game PM* immediately after. "That was cheap and unprofessional," panelist Richard Dawson opined years later. "I'm surprised nobody quit. Including myself."

Match Game's famous open bar was heavily used by the time the *PM* version was ready to tape. "Miss [Brett] Somers in particular had to be shall we say escorted," said Dawson, "to her seat for our syndicated filming. More than once . . . my, yes."

As time passed, Bill Todman attended fewer creative meetings, which Mark Goodson not only dominated but could also make uncomfortable for him. Company producer Ira Skutch noted that if Todman ventured to add an idea to "a format in development, Goodson would harshly rebuke him by barraging him with several questions in a row. When Todman hesitated in answering one, Goodson would invariably say, 'See that? You don't really understand what we're talking about.'"

Insiders believed Goodson, whose parents weren't affluent, resented Todman, whose father was a Wall Street accountant whose clients included the New York Stock Exchange, Chase Manhattan Bank, and Eastman Kodak. Game show announcer Randy West (*Supermarket Sweep, Trivial Pursuit*) stated, "Todman was a master salesman, adept at the art of the two-martini lunch that lubricated commerce in the TV and ad industry at the time. Goodson was always self-conscious about his not fitting in with that crowd."

Over the decades, the tensions between the two men grew. Some said Goodson wore Todman down. The more energetic Mark continued pursuing new game shows and rebooting their hits and also appeared in public when the occasion arose. Todman, who'd secured the company's financial footing, gradually slowed down. Gene Rayburn felt Bill was "emasculated" by Mark, who eventually hired another financial expert to take over most of Todman's duties. Todman moved to Florida and died in 1979 at 62. His name remained part of the company name until 1982 when Mark bought Bill's share of the company from his heirs, and it became Mark Goodson Productions. Goodson died in 1992 at 77.

Son Jonathan Goodson took over in 1993. He began his TV career as chief counsel for Goodson-Todman in 1973 and produced various game shows. His Jonathan Goodson Productions mostly did state-based lottery games like *Illinois Instant Riches*, one of two state-based lottery game shows that aired nationally via Superstation WGN.

In 1995 Mark Goodson Productions was sold to All American Television, in 1998 to British-owned Pearson Television, and in 2000 to Fremantle, owned by the German Bertelsmann conglomerate. His corporate name has long since disappeared.

"I think to be number one at anything you have to be a little ruthless," volunteered *Match Game* regular Charles Nelson Reilly, who considered Mark Goodson a friend. "I cannot fault the Goodson-Todman output . . . it's matchless, no pun intended."

Among the Mark Goodson-Bill Todman Productions: *Beat the Clock*; *It's News to Me*; *What's My Line?*; *The Name's the Same*; *I've Got a Secret*; *Two for the Money*; *Judge for Yourself*; *What's Going On*; *Make the Connection*; *The Price Is Right*; *Choose Up Sides*; *To Tell the Truth*; *Play Your Hunch*; *Say When!!*; *Number Please*; *Password*; *Missing Links*; *The Match Game*; *Get the Message*; *Call My Bluff*; *Snap Judgment*; *Tattletales*; *He Said, She Said*; *Now You See It*; *Showoffs*; *Family Feud*; *Double Dare*; *The Better Sex*; *Card Sharks*; *Mindreaders*; and *Password Plus*.

5

You Bet Your Life!

You Bet Your Life WAS THE FIRST QUIZ SHOW TAILORED MORE TO A host's personality than its Q and A format. That stellar personality was Groucho Marx (born Julius; who would name a baby Groucho?). The Marx Brothers' standout character enjoyed a successful solo career after the siblings' acclaimed movie career with *You Bet Your Life* on NBC-TV prime time, sometimes twice a week, from 1950 to 1961. Its summer reruns were titled *The Best of Groucho*. After its 10th season, *You Bet Your Life* was renamed *The Groucho Show*.

For reasons of ego, Manhattan's weather, and possible boredom reciting questions and performing hosting duties Marx initially declined radio producer John Guedel's offer to host a quiz show. Also, Groucho, whose solo film career wasn't A-list, had vainly attempted his own successful radio show (which was not a quiz-type show) four times. Guedel reassured the comedian that the show's quiz portion wasn't that important(!). The main event would be Groucho chatting with contestants, usually a man and woman, while employing his wit and flair for innuendo—"Innuendo, isn't that Eye-talian for suppository?"

Guedel had observed a recent radio skit pairing Marx with Bob Hope. When the latter dropped his script on the floor, Groucho did the same, accepting the challenge and outshining the younger man with quick ad-libs and toppers. Guedel advised that if *You Bet Your Life's* contestants were bright they would elicit laughter, which Groucho could build on, and if they were dull, Groucho would score laughs off them. (Announcer

George Fenneman introduced the star as "The one, the *only*, Groucho" and served as his admiring right-hand man.)

You Bet Your Life was a rare quiz show that originated in Hollywood, where Marx lived. Its musical theme was "Hooray for Captain Spaulding" from the Marx Brothers movie *Animal Crackers*. Its logo was Julius, a stuffed, bespectacled, mustachioed, bow-tied duck alter ego of Groucho. Julius descended from the rafters each time "the secret word" was spoken. The secret word was shown to the audience before the contestant interviews and inadvertently saying it earned the player $100 cash. The secret word on the first TV airing was "wall."

The program started on radio in 1947 and lasted until 1956, one of NBC's last big radio shows. Interviews before the quiz generally took up 75 percent of airtime. Unlike most early television offerings, the TV program wasn't live. Groucho, who habitually adjusted his "act" to audience reactions, disliked time restrictions. He insisted his show be filmed, primarily so his performance could be tip-top. Typically, 60 to 90 minutes of show were prerecorded, from which the editors culled the best 30 minutes.

Groucho's repartee was partly ad-libbed and partly scripted. Often during a joke he would roll his eyes so as to read an upcoming line or "ad-lib." Jokes were prepared on cue cards that he read off a small TV screen situated immediately above head level. During a decade when TV star Milton Berle elicited major yuks by walking in women's shoes turned sideways, Marx was widely considered the wittiest man on television. His show's popularity was a launching pad for some guests' careers. For instance, Marx couldn't get over the double surname (a Hispanic custom because everyone has two parents) of Pedro Gonzalez Gonzalez, who took the ribbing good-naturedly.

John Wayne was watching that episode and hired Pedro for a small part in an upcoming movie. Gonzalez Gonzalez ended up acting in a dozen pictures, most starring Wayne (all of whose wives were Hispanic). In 1958 a middle-aged housewife and mother of five trying to become a stand-up comic guested on *You Bet Your Life*, later rating her appearance a nervous disaster. Nonetheless Phyllis Diller's jokes and madcap personality made an impression, and she surged forth into a multidecade comedy career.

In 1960 writer William Blatty (later William Peter Blatty) won a $10,000 jackpot and informed Groucho he would use it to take a year off from work to write a novel. He eventually wrote *The Exorcist*.

Marx enjoyed verbally sparring with a variety of guests, from 600-pound wrestler Haystacks Calhoun to the inevitable young pretties he could still leer at. As his show's popularity grew, more notables were willing to be confronted by Groucho and share a national spotlight. Among them, Harland Sanders the Kentucky Fried Chicken entrepreneur, Tor Johnson of director-Ed-Wood movie infamy, former Tarzan Johnny Weissmuller, boxing champ Joe Louis, and army general Omar Bradley. An especially memorable guest was Harpo, the silent Marx Brother, who was lowered from the rafters like Julius the Duck.

Ever-competitive, Mark Goodson-Bill Todman Productions took aim at *You Bet Your Life* in 1952 with *Two for the Money* on NBC, Groucho's network. In its second season *Two* switched to CBS. Its host was a former harmonica player, Herb Shriner, described as mild-mannered and unsophisticated. The Goodson-Todman show featured a live band headed by an accordionist and gave away more money than Groucho's show—as if that in itself would draw viewers.

The producers weren't happy about the amount of money being disbursed, partly thanks to a staff that found it hard ascertaining some questions' difficulty. For example, during one episode a winning couple reached a point where each correct answer was worth $350. Their question: Name as many words as you can that end with -th (during rehearsals, staffers only came up with a few, including "zenith"). When the clock began ticking, one contestant announced, "13th," then her partner continued, "14th," and they kept going until time ran out and they'd given 14 correct answers for a total of $4,900.

Two for the Money lasted about five years, due partly to scheduling. CBS placed it after *The Jackie Gleason Show* on Saturday nights, where the shows performed well enough to see cancellation of NBC's *Your Show of Shows* a year later. Pressure, or the lack of it, may have played a part in Groucho's show outlasting its rival. When Marx began hosting his show's radio version he was 57, already a national figure, and the 14 years of *You Bet Your Life* were gravy. Groucho's attitude of what-me-worry? afforded him a less strained air and more risk-taking.

Herb Shriner, age 34, believed his quiz show was stifling his career. In 1956 CBS dropped *Two for the Money*, and Herb gladly contracted to do a variety show instead; it ran three episodes. CBS soon brought back *Two*, hosted by author-humorist Sam Levenson, but the show was finished within six months.

Two for the Money's judge, Dr. Mason Gross, was later president of Rutgers University for 12 years. His vacation substitute was Walter Cronkite. Another future success was Sam Levenson's announcer Ed McMahon, who would become a game show host but more famously enjoy a three-decades-plus partnership with Johnny Carson, starting with the game show *Who Do You Trust?* in 1958. That program (which began as *Do You Trust Your Wife?* in 1957) was, like *You Bet Your Life*, structured more closely around the host-contestant interchange than the actual game.

Groucho Marx was reportedly devastated by the cancellation of his longstanding show. Enough viewers protested that he received a variety of offers, among them two Broadway shows (one, the future hit *A Funny Thing Happened on the Way to the Forum*) and the possibility of replacing Jack Paar as *The Tonight Show*'s host. At 71, Groucho felt he was too old to do either but offered to host a week a month (NBC chose full-time Johnny Carson). In 1962, less than four months after his cancellation, Marx tried again with *Tell It to Groucho* on CBS.

The format was similar but popular straight man George Fenneman was replaced with two teens, a boy and a girl. The concept shifted to contestants telling their problems to Groucho and hoping for monetary aid to solve them. The show aired less than five months.

Years passed, as impatient novelists say, and 1980 brought a syndicated *You Bet Your Life* via Universal's television arm and Hill-Eubanks, the short-lived production company partnering *Newlywed Game* host Bob Eubanks. The show starred twist-mouthed comic and former policeman Buddy Hackett. It lasted a season. TV critic and lecturer David Sheehan felt, "Hackett was no Groucho, in any sense. . . . His humor was invariably flat-footed, often crude, and the audience he amused most was an audience of one, himself." The consensus was that Universal's muscle (and pride?) kept the program going as long as it did.

In 1988 former *Family Feud* host Richard Dawson did an NBC pilot for a new *You Bet Your Life*. Wittier and more articulate than Hackett, Dawson seemed a promising successor to Groucho. Alas his reputation for being difficult and controlling probably kept the pilot from being picked up. After *Family Feud* became a huge success, the Englishman's ego blossomed, and his relationships wilted. He'd had the show's producer barred from the set and replaced with his own daughter-in-law.

A more moderate bet seemed to be the 1992 *You Bet Your Life* starring Bill Cosby, who years earlier had received encouragement from Marx. This syndicated version was offered by Marcy Carsey and Tom Werner, producers of the 1980s hit *The Cosby Show*, and Cosby's own company. Despite the sitcom's eight-year success, NBC didn't get behind the comedian's new effort. It too lasted one season. Where Hackett's duck was renamed Leonard, Cosby's became a black goose sporting a Temple University T-shirt (Cosby's alma mater).

The winning team on the Hackett show got to meet Leonard the Duck and select one of his eggs (male ducks lay eggs?) for an additional prize. Inflation was proven on Cosby's show, where a player uttering the secret word won $500.

Why didn't the reboot fly? Theories abounded: Viewers weren't used to seeing Cosby in a game show or as a host (in 1976 he'd hosted *Cos*, an unpopular variety show). Or the show was dull, or the host was dull or tired. He'd become a father figure; whatever else Groucho was, he wasn't a father figure. Father figures after their popular sitcom are taken for granted and limited. (After *Brady Bunch*, Robert Reed groused, "That 'dad' box just about killed my career.")

The show was shot in Cosby's hometown of Philadelphia, and many of the contestants weren't too bright. Bill said wife Camille thought they "damn near served as buffoons. She thought it was embarrassing to like people and then hear a question that was very simple, and these people were struggling to answer." Also, *You Bet Your Life*'s daily pace couldn't accommodate anything like director Jay Sandrich's artful weekly editing of Cosby's riffs that had enhanced his sitcom.

Another probable negative was most viewers' desire to see a star reprise his most long-running success—as with Groucho's follow-up effort, *Tell It to Groucho*. "Television audiences are mentally unreliable," said Marx in later life. "You add a little bit of change or difference, it can upset them . . . makes them change the dial to see something totally different."

Time will sum up the staying power of Jay Leno's 2021 *You Bet Your Life*, which Fox renewed for a second season. Nice-guy Jay (as "Cos" was then thought to be) insisted he would avoid controversy or angering viewers (specifically, antimask, antivaccine Trumpites). But genial chat wouldn't seem to channel the legacy and success of Groucho's pioneering show (the more acerbic David Letterman might have been a more apt hosting choice).

One critic found the fourth *You Bet Your Life* "resembling *The Tonight Show* standing up, with cash-value questions and answers." Not too much cash; Leno didn't wish the show to be "primarily about the money . . . you know, 'big bucks! big bucks!'" Possibly the first *You Bet Your Life* was so seamlessly tailored to its star that any reboot is doomed. Then again, a combination of talk show with a likeable, soft-spoken host and quiz show that's light on intellect, pressure, and "big bucks" could prove a popular contemporary format.

Groucho Talks

Groucho (1890–1977): I still remember how I enjoyed your western movies when I was just a little kid.

Former cowboy star Hoot Gibson (1892–1962): Thank you, Groucho. I enjoyed your pictures when I was a kid.

Groucho: How old are you, Barbara?

Barbara Schmidt: 18.

Groucho: 18, huh? A lovely age for a girl. In fact it's a lovely age for a woman of 40.

Groucho: What do you consider a funny joke?

Entertainer Aki Aleong: Well, um. . . . What did the two flies say after they flew off of Robinson Crusoe?

Groucho: I haven't the faintest idea.

Aleong: Well, they said, "So long. See you on Friday."

Groucho to housewife Maryanne Badger: Your name was Wolf and you married a Badger? Well, it could be worse. One of my neighbors claimed she married a skunk. It isn't true because I know him and he hasn't got a cent.

Steve Cory: If I told you everything that happened in my life, Groucho, it would take about eight hours.

Groucho: If I told you everything I did in my life, I'd get 30 years.

Groucho, to a Dr. Paul Saltman: You look like an educated Jerry Lewis.

Groucho: Ruth, where are you from?

Ruth Elder: Alabama.

Groucho: Have you got a banjo on your knee or, uh, what have you got on your knee—anything?

Elder: Water.

Groucho to spunky elderly lady: Now let's talk to you, okay, Mrs. Sackett?

Miss Sackett: Miss Sackett, if you please.

Groucho: Miss Sackett.

Miss Sackett: Thank you.

Groucho: Oh, I'm terribly sorry.

Miss Sackett: You may be sorry, but I'm not. (Pause.) And if you'll dispose of the cigar, I'll thank you.

Groucho: Is it Miss or Mrs.?

Jean Rosenthal: Well, I'm afraid it's Miss.

Groucho: Well, if you're afraid, I'm not surprised it's Miss.

Groucho: I play golf too, you know. What is your handicap?

Golf pro Jim Ferrier: Well, as a pro, I don't have a handicap.

Groucho: Well, congratulations. How is it a tall, handsome man like you isn't married?

Ferrier: Oh, I'm married. I have a wife.

Groucho: You just said you didn't have a handicap.

Groucho: May I kiss your wife?

Husband: That would have to be over my dead body.

Groucho: Have it your way. Fenneman, get the gun!

Groucho: If we got together as an act, what would it be called?

Pedro Gonzalez Gonzalez: It would be Gonzalez Gonzalez and Marx.

Groucho, to audience: Do you believe that? Two men in the act and I get third billing!

Groucho: What kind of a deal do you get with Washington now?

Ballplayer Chuck Dressen: Well, I got what I wanted with Washington. I got a two-year contract with the Senators.

Groucho: Chuck, they slipped one over on you. All the other Senators get six years in Washington.

Groucho: What are the requirements for an umpire?

Jack Powell: An umpire must have honesty, integrity, good eyesight, and plenty of intestinal fortitude.

Groucho: Wouldn't it help if you knew a little about baseball?

Jack Powell: We have 14 umpires and when all the teams are playing, there's only four places they can go.

Groucho: You're wrong. There's five places they can go.

An ordained minister: Groucho, I want to thank you for all the enjoyment you have given the world.

Groucho: And I want to thank you for all the enjoyment that you have taken out of it.

Groucho, to a Mrs. Story who had 20 children: Why do you have so many children?

Mrs. Story: Well, because I love children and I think that's our purpose here on Earth and I love my husband.

Groucho: I love my cigar too, but I take it out of my mouth once in a while.

6

Record-Breaker: Bill Cullen

MOST AMERICANS DURING THE 1930S AND 1940S DIDN'T KNOW THAT four-term president Franklin Delano Roosevelt (FDR) was crippled by polio. They didn't get to see him walk or confined to his wheelchair. FDR was stricken with polio as an adult in summer 1921. So was a one-year-old in Pittsburgh named William Lawrence Cullen. Future record-breaking game show host Bill Cullen had to wear a brace on his left leg until age 10. For the rest of his life he had a definite limp in his left leg.

TV game show audiences didn't get to see Cullen walk. He was always positioned standing at a podium or sitting. A likeable, good-humored, quick-witted radio star, Cullen initially avoided television because he was plain, had a poor complexion, wore thick eyeglasses, and limped. But by the time he retired in 1988 he'd appeared in more than 30 TV programs as a host or panelist and almost two dozen radio shows.

Cullen logged some 25,000 individual radio and television episodes during his 49-year broadcasting career. And he hosted more game shows than anybody else: 23 of them.

He enrolled as a premed student at the University of Pittsburgh in 1938 but financial hardship resulted in his leaving college to work in his father's garage as a mechanic and tow-truck driver. When a local radio executive became a customer, Bill offered to work at his radio station for free. He was hired as an unpaid announcer working six hours a day, seven days a week at WWSW. After two months, he was earning $25 a week, and then switched to local KDKA as a sports announcer, disc jockey, and variety show host. He returned to college and earned a fine arts degree.

By early in the 1940s, Bill was earning $250 a week. From 1942 to 1944 during World War II he was a civilian flight instructor and patrol pilot for Civilian Air Defense. He was ineligible for military service, as he had been for most sports during high school. In 1949 he launched Appointment Airlines after buying three small airplanes and renting four others. By 1953 he was down to one plane and shuttered his airline but kept a Beachcraft Bonanza four-seater and flew other small craft until late in the 1970s. "I love flying. It's like becoming more spirit than body."

Cullen moved to New York City in 1944 and, partly due to the war's manpower shortage, was soon working at CBS Radio announcing ads, dramatic shows, and a successful 1946 quiz show, *Winner Take All*. When its host quit, Cullen took his place. In 1949 he debuted as a TV game show host with *Act It Out*, a NYC program. It employed actors to enact scenes. A home viewer—there weren't many yet—received a telephone call and was invited to sum up a given scene in one word. If successful, the viewer won a prize. The show lasted half a year.

The Q and A *Winner Take All* was the first Mark Goodson-Bill Todman game show on TV in 1948. It was canceled in 1950, brought back in 1951, canceled the same year, and then revived for two months in 1952 with Bill Cullen as emcee, his national TV hosting debut. It was the first game show to feature a returning champion who remained until defeated by a newcomer. It was also the first game show to introduce the dreaded—by contestants—lockout device later known as the buzzer.

(As this writer learned on *Jeopardy!*, if you press it a fraction of a second too early, you're locked out, and a fraction of a second later than another contestant, you're locked out until and if that person answers incorrectly.)

In summer 1952, Cullen began a 15-year run as a panelist on CBS's *I've Got a Secret* (hosted by Garry Moore). Bill thrived on work and, by 1954, was also hosting *Place the Face* for CBS, *Bank on the Stars* for NBC, and *Professor Yes 'n No*, a syndicated 15-minute quiz show. He also hosted a radio quiz, *Walk a Mile*, and *Road Show*, a radio program offering news, music, contests, weather, and driving tips. Before year-end, the bicoastal commuter was also hosting *Name That Tune* on CBS prime time and CBS Radio's *Stop the Music.*

Cullen was earning a then-impressive $150,000-plus a year, but the pressing schedule put an end to his 1949 marriage in 1955. On Christmas Eve that year he wed Ann Roemheld and that marriage lasted until his death in 1990. Bill, who generally avoided parties, met Ann at a party hosted by her brother Jack. Thus, his brothers-in-law were game show hosts Jack Narz and Tom Kennedy (né Narz).

Marriage didn't slow Bill down. In 1956 he initiated *The Bill Cullen Show* on WRCA in New York City. It aired four hours weekday mornings and two hours Saturday, with a mix of music, news, weather, and contests.

Partly because he hosted so many game shows, Cullen isn't as closely associated with one show as, say, Gene Rayburn with *The Match Game* or Allen Ludden with *Password*. His longest-running hosting job was *The Price Is Right*, which debuted in 1956 and ran to 1965. Meantime he appeared on the cover of *TV Guide* seven times, a record for a game show emcee.

During the 1956 and 1957 seasons, he was sportscaster for radio's Army football games and did commentary for hockey, basketball, and his hometown's Pittsburgh Steelers. By 1958 he was earning more than some movie stars: $300,000 a year. *The Price Is Right* was going great guns on daytime and nighttime, and Bill was no longer spreading himself thin. He still did radio; his eponymous show had been retitled *Pulse* and WRCA was now WNBC. Both his shows were done in Manhattan. Bill informed *Look* magazine, "Between *Pulse* and *Price* I have a costume change. I straighten my tie."

With *Price*'s cancellation in 1965, he was left with only his *I've Got a Secret* panel duties. But the following January he emceed *Eye Guess*, created by colleague and former Goodson-Todman producer Bob Stewart. The show combined a test of memory with humor and was an NBC hit for three years. One winning 1968 contestant was Michael King of King World, which later syndicated TV shows like *Jeopardy!*, *Wheel of Fortune*, and *The Oprah Winfrey Show*.

The very month in 1969 that *Eye Guess* terminated, Bill started a nine-year stint as panelist on a syndicated revival of *To Tell the Truth*. In 1971 he was hosting again, via *Three on a Match*, comprising true-or-false questions and game-board squares that hid prizes. Meanwhile he was one of the rotating hosts of NBC Radio's *Monitor*, described by media historian David Baber as "a combination of news, music, skits, and chatter." When *Three on a Match* ceased in 1974, Bill commenced five years hosting *The $25,000 Pyramid*, a syndicated weekly edition of ABC's *The $10,000 Pyramid* (hosted by Dick Clark).

During the mid- to late 1970s, Cullen hosted such shows as *Winning Streak*, *Blankety Blanks*, *I've Got a Secret* redux, and *Pass the Buck*. He and Ann had long wished to move to California, partly for the weather, but show after show after show kept him Manhattan-bound. Finally they moved. Bill's first LA show in 1978 was the syndicated *The Love Experts* for Bob Stewart Productions. The one-season program featured four celebrity "love experts" brazenly offering advice on love, romance, and by implication, sex to contestants. At show's end, the quartet chose the contestant with "the most unique or interesting love problem." Said winner was awarded a prize or trip. The "experts" included Peter Lawford (who was married more than once and former brother-in-law to President John F. Kennedy), Soupy Sales, Jamie Lee Curtis, game show host Geoff Edwards, and David Letterman.

In 1980 Cullen was back hosting NBC's *Chain Reaction* and temporarily hosting *Password Plus* while Allen Ludden underwent cancer surgery. Late in 1980, Bill hosted *Blockbusters*, a Goodman-Todman entry focused on knowledge that pitted a lone contestant against a family pair. The title referred to hexagonal "blocks" the players used to form a winning chain across the game board. Though popular for its *Jeopardy!*-esque content and Cullen's mirthful banter with contestants, *Blockbusters* vanished in 1982.

So Bill turned up late in 1982 hosting CBS's *Child's Play*, a distinctive concept in which contestants tried to guess particular words as defined by children five to nine during prerecorded segments. To promote it, Cullen paid a surprise visit—host Bob Barker seemed surprised—to the set of *The Price Is Right*, which he'd departed in 1965 (*Play* and *Price* were both Goodson-Todman shows). The emcees reminisced about hosting the long-running *Price*. Bill's entrance onto the set aboard a miniature train driven by model Janice Pennington was both novel and avoided his having to walk onto the set.

After *Child's Play* ended in 1983, Bill pondered retirement but accepted NBC's offer to host *Hot Potato* (1984) via Barry & Enright Productions. It was similar to *Family Feud* in terms of guessing common answers to questions previously posed to a large sample of respondents. Four months into its five-month run the program became *Celebrity Hot Potato*. (Singer-actress and "disgraced" Miss America Vanessa Williams made her game show debut on the retitled show.)

After host-producer Jack Barry died unexpectedly in 1984, producer Dan Enright tapped Bill Cullen to take over Barry's hit show *The Joker's Wild*, which he did until its 1986 cancellation. Bill's swan song was a return to radio, somewhat ironically (in view of having no children), offering parental advice during a series of short programs titled *The Parent's Notebook*.

In 1968 a pancreatic condition had caused an end to alcohol consumption; however, Cullen remained a heavy smoker until giving it up in the mid-1980s. In summer 1989, a routine X-ray disclosed a cancerous spot on his lung. Bill declined hospitalization and chemotherapy with its ensuing hair loss by jocularly informing the doctor, "I'll have to turn [it] down because I promised to leave my hair to Bob Stewart," who was bald.

Until his final month, Cullen fought the spreading cancer and lived as normally as possible. When he died at age 70 on July 7, 1990, his wife Ann was holding one of his hands, and his best friend, Bob, the other. The latter commented, "I could name a batch of successful hosts who look and act like menswear mannequins come to life. They're fairly interchangeable and pretty forgettable. . . . If you've seen Bill Cullen host something, you remember him. He was one of a kind, fun, and funny, a total pro. . . . In our business he was known as the Dean of Game Show Hosts. He's tops."

Handsome Peter Tomarken, who wore several hats during his varied career and experienced only one real hosting hit (*Press Your*

Luck), said shortly before his death at 63, "I'm not sure I'd want to have spent my whole working life in game shows. But if I had, the one person I could most envy would be Bill Cullen."

"Bill set a record for how many game shows he hosted," eulogized TV producer-director Ira Skutch. "He set another record, at least as important. There was nothing bad you could say about him. I never once heard anyone say anything bad about Bill."

7

The Two Neediest

QUEEN FOR A DAY WAS THE MOST FAMOUS GAME SHOW OF ITS KIND. What kind? The kind that today would induce cringing but was once a huge hit on radio from 1945 to 1957. It launched nationally on TV in 1956 via NBC until it switched to ABC in 1960 until 1964 and then was syndicated in 1969–1970. Mustachioed Jack Bailey, a former world's fair barker in the 1930s who also voiced Goofy the Disney character, hosted the show on radio and from 1956 to 1964 on TV. He famously opened each show peering into the camera, yelling, "Would *YOU* like to be Queen for a Day?"

Heaven forbid.

The show's original radio title was *Queen for Today*. In 1951 there was a *Queen for a Day* movie starring Bailey, with Darren McGavin and Leonard Nimoy in supporting roles. In 2012 a *Queen for a Day* musical opened in Toronto, starring Canadian actor and host Alan Thicke as Bailey.

Queen for a Day was filmed in a Hollywood theater-restaurant on Sunset Boulevard called the Moulin Rouge. Its live audience was female, and it presented a daily fashion show narrated by Jeanne Cagney, actor James's sister. Despite the fancy trimmings, *Queen* was blue collar with a vengeance.

Bailey would welcome four women who sat at a "royal" dais in front of the throne that only the neediest among them would occupy, as decided by audience applause (the 1969–1970 version, hosted by Dick Curtis, substituted an electronic voting machine for the sound of clapping).

The show's contestants included destitute widows, women with too many children, women with incapacitated husbands, women requiring major surgery, women with children whose husbands had left them, mothers of disabled offspring in need of care and funds, women who'd been in accidents or suffered major financial losses, and so on. TV historians wrote that *Queen for a Day*'s goal seemed to be deciding "which contestant had the saddest life." One suggested the show's title should have been *Dire Straits*. Another called it "a wallow for people who chose to watch people more miserable than themselves."

Host Bailey could be smarmy or condescending, not to mention sexist, remarking about more than one adult contestant, "Poor little girl." During a 1958 episode he told a woman named Dorothy Lacey, "You look so cute and shaky. Don't you worry about a thing." Then he asked, "Is that a new dress? It looks wonderful." Lacey, who lived in a trailer with her four daughters, was on the show to ask for the materials to build two sets of bunk beds, plus four mattresses. A competitor whose son had polio requested a gurney so she could wheel her 15-year-old outside for fresh air. Another contestant, who looked at the floor almost the whole of her interview, asked for an encyclopedia set so her kids could finish high school.

So popular was *Queen for a Day* that NBC lengthened it to 45 minutes to sell more commercials. Accused of popularizing bad taste, the sob show was defended by its producer, Howard Blake. "It was exactly what the general public wanted. . . . Five thousand queens got what they were after and TV audiences cried their eyes out." It took time for the general public to stop crying and start cringing.

To extend its popularity *Queen for a Day* added theme episodes, including "King for a Day." "Baby Day" afforded a six-month-old with a foot deformity requiring special shoes a supply of shoes to last her until age five, as well as new clothes, a crib, talc, soap, a year's supply of evaporated milk, and a $2,000 scholarship. "Newsboys Day" featured a winner whose mother had recently died; he wanted and got a new room built onto the family home so his brother could move in.

Far from being embarrassed, most *Queen for a Day* winners were proud of their achievement. For half a century there was a Queen for a Day Club of past queens who convened at luncheons in Los Angeles and Las Vegas wearing the crowns they'd won, paying court to each other as Your Majesty or Your Highness and initiating fundraisers for charity.

Occasional substitute TV host Dennis Day claimed, "Most viewers were very happy for the winners. It was a heartwarming thing and in ways very inspiring."

Why did *Queen for a Day* fail when revived in 1969? "Public embarrassment finally kicked in," felt not-easily-embarrassed game show producer Chuck Barris. "Like, who's the poorest of them all? Who's the most miserable? Come *on*."

During its live nationwide tour in 1947, tickets for the radio show were in such demand that *Queen for a Day*'s Dallas stop took place at the 45,000-seat Cotton Bowl. "By the late '60s," noted Dr. Joyce Brothers, "words like 'exploitation' and 'sexism' were filtering through to the masses. . . . The spectacle of pitting four sadly deserving women against each other and rewarding one was no longer automatically considered entertainment."

During a less affluent past, poverty was sometimes a part of mass media. In 1938, Lucille Ball was listening to a nighttime radio show comprising interviews with jobless people seeking employment from a possible caller-in. Lucy heard the voice of Harriet, "a colored girl my age [27] who wanted to be a ladies' maid. She said she was honest, loyal, a hard worker . . . and her mother had trained her." Harriet's mother worked in the Jack Benny household. Benny and Ball would later become next-door neighbors in Beverly Hills.

Lucy hired Harriet. "She wasn't my maid, she was my friend." They kept in touch until Harriet's death in 1984 (Lucy died in 1989).

Strike It Rich debuted on CBS Radio in 1947 and became a CBS TV show in 1951; months later, it added a nighttime edition. Host Warren Hull had enacted Spiderman and Mandrake the Magician in several 1930s movie serials. Like most shows at the time, *Strike It Rich* (1951–1958) originated in New York City. It billed itself as "The Quiz Show with a Heart."

Contestants of both genders were in dire straits financially. Each was given $30 that could be bet in part or entirely on the player's hopes of answering four general knowledge questions. If that didn't pan out, a contestant could rely on the Heart Line, whereby viewers phoned in with a pledge to donate merchandise or money.

Guest hosts included Todd Russell, Monty Hall, and actors Don Ameche and Robert Alda (Alan's father). Hall, later of *Let's Make a Deal* fame, offered, "The concept sounds gauche these days [the 1990s]. But times were different. . . . The program was handled with a finesse that prevented its being maudlin. . . . In any case, audiences were enthusiastic."

New York, where *Strike It Rich* was shot, was not. The state's welfare commissioner labeled the show "a national disgrace." Its rising popularity induced indigent families to move to New York and try for the show; when they failed to make it, they often stayed put and sought government aid. One Maryland family with 11 children applied for welfare, but the state arranged for them to return to Maryland.

Ultimately, New York State employed threats against the show whose soliciting viewers for money amounted to panhandling. Show producer Walt Framer modified the rules concerning the Heart Line and the manner in which viewers could contribute. Although *Queen for a Day* shouldered its share of criticism, there were two big differences: It involved "just" women—men shedding their dignity for possible gain was viewed more seriously—and the Bailey show was daytime, when most viewers were "just" women. *Strike It Rich* also aired at night and, therefore, was more important. Though government criticism diminished, media and public criticism continued and resulted in CBS canceling the prime-time version in 1955.

There would have been more controversy had Walt Framer had his way. The ambitious ad man and writer formed his own production company before 1950. His specialty was what rival producer Louis G. Cowan labeled "a microscope on misery." The game show industry looked down on Framer and his shows. In 1953 he asseverated, "I'm producing *Strike It Rich* for the benefit of Mr. America, the poor guy who works all day, comes home, eats his dinner [and] doesn't want *Studio One* or some artsy show.

"He's looking for [*I Love*] *Lucy* or [*Strike It*] *Rich*. He has simple, elemental tastes. . . . If I don't put on a real needy case, I get a dirty, nasty letter from Mr. America."

Framer believed *Strike It Rich* displayed restraint. Buoyed by its success, he hoped to produce a novel game show titled *Behind Closed Doors*. Its contestants would have been mentally ill people competing to win psychiatric help.

Some game shows were of their era without being condescending or cringeworthy. NBC's *Feather Your Nest* ran from 1954 to 1956 and was hosted by Bud Collyer. At the time, many young couples had to live with their parents or in-laws, and the luxury of a new car at 16 (or 18 or 20) wasn't widespread. In *Feather Your Nest*, three couples played a Q and A quiz to win furniture for their own home. Each piece of furniture cost a particular number of points, and the show's three competition levels were represented by feathers colored red, yellow, and green. If a couple proceeded to the jackpot and won it, they earned an entire room's furnishings.

By late in the 1960s, affluence was within general reach in the US. *Dream House* debuted in 1968 on ABC (until 1970), hosted by Mike Darrow, and returned in 1983–1984 on NBC with Bob Eubanks. It too was a Q and A show featuring husband-and-wife teams, but the grand prize was a house. Before that possibility, each game was played for a room of furniture.

"We can carp about TV today," said journalist Harold Fairbanks. "But there's less emotional manipulation on game shows. To me, game shows and heartstrings shouldn't mix. Remember *The Girl in My Life*?" It aired from July 1973 to December 1974 on ABC and was hosted by Fred Holliday. The sentimental show was about doing good. Three or four profiles per episode highlighted a "girl" (no matter her age) who'd made a big, positive difference in someone's life. At the end of each vignette her "sponsor" would declare, "My name is (blank) and the girl in my life is (blank)." The woman then entered the set, was interviewed by Holliday, and then was awarded a modest prize.

"Some called it a game show," continued Fairbanks. "Some said it wasn't. But it was often a tearjerker, clearly descended from *Queen for a Day*. . . . If it had been popular there'd have been a bunch of similar shows. Popularity is an excuse for almost anything." *The Girl in My Life* was spoofed on *The Carol Burnett Show* as *The Girl That We Like*.

The popularity and profits of game shows "with a heart" inspired an attempted 1987 *Queen for a Day* revival to be hosted by Monty Hall and a one-time-only 2004 cable-TV special with Mo'Nique, but it was too late. An unnamed Game Show Network executive stated in 2011, "Some of us are eager to do a show titled *Strike It Rich* . . . a few of us like the drama of that 1950s show. But it seems to clash with national pride and current sensibilities."

It's worth remembering that *Queen for a Day*, unlike nearly all game shows, didn't involve playing a game (e.g., answering questions, puzzling something out, or enduring stunts). All a woman had to do, and that was plenty, was present a worse true tale of woe than her "competitors." The show itself could be faulted, but not its queens nor, let's say, its princesses.

8

Rigged!

GAME SHOWS INVOLVE THE TRANSFER OF MONEY, SOMETIMES CONSID-
erable amounts, and there's room for hanky-panky. Unlike banks,
early quiz shows were governed by virtually no rules concerning the
disbursement of their dollars. After game shows took off on television,
the FCC tried to ban them but was overruled by the Supreme Court in
1954—four years before the national scandal over rigged shows.

It started with greed for higher ratings and bigger profits on the
parts of sponsors, networks, and quiz show production companies. The
larger the audiences watching, the greater the temptation to fix things
so their numbers wouldn't decrease, which in time they're bound to do.

As with so much about early television, it began with radio. In 1940
a new CBS quiz show, *Take It or Leave It*, introduced an element of risk
that intrigued listeners. Host Bob Hawk withdrew names of audience
members from a fishbowl. From a blackboard on the stage, members
chose a knowledge category and began answering questions. The first
correct answer was worth a dollar. Each subsequent question's value
doubled until the seventh question was worth $64. But answering each
new question meant giving up any money already won, ergo the title. So
popular was the show that 20th Century-Fox built a B movie around it
in 1944, *Take It or Leave It*.

Louis G. Cowan had partnered with Mark Goodson on radio's *Stop
the Music*. He proposed a new TV quiz show based on *Take It or Leave
It* (Goodson passed) and asked Garry Moore, who'd become its host
in 1947, to emcee *The $64,000 Question*. Moore was aghast at the sum

and declined, correctly guessing that as quiz show jackpots got bigger, someday there would be a scandal he wished to be no part of.

For host, Cowan secured reluctant actor Hal March (né Harold Mendelson). *The $64,000 Question* premiered on June 7, 1955, and was an instant sensation. Cowan, an adman at CBS, had gotten Revlon to sponsor it. When the cosmetics company's sales soon rose by 154 percent, boss Charles Revson took charge. He held regular meetings to discuss the show's ratings and contestants—those he liked and those he disliked.

The public was enthralled by the risk and high stakes (the average US household's income that year was $4,400). Publicity revved up when *$64,000 Question*'s ratings surpassed TV's number one program, *I Love Lucy*. Big money became the rage. Prize amounts had already been increasing, but this was a new ratings-conscious era of fiercer competition. *Name That Tune*, which had touted the possibility of winning $1,600 in its Golden Medley, now offered a possible $25,000 in its retitled Golden Medley Marathon.

Break the Bank on radio had been notable for its generous prizes averaging $7,000. It remodeled itself and became *Break the $250,000 Bank*. Groucho Marx spoofed the trend on *You Bet Your Life* by gleefully asserting that the Secret Word (which awarded players a $100 bonus if they happened to say it) would now be worth more than it ever had been before: $101.

Revson was concerned that certain contestants might diminish audience interest in his show and products. He did everything he could to get rid of winning contestants he didn't like. That was possible because after reaching the $4,000 level, a contestant returned home and then appeared on the show to answer one question per week until the $64,000 level.

Revson especially disliked young psychologist Dr. Joyce Brothers, who wasn't glamorous and didn't wear makeup. As she kept on winning, he feared she would harm his company's aesthetic image. But try as he might, he couldn't prevent her becoming the second person and first woman to win $64,000 (eventually she won twice; see sidebar in chapter 19). Ironic that the self-described "nice Jewish girl" chose boxing as her field of knowledge.

The $64,000 Challenge was TV's first game show spin-off, in April 1956. In November another spin-off, *Giant Step*, presented 7- to 17-year-old contestants. The prizes were 4-year college scholarships. Alas, that show only survived 6½ months.

The $64,000 Question wasn't the primary focus of fixed-show publicity and charges. *Dotto* and *Twenty-One* were, though it later came out that for instance Richard McCutcheon, *$64,000 Question*'s first big winner, was given a preshow "warm-up session" to "relax" him. While on stage in the famous isolation booth (used once a player attained the $8,000 level), McCutcheon was astonished to find that each question thereafter given him, including the $64,000 one, had already been given (and answered) during a backstage session.

That final question asked which were the five entrées and two wines served at a 1939 banquet presided over by king George VI, honoring French president Albert Lebrun? Some people wondered how anyone could be expected to know that? Exactly. McCutcheon eventually acknowledged the deception.

Initial contestant revelations about rigging were mostly by those who'd been acted against. And they were not believed. At first. Director Robert Redford's 1994 movie *Quiz Show* highlighted the fall of Herbert Stempel and the rise of Charles Van Doren on *Twenty-One*, *$64,000 Question*'s leading competitor. The NBC show, sponsored by unglamorous Geritol, was the brainchild of Barry-Enright Productions, partnering host Jack Barry and Dan Enright. It debuted in September 1956.

Twenty-One's opening show wasn't suspenseful. Its contestants missed 17 questions. But tough questions couldn't be scaled down without the program seeming less competitive than its rival. Geritol's manufacturer, Pharmaceuticals, Inc., warned Barry-Enright they did not want another such episode. The decision was made to "fix" it.

On rigged shows, contestants were coached to take long pauses or stammer, or both, while delaying the correct answer. They were assigned various facial expressions to convey assorted emotions. The heat in the isolation booths was turned up so audiences could see a "nervous" player sweat; contestants were instructed not to mop their brows.

In October 1956, Herb Stempel, a 29-year-old Army vet attending City College of New York, appeared on *Twenty-One* and went on to defeat one contestant after another over the next several weeks. Ratings rose and Stempel became famous. Late in November his newest competitor was Charles Van Doren, an English professor at Columbia University. Van Doren was likewise coached and given answers in advance. *Twenty-One* then decreed it was time to dump Stempel in favor of the handsomer, unbespectacled WASP.

During their first match, the score ended in a tie. During their second match on December 5, Stempel was told to miss a question whose answer he knew. One of his favorite films was *Marty*, and the question was: Which 1955 movie won the Oscar for Best Picture? The answer was *Marty*, but Herb was ordered to reply *On the Waterfront*—and did. Why would a winning contestant throw a game? Some players were offered money to do so, or it was otherwise suggested it would be worth their while.

On-the-air pressure and intimidation, the feeling that big money and Big Brother knew best, was hard to ignore. One of Stempel's losing opponents told the district attorney she felt scared when moments before going on stage, she was warned, "Don't ask for any questions worth more than eight points, or *else*."

Stempel left *Twenty-One* with $49,500, but golden boy Van Doren was better rewarded. At the time of his defeat in March 1957 (by Vivian Nearing, an attorney) he'd raked in $129,000 and was given a three-year, $150,000 NBC contract whereby he became *Today*'s cultural correspondent. The Stempel–Van Doren rivalry—*Time* put the professor on its cover, solo—upped *Twenty-One* to number one in the ratings, beating its Monday night competitor *I Love Lucy*, whose run ended with the 1956–1957 season.

(Despite Van Doren's popularity and publicity, he wasn't *Twenty-One*'s biggest winner. That was Elfrida von Nardroff, a professional woman with several job titles, in spring 1958: $220,500. She insisted the show was not rigged.)

Herb felt humiliated. He'd been made to seem awkward and ungainly (e.g., directed to address host Jack Barry as Mr. Barry and being made to wear oversized suits). But when he tried to tell the truth about *Twenty-One*, he was dismissed as a sore loser.

Dotto, based on the children's game Connect the Dots, was a new 1958 CBS game show that ended that same year, though it quickly became daytime's top-rated program. It was the first casualty of the rigging scandal. On May 20, 1958, Ed Hilgemeier was waiting backstage to go on while returning champion Marie Winn was on stage. Prior to that, she'd been reading from a notebook—studying for a test, she explained. Winn left the notebook behind when she walked onstage. Hilgemeier picked it up and saw that it contained the answers to the current round's questions.

Dotto's producers offered Ed $4,000 to keep quiet. He refused. He'd made copies of the notebook's pages and showed them to an attorney. The producers offered to place him on the show's new prime-time edition, premiering in July, with the tacit understanding that Ed would win big on it. He refused.

In August, the Federal Communications Commission informed CBS that Ed Hilgemeier had filed a complaint about *Dotto* and presented evidence. The show was canceled that month.

Meanwhile, contestants beside Stempel and Hilgemeier were trying to bring the shady truth to light. One contestant on *Tic Tac Dough* said she'd been led to a room whose filing cabinets she was invited to look through, any knowledge category she liked, to "trigger her memories" on particular subjects and make her more comfortable for the show.

While on the show, she realized the questions being asked were from the files she'd gone through. The next time she was instructed as to which categories to pick and in what order. On air and nervous, she ordered the categories erroneously but won anyway though her errors had implied a tie. Before her third game she received no orders or special attention, and her opponent easily mowed her down.

Tic Tac Dough's popularity spawned a nighttime musical version, *Dough-Re-Mi*, via Barry-Enright. Jack Barry was concurrently hosting their company's *Twenty-One*, *Tic Tac Dough*, and *High Low*. NBC was so pleased with the hit-spinners that it bought their company and then paid them to produce the shows.

Name That Tune, not via Barry-Enright, had a producer, Harry Salter, with the habit of making his way onstage and whispering song titles in the ears of contestants he wanted to win. "It was easily contagious," said game show host and producer Jan Murray. "Crooked sponsors, amoral networks . . . you could guess what was going on."

When authorities finally moved to investigate the quiz shows, some assumed that contestants might have bribed producers to get on their shows. No such evidence turned up. But Barney Martin, associate producer of Murray's *Treasure Hunt*, was found to have promised possible players to book them if they gave him a percentage of their winnings. When Jan found out, he fired Martin on the spot.

Herb Stempel, still smarting from having been cut off during his winning streak, had met with Dan Enright and threatened to expose the company and *Twenty-One* unless he was paid what he believed he would have won anyway. Enright secretly taped their conversation and then used it to paint Stempel as a blackmailer. Regardless, other *Twenty-One* contestants came forward, and New York's District Attorney got involved. NBC said it would investigate. The network and Jack Barry then publicly announced there was nothing irregular about their quiz shows. A few former contestants came forward to support their lie.

Stempel insisted Van Doren must have been in on the con too, otherwise it wouldn't have worked. Van Doren denied it to a grand jury and then denied it in a meeting with NBC executives. The mounting revelations and evidence couldn't be ignored, yet official action was slow, mostly because no actual laws had been broken. Laws governing game shows didn't exist because it had been assumed they were and would continue to be run honestly.

When the general public learned the truth, it felt betrayed, and the whole game show genre fell out of favor and into disgrace. NBC fired Dan Enright and Jack Barry. The latter was off national TV for seven years (see chapter 23), and Enright moved to Canada to continue his career, albeit honestly. In 1958, numerous shows, including *Twenty-One*, *$64,000 Question*, and *Dotto*, were canceled.

The public followed the congressional hearings on quiz shows in October and November 1959 as closely as those on Watergate and

Nixon in the 1970s. One of the contestants testifying was child actor Patty Duke, who'd competed on *The $64,000 Challenge*. She cheerfully, perhaps too cheerfully, denied that her games were fixed. Then a friendly congressman gently and sweetly asked, "Now, Patty, was everything that you just told us the truth?"

She broke down in tears and confessed that it wasn't.

At the time of the hearings, Charles Van Doren went into hiding. He soon reappeared with a prepared statement he publicly read, pleading guilty to lying under oath and stating, "I've learned a lot about good and evil." Many praised him for coming clean. Others felt it was high time he did so. NBC fired him. He received a suspended sentence. Nobody involved in the quiz show scandals went to jail. And Herb Stempel completed college on his GI Bill and became a New York City schoolteacher.

The hearings resulted in new federal laws, the first of which begins, "(a) It shall be unlawful for any person, with intent to deceive the listening or viewing public," to do 1, 2, 3, 4, and 5, concluding: "(c) Whoever violates subsection (a) of this section shall be fined not more than $10,000 or imprisoned not more than one year, or both."

Limits were mandated as to how much money game show contestants could win and how often. Also, corporate sponsors no longer controlled a show; rather, a given program had a number of sponsors.

Quiz show ratings had been dropping as audiences grew accustomed to the big-money shows. During Van Doren's late-1956/early-1957 heyday, Trendex ratings indicated 54.7 percent of homes with television were watching. By autumn 1958, the percentage was 10.3. Virtually all game shows suffered a decline in popularity. Audiences were wary, bored, and fed up. The big-money era was over (basically until 1999 and *Who Wants to Be a Millionaire?*).

Remaining game shows were more modest in scope and rewards, and questions were easier to realistically answer. The 1960s would usher in a spate of less serious, more fun, and often more risqué shows, many of which are still around.

Lights! Camera! Big Bucks!

Not illegal but scandalous and still semi legendary was the episode of an unemployed ice cream truck driver from Lebanon, Ohio. His adventure played out during the first of three seasons of *Press Your Luck*, a CBS daytime hit that debuted in 1983. Michael Larson had plenty of time to watch the show and study it. *Press Your Luck* featured a giant flashing-lights game board with 18 squares representing a shifting collection of cash, prizes, and Whammys. Whenever one of the wee devils inevitably appeared, it erased a contestant's entire winnings.

The bouncing lights that settled on given squares seemed random but weren't. For weeks, Larson focused on the board's light patterns with the aid of a VCR and its pause button. Taking notes and using slow motion he determined that five light patterns repeated over and over and over. After memorizing them he traveled to Los Angeles and auditioned for *Press Your Luck*, which was hosted by Peter Tomarken (see chapter 23).

Contestant coordinator Bob Edwards later said he'd felt vaguely uneasy about Michael Larson. But director and executive producer Bill Carruthers liked him, so Larson got on the show. At CBS Television City on May 19, 1984, he appeared on the fifth show taped that day, a Saturday. The canny contestant played unremarkably during the first round and even landed on a Whammy on his initial spin. Michael was in third place out of three before the show's second round began.

That's when he initiated his unparalleled winning streak. He used his light knowledge to land on the big-money squares and get extra spins. Because he knew how to avoid the dreaded Whammy he just kept going without using his extra spins. Larson ran a seemingly impossible 40 spins in a row, no Whammys, and initially amassed over $50,000, more than any previous *Press Your Luck* winner.

Host Tomarken recalled, "I knew he was doing something. What it was, I didn't know. I wasn't privy to [the secret of the game board's light patterns]. I just figured that pretty soon I'll be working for him instead of CBS."

The show's staff were dumbfounded, and the control booth froze in panic as Larson proceeded to win $110,237, a record for a single day on any game show. The network aired the spectacular show in two parts on Friday June 8 and Monday June 11. However, CBS charged Larson with cheating and initially declined to pay him his winnings. Attorneys soon determined that the contestant, who'd surely done his homework, had done nothing illegal.

Larson invested most of his earnings in a real estate deal that went bad and was then burglarized of what remained. After he outwitted *Press Your Luck* and its Whammys, the show's game board was reprogrammed with 32 light patterns.

Larson, who wound up working at Walmart, died of throat cancer in 1999 at 49.

From April 2002 through December 2003, the Game Show Network (GSN) aired *Whammy! The All-New Press Your Luck* (hosted by Todd Newton). One March 2003 episode was a rematch that included a tribute to the ebullient Michael Larson and pitted his brother James against the two runners-up from 1984. James won, unspectacularly but minus any competitive advantage. GSN also devised a two-hour documentary titled *Big Bucks: The* Press Your Luck *Scandal.*

9

Password and Allen Ludden

"I LIKE WORD GAMES BEST, AND *PASSWORD* IS DEFINITELY THE BEST word-game show," said celebrity guest Elizabeth Montgomery of *Bewitched*. "It's simple yet smart and entertaining."

An instant hit, *Password* debuted in 1961 on CBS, pitting two teams of contestant and celebrity against each other, using one-word clues to guess the password that was shown to the audience and home viewers. Presiding over the cerebral yet frequently mirthful proceedings was bespectacled, debonair Allen Ludden, a former high school teacher. He hosted *Password* from 1961 to 1967 (daytime and prime-time versions), also from 1971 to 1975, 1979, and 1980.

Guest star and movie actor Barry Sullivan tendered a reason for the show's popularity. "When you watch *Password* you can hardly avoid blurting out your own clue. . . . Alone or watching with someone else, you're soon playing along."

Password required a decent to good vocabulary. "Some people know more words than others," said guest Carolyn Jones (*The Addams Family*), "but on *Password* it's also about thinking fast—coming up with a clue right away. It's also a chance to expand your vocabulary. Let's face it, people judge you by the words you use."

Password sometimes attracted bigger-than-usual stars who enjoyed the challenge and the show's quiet dignity, owed in large part to its host. "Allen's a very smart gentleman," remarked guest Lucille Ball. Other major-star guests included Henry and Jane Fonda (separately) and James Stewart.

In 1962 Milton Bradley, the number one board-game manufacturer, put out a *Password* home game that sold two million copies its first year. There were eventually 25 editions, the second-best-selling 1960s game after *Monopoly*. *Password* on TV also proved popular in Britain, Australia, and New Zealand, and in their own languages in Brazil, Portugal, and Vietnam.

Ludden attributed some of the US show's "non-threatening intellectuality" to its calming, unobtrusive theme music by Robert Cobert, who also created the themes for *To Tell the Truth*, *Blockbusters*, *Chain Reaction*, and the gothic soap opera *Dark Shadows*.

Password's daytime version proved the more durable, with consistently good ratings until they were worn down by ABC's *The Newlywed Game* in 1966. Even so, they were respectable. CBS executive (later head honcho) Fred Silverman disliked game shows and reportedly hated *Password*, which was canceled in 1967 and replaced with a new soap opera, *Love Is a Many Splendored Thing*. The sudser never achieved *Password*'s lowest ratings.

In 1971 ABC reintroduced *Password*, which remained a hit until the network erred by switching it from late afternoon to noon, in direct competition with NBC's *Jeopardy!* In 1974, ABC almost canceled *Password*, but a series of summertime specials boosted its ratings. Among the special programming: a week of Monty Hall hosting *Password* while Allen Ludden and wife Betty White were players.

The network renewed the show for half a year but changed the format to all-celebrities and the title to *Password All-Stars*, which depressed the ratings. Executives forgot that the show's average viewers identified with contestants more than celebrities. The show was canceled in June 1975.

In 1979, it was NBC's turn to revive *Password*, as *Password Plus*. The rebooted show made each password into one of five clues that together named a thing, person, or place. The first team to guess the puzzle won the round. Over the years, the show was kept fresh by features like a lightning round in which the winning team tried to come up with, say, 10 correct answers in 60 seconds to win the contestant a jackpot.

In 1980, Ludden was hospitalized, missing numerous taping dates between March and May. The public was told he was ill but given no details. The durable and popular Bill Cullen assumed Ludden's role while also hosting *Chain Reaction*. When Allen returned to the show, he thanked viewers for the flood of cards and letters they'd sent, and Cullen did a week of shows as a guest.

Ludden's hosting came to an end in October 1980. His cancer operation hadn't been a complete success, and there were complications. He was replaced as host of *Password Plus* by Tom Kennedy (Bill Cullen's brother-in-law). The show was canceled in March 1982.

Two years later, NBC brought back the show as *Super Password*, hosted by Bert Convy until 1989. On January 11 and 12, 1988, a contestant by the name of Patrick Quinn won $58,600, the show's biggest-ever jackpot. A viewer in Anchorage, a bank manager, identified "Quinn" as Kerry Ketchem, a previously convicted felon wanted in Alaska for involvement in a mail-order scheme, wanted in California for mail and insurance fraud, and wanted in Indiana for "the fraudulent purchase of a luxury car."

Two days after the "Patrick Quinn" shows aired, Ketchem was arrested by agents of the Secret Service (originally established to fight counterfeiting). When *Super Password* refused to pay Ketchem his winnings, he tried to sue, arguing that he'd played the game honestly, and his illegal activities had nothing to do with the show. But prior to appearing on-air he'd signed a mandatory agreement in which he gave a false name and Social Security number, thus invalidating the contract. Ketchem was subsequently sentenced to five years in prison.

When *Super Password* was canceled in 1989, host Bert Convy gave Betty White the chance to deliver its final words, stating it was "her show" because it was her fifth appearance on a final episode of *Password*.

A planned 1998 syndicated resurrection of *Password* never materialized, but in 2008, CBS supersized *Password* into *Million Dollar Password*, a dozen episodes of which ran over two seasons, emceed by Regis Philbin, already known as host of *Who Wants to Be a Millionaire?* In 2021 a new edition of *Password* was planned by Fremantle, the European company with rights to a surprising number of classic US game shows. Minus a premiere date, NBC announced that late-night talk host Jimmy Fallon would serve as its executive producer. Fallon and sidekick Steve Higgins now and then played *Password* on *The Tonight Show* with celebrity participants.

Allen Ludden is today remembered almost exclusively for *Password* though he had a long run hosting the *G.E. College Bowl*. It would surprise most people how musically inclined he was. In 1964 RCA Records released *Allen Ludden Sings His Favorite Songs*, which was too antithetical to his image to become a success, let alone launch a singing career. "Some folks thought the album was meant as a joke, sort of like with Mrs. Miller," said *Password* guest Marcia Wallace of *The Bob Newhart Show*. "They never heard Allen's rather charming singing voice."

In 1968, while *Password* lay dormant, Ludden hosted the musical game show *Win with the Stars*. Its two celebrity-and-contestant teams tried to identify several songs within 45 seconds and then had to warble the opening two lines of song lyrics, gaining points for each identified song and each word correctly (if not necessarily tunefully) sung. The show lasted one season.

In 1969, Allen starred in *Allen Ludden's Gallery*, a variety/talk show that Betty White later described as his favorite of all his shows. It was produced by Eltee Productions (as in L.T.), which partnered Ludden with longtime friend Grant Tinker (later married to Mary Tyler Moore and head of MTM Enterprises). The show afforded Allen a chance to sing regularly to an audience. Unfortunately Ludden's pet project was canceled after a few months.

In 1970, Betty White devised her own syndicated show, *The Pet Set*, with Allen as producer and announcer. Animal lover White's guests visited her set along with their pets, most frequently dogs. They included Doris Day, Carol Burnett, Burt Reynolds, Vincent Price, and Merv Griffin. The show lasted 39 weeks.

To backtrack, Ludden was born Allen Ellsworth in 1917 in Mineral Point, Wisconsin. Two years later, the only child's father died at 26 in the global influenza pandemic. Allen's mother remarried, and he took his stepfather's surname. At nine his family moved to Texas, where Allen received his degrees and taught high school in Austin. Serving in the Army during World War II he worked in the Special Services group under English stage actor Maurice Evans (later best known as Samantha's father on *Bewitched*). The men became friends, and Ludden later served as Evans's theatrical manager.

In 1943 Allen married former classmate Margaret McGloin. They had three children. Through Maurice Evans, he began lecturing, which in 1947 led to hosting a radio show focusing on teenagers titled *Mind Your Manners*. In 1951, the program was brought to television by NBC. On its cancellation in 1952, Allen was hired by the New York City Board of Education to produce and host the educational shows *Inside Our Schools* for WNBT-TV and *On the Carousel* for WCBS-TV.

In 1953, producer Grant Tinker interested Allen in hosting a radio quiz program titled *College Bowl*. It originated in Manhattan and via a three-way hookup involved two student teams of four undergraduates each, competing from their campuses. Knowledge was the topic, and scholarship grants for the winning school were the prizes. Allen held other TV jobs during *College Bowl's* run. One was *Dance Time*, a 1954 show on WPIX-TV at 5:00 p.m. featuring high school students dancing to the latest hits. Not long after, he was hired by CBS as a radio program director and as Creative Services Consultant for its TV news.

In 1959, Ludden became nationally visible hosting *G.E. College Bowl*, which CBS introduced to television under the sponsorship of General Electric (GE). The show had the same format as the radio version but more generous scholarships. In 1960 it became the first TV game show to win the Peabody Award for excellence in broadcasting. Its popularity inspired hundreds of high schools to present their own versions of the game. (In 2021, the TV show was revived as *Capital One College Bowl*.)

The following year brought triumph and tragedy. *Password* debuted in 1961, but Margaret, who'd had cancer for four years, became gravely ill. Allen's family opposed his choice of signing with *Password* and giving up his executive position at CBS. He did it for the bigger salary needed for his wife's mounting hospital bills. Allen continued hosting *G.E. College*

Bowl on Sundays, affording him TV exposure six days a week. He had to give up the *Bowl* in 1962 when *Password*'s nighttime version moved to Sunday nights. GE objected to Ludden hosting two shows on the same night and made him choose. Margaret Ludden died on October 31, 1961.

Allen had already met Betty White when she guested on *Password*, but they didn't socialize until May 1962 when they costarred as husband and wife in the play *Critic's Choice* (the film version starred Lucille Ball and Bob Hope). Their first kiss was on stage when their characters kissed. They wed in Las Vegas on June 14, 1963. There was no honeymoon because Ludden had used up all his vacation time, and the day after the wedding they flew to New York to tape *Password*.

In the mid-1960s, the business partners traveled to Columbus, Ohio, to demonstrate QUBE-TV, a TV setup that would give viewers an "unprecedented" 32 channels to choose from. But the idea, tested in Columbus, was ahead of its time. In an era when there were only CBS, NBC, ABC, and a public television channel, the idea of 30-plus TV channels seemed rather preposterous.

After *Password*'s cancellation in 1967 and before its resuscitation in 1971, Allen hosted the aforementioned *Win with the Stars* and *Allen Ludden's Gallery*. Following *Password*'s 1975 cancellation, he hosted a game show similar to *Password* titled *Stumpers*. Its two teams comprised two contestants and a celebrity guessing phrases via three clues. *Stumpers* lasted 13 weeks.

Ludden replaced Bill Armstrong in 1977 as host of *Liar's Club*, in which four contestants had to guess which of four celebs wasn't lying about the function of an unusual object shown at the beginning of each round (the prevaricators included Betty White and future talk host David Letterman). The syndicated show had begun in 1969, hosted by Rod Serling of *Twilight Zone* fame but lasted only six months before returning in 1976. Ludden hosted until its (not final) demise in 1979.

Things were looking up for Allen in 1979 with the revived *Password Plus*. He and Betty White decided to build a vacation house in Carmel, California. However, his health started fluctuating, and in March 1980, he was diagnosed with stomach cancer. Although his operation didn't remove all the cancer, Ludden then felt better than he had in a long time.

The cancer was kept from the public, and Allen returned to hosting his signature show on May 13, 1980.

Construction on the second house continued that summer. On October 7, two days after turning 63, Allen collapsed in Carmel and was in a coma for six days. Doctors found that he'd undergone a stroke-like reaction to the steroid medication used to treat his cancer. Within weeks he was well enough to be moved to Los Angeles's Good Samaritan Hospital. His hosting days were over; his final *Password Plus* episode, taped before the collapse, aired on October 28, 1980. NBC chose to continue the program without him. At Allen's suggestion, his friend Tom Kennedy took his place.

Ludden's swan song was doing radio commercials early in 1981 for the Southern California Gas Company. He died at 63 on June 9, 1981, at the Good Samaritan Hospital.

After the TV networks denied her a hosting position in the 1950s, the 1960s, and the 1970s, Betty White bowed in 1983 as a game show host with *Just Men* on NBC. At the time, female hosts were rare. The show featured two female contestants guessing how a panel of seven male celebs would reply to assorted personal questions. The show lasted only three months but yielded White an Emmy for hosting. Her greatest success (yielding fifth and sixth Emmy wins) commenced in 1985 with the seven-year NBC sitcom *The Golden Girls*.

In 1994, the Game Show Network began televising episodes of the Allen Ludden–hosted *Password* and *Password Plus* to excellent ratings (it later aired and airs on the Buzzr cable channel), and in January 2001 a *TV Guide* poll of "Hosts We Love the Most" was headed by Allen Ludden.

10

Games People Play

UMPTEEN TV GAME SHOWS WERE BEGAT BY POPULAR GAMES. FEWER were inspired by popular board games. Too often the result was or is disappointing. For one thing, board games are do-it-yourselves. Can watching strangers in a TV studio play a necessarily, and sometimes heavily, modified version of a household favorite compare with the gratifying involvement of playing, say, Monopoly at home?

Among board games that bored or scored as TV game shows were *Scrabble* in 1984 and 1993, both hosted by Chuck Woolery but each having little to do with the popular home game. *Boggle* in 1994, from the hidden-word game, had Wink Martindale hosting and was notably complex (his reading the rules at show's opening took a good 90 seconds).

Yahtzee, inspired by the dice game and hosted by Peter Marshall, lasted eight months in 1988 and began with Q and A. Correct answers led to control of the dice. The most memorable thing about the show was coproducers Larry Hovis (of *Hogan's Heroes*; Hovis was also the game show's announcer and a panelist) and Gary Bernstein being arrested for allegedly trying to steal game show property and the ensuing lawsuits. "Game shows," declared Hovis, "are fun for people sitting watching in their dens. They're not really fun and games for the people who bring them into your den or rumpus room."

Monopoly in 1990 was an almost predestined disappointment to the board game's fans. It became basically a Q and A show and lasted three months, leaving behind just a memorable theme song. Its handsome and personable intended host Peter Tomarken was replaced with a contestant (!) by producer Merv Griffin after Tomarken stood up for decent treatment of the female little person playing Mr. Moneybags. That character was gone by the time the show aired. (For more on Tomarken versus Griffin, see chapter 23.)

Pictionary, the visual charades-type game, became a syndicated kids' game show in 1989 hosted by actor Brian Robbins (*Head of the Class*). Additionally, Julie Friedman was "Felicity." Mostly she kept score by means of an instrument resembling a faucet that emitted colored balls into a tank. And arm wrestler Rick Zumwalt was the show's enforcer/judge, "Judge Mental." It lasted less than three months.

Pictionary returned as a syndicated adult game show in 1997, hosted by Alan Thicke. It lasted a whole season. "The financiers think if you have a name-recognition property, be it a board game, bestselling novel, or Broadway hit, they'll have more chance at a hit adaptation. Except look at all the flop movies from popular sources or . . . look at *Pictionary*."

Trivial Pursuit adapts perfectly to a televised Q and A format but didn't have a long run on the Family Channel in 1993–1994, which was hosted by Wink Martindale (early on sometimes billed as Win and sometimes Wing because one network deemed "Wink" too flirtatious). The show resumed on ESPN in 2004 for a season and as *Trivial Pursuit: America Plays*, syndicated in 2008, another season. An Entertainment One (eOne) 2022 version looms with host and coproducer LeVar Burton of *Roots* and *Reading Rainbow* fame.

Is Bingo a board game? If so, it's the easiest one there is. It originated in Italy in the 1500s before spreading to France and then England. It may first have been called Bingo in the US in 1929. Earlier, one name for the game was Beano because beans were used to mark the numbers. Supposedly, an excited winner accidentally yelled "Bingo!" and the name caught on. Over the decades the game has inspired game shows like the following.

- TV bingo was seen in New York City on *Bingo At Home* (1958), an interactive show before there was "interactive." It lacked but didn't miss a studio audience because host Monty Hall called out bingo numbers that home viewers attempted to match with their phone numbers' last five digits.

- *Lingo* combined chance, as in Bingo, and word guessing, specifically five-letter words. Taped in Canada, it debuted in 1987 and was a daily syndicated show cohosted by Michael Reagan, adopted son of Ronald, and Dusty Martell. It lasted half a year; TV critic Ava Mandal blamed its demise partly on the male cohost's "personality-minus."

  In 2002 it was rebooted by the Game Show Network (GSN), and with host Chuck Woolery, it ran six seasons. It was modified by GSN in 2011 (with host Bill Engvall) but expired after two months. Early in 2022 CBS announced its own reboot for later in the year, with RuPaul as host.

- *Trump Card*, a syndicated daily program that debuted in September 1990, was adapted from a UK show called *Bob's Full House*. Donald Trump's entertainment team intended it to stir interest in his three Atlantic City tourist properties by filming at Trump Castle Casino Resort by the Bay (later renamed the Golden Nugget Atlantic City). Emceed by former football star Jimmy Cefalo, the program and its backer had delusions of grandeur, recalled by game show producer Mark Maxwell-Smith (not affiliated with Trump). "The sales pitch for that show was such a bizarre thing.

  "They were touting that Donald Trump himself would occasionally appear on the program. Wow, this real estate investor will occasionally come onstage and take a bow—I'd better circle that in *TV Guide*. Are you kidding?"

  Trump briefly materialized on the premiere show, which involved three players who were given a bingo-style card with 15 numbers in three rows of five that they competed to fill in by answering questions. The show called itself a "non-stop game of knowledge." It stopped in May 1991.

Since the 1980s, Trump had produced and hosted the reality series *The Apprentice* and *The Celebrity Apprentice* (he was replaced as host on the latter by Arnold Schwarzenegger, who later departed due to his feud with the man who alienated most everyone he associated with). Trump also made dozens of cameo appearances in movies, TV shows, and ads while gathering publicity and momentum.

- The steady increase in Bingo's popularity lent ABC high hopes in 2007 for *National Bingo Night*, which was hosted by UK actor and carpenter Ed Sanders, noted for his work on *Extreme Makeover*. Players, selected from the audience, competed for $5,000. The energy level was high despite the program's 60-minute length, but cancellation occurred after six episodes. However, the show was sold to GSN, who reformatted it and retitled it *Bingo America*. The host was Patrick Duffy of *Dallas* and later Richard Karn of *Home Improvement*.

  The new format made it a quiz show that featured drawing balls from a hopper and competing for the letters in the word "Bingo." Correct answers yielded a letter. A contestant could win up to $100,000. Also, home viewers could play via computer technology and win up to $50. Even so, viewership didn't match GSN's expectations and the show ended in 2009.

Several TV game shows derived from Charades. One was *Body Language*, which was hosted by Tom Kennedy. It ran a year and a half from 1984 in daytime on CBS. Its two teams each comprised a contestant and a celebrity, one acting out charades and the other guessing. The charades represented five words in a puzzle with seven blanks. First team to solve the puzzle won.

One fan of the show was Bert Convy. "Charades in your living room is easy. . . . When it's transferred to television you have to supply a new twist, otherwise everyone's doing and watching pretty much the same program."

A frequent celebrity guest on *Body Language* was Lucille Ball. Husband Gary Morton said, "Charades went into a decline once things got more hip . . . rock 'n roll and all that. The kids thought it was for grown-ups and squares. But on her shows, especially in the 1960s, Lucy helped popularize it all over again. . . . She loved playing it. It's a chance to be imaginative and funny and physical."

Bert Convy hosted and coproduced the first two years of the syndicated *Win, Lose or Draw* (1987–1990), a Burt and Bert Production. Convy's partner and pal Burt Reynolds often guested on the show, whose set was patterned after Reynolds's living room. The show's twist on Charades was visual, "sketchpad charades." Players used an easel to draw a clue to help their team guess correctly—within 60 seconds. The two teams each comprised a contestant and two celebrities.

Win, Lose or Draw's two-year NBC version was hosted by Vicki Lawrence (*The Carol Burnett Show*) and its third, syndicated year by Robb Weller (*Entertainment Tonight* cohost). Friends of Burt Reynolds such as Charles Nelson Reilly, Rip Taylor, and Dom DeLuise considerably enlivened the show.

The longest-lasting Charades game show began as *The Game* in 1939 on W6XAO, an experimental TV station atop a car dealer's garage in Los Angeles. It was the pet project of future host and producer Mike Stokey, attending LA City College at the time. In 1947, it became *Pantomime Quiz* on KTLA TV, which began commercial broadcasting that year. In 1949 WCBS in New York started broadcasting it, and the show went national in 1950 via CBS as a summer replacement.

Pantomime Quiz lasted through the 1950s as a summer program, airing eventually on all four commercial networks: ABC, CBS, DuMont, and NBC. (Its theme song was "Huckleberry Duck.") In 1953 Stokey moved it from Los Angeles to New York City. Two teams of four players competed to guess a name, phrase, or quote in the least time possible. Celebrity regulars included Carol Burnett, Robert Clary (*Hogan's Heroes*), Jackie Coogan (former silent child star and Uncle Fester on *The Addams Family*), Angela Lansbury, Vincent Price, Robert Stack (*The Untouchables*), and Dick Van Dyke.

Pantomime Quiz was the first TV show to win an Emmy Award. It won Most Popular Program on Television in 1948. (Of course, there wasn't much competition yet.)

The show returned in 1962 on CBS for one season and was renamed *Stump the Stars*. It was still via Mike Stokey Productions and still emceed by him after Pat Harrington Jr. hosted the first 13 weeks. Among the debut guests were Jayne Mansfield, British bombshell Diana Dors (married to Richard Dawson), Ross Martin (*The Wild Wild West*), and Jerry Lewis.

Stokey returned with a syndicated *Stump the Stars* in 1964 that lasted slightly more than half a year. Debut guests included blonds Tab Hunter, Mamie Van Doren, Joyce Jameson (of Roger Corman comedy-horror fame), and Connie Stevens. A syndicated 1969 *Stump the Stars* lasted a year. Modeled after Mike Stokey's series was the syndicated all-celeb (the game was played for charity) *Celebrity Charades*. It too lasted a year and was hosted by ventriloquist Jay Johnson and his dummy Squeaky (Johnson costarred on the sitcom *Soap*).

In 2005, *Celebrity Charades* revived, for five episodes anyway (also played for charity), on the AMC channel. It was inspired by parties at the home of then-married actors Hillary Swank (two-time Best Actress Oscar winner) and Chad Lowe (he hosted).

Cards and Las Vegas–style games have inspired numerous game shows, though most formats necessarily include some form of Q and A.

- *Card Sharks* cards were the size of movie posters, but the program was simple: two players in a game of five-card High Low. Control of the board went to the contestant who more closely guessed—higher or lower—than their opponent how 100 people polled answered a given question. It premiered on NBC in 1978 and lasted 3½ years and was hosted by Jim Perry. From 1986 to 1989 on CBS its host was Bob Eubanks and, in syndication from 1986–1987, Bill Rafferty. It reemerged for a few syndicated months in 2001 with Pat Bullard and was revived in 2019 on ABC prime time with Joel McHale.

    "For contestants," said Perry, "this is about as easy as a show gets. . . . Cards still hold a certain glamour, and guessing outcomes is as old as civilization. . . . *Card Sharks* isn't high-brow, which is part of its appeal. It demonstrates the importance to a popular show of appealing visuals, enthusiastic players, and a host who tries to treat his players like personal guests."

- *Gambit* was based on blackjack, where players try to obtain cards with a face value totaling 21 and no more. Dick Clark auditioned for the 1972–1976 CBS show, but the job went to Wink Martindale (who had a 1959 song hit with "Deck of Cards"). Two husband-and-wife teams answered general knowledge questions. If correct, they could retain or discard a playing card from an oversized deck. If a duo didn't achieve an exact score of 21, they had to come as close as possible without exceeding that number before the other duo did.

  The first team to win two games won and proceeded to the Gambit Board of 21 cards where they could win prizes. So why wasn't the show titled *Twenty-One*? Because the unrelated show with that title had been a major player in the 1958 quiz show scandals.

- "The game where knowledge is king and lady luck is queen" was *The Joker's Wild*, a major comeback in 1972 for host and coproducer Jack Barry, who'd been disgraced in 1958. In 1969 and 1971, he got to host two shows that lasted but 13 weeks each. This Q and A show's categories were supplied its two contestants by what looked like a slot machine. If one of the board's three windows displayed a Joker, the $50 question's value doubled. Two Jokers increased the value to $200, and three Jokers were an automatic win. The first contestant to earn $500 won and got to play the Bonus Game.

  Spicing things up were the Bonus Game's Devils, whose appearance, like Whammys on *Press Your Luck*, eliminated the winner's Bonus winnings. However, the winner had the choice to quit at any time.

  CBS dropped the show in 1975, but a syndicated version ran from 1977 to 1986. Barry hosted until his sudden death in 1984 (see chapter 23). He was replaced by the Dean of Game Shows, Bill Cullen. A syndicated edition in 1990 with Pat Finn lasted one season. On TBS in 2017 and TNT in 2018, it was hosted by Snoop Dogg, whose favorite game show it was while growing up. It was canceled in 2019

- *High Rollers* with Alex Trebek and *The Big Showdown* with Jim Peck both premiered in 1974 (the latter on ABC for one season). Each was dice-inspired and featured large dice and a Vegas-y look. Control of the dice on *High Rollers* was determined by two players answering a toss-up question. The object was to eliminate all nine numbers on the game board through any combination of numbers on the rolled dice. For example, if one rolled nine, one could eliminate the nine or a combination like five and four. A player lost by rolling an already displaced number; thus, one could cede the next roll to the competition to avoid rolling a possibly losing number.

High Rollers ran on NBC from 1974 to 1976 and 1978–1980, and was syndicated in 1975–1976, all hosted by Trebek, and one syndicated season in 1987 with Wink Martindale. During its first run, the dice were rolled by female "assistants" who included Ruta Lee, Elaine Stewart, Leslie Uggams, and Linda Kay Henning of *Petticoat Junction*.

Big Showdown was oriented more like Q and A. A target number of points was given at the game's start. Correct answers earned points. One of three contestants was eliminated before the Final Showdown. Its winner was escorted to a dice board to roll special dice—one die had the word SHOW on one of its faces, and the other had DOWN. If the player rolled up SHOW and DOWN the prize was $10,000. At best the odds were 1 in 12 that that would happen, so when it didn't, the player got 30 seconds to keep rolling, trying for the lucky combination that would then bring $5,000. It didn't happen often.

That fact and the game's lack of suspense compared with *High Rollers* may have worked against *The Big Showdown*. Another possible limiting factor was that *High Rollers* had a significantly bigger production entity behind it (the men who produced *Hollywood Squares*).

And then there are more recent game shows that don't restrict themselves to one type of game. Nor, in these two cases, to heterosexual hosts. In 2013 Jane Lynch emceed *Hollywood Game Night* on NBC. It was cocreated and coproduced by Sean Hayes, the gay actor who played one of the two gay characters on the pioneering sitcom *Will and Grace*.

The cocktail-party-style show presented a casual game night while boasting six celebrities and two contestants—two 4-person teams. Each episode lasted 42 minutes (ergo an excessive 18 minutes for the hour's commercials). There were five games per episode, involving knowledge, questions, visual and audio clues, wordplay, and "*guessing*, the core of most games," reminded TV critic David Sheehan. "If you guess and you have at least one other individual to compete with, you've got a game. How long its fun lasts, that depends."

Unofficially, *Hollywood Game Night* probably ran six seasons due to a break during COVID, after which more episodes were ordered. NBC didn't formally renew the show (2013–2020) for a seventh season.

In 2017, Ellen DeGeneres spawned *Ellen's Game of Games*, which ran four seasons on NBC prime time. It ceased when she concluded her eponymous talk show's 19-year run. The sometimes goofy and over-the-top show derived from game segments of Ellen's daytime talk show. They included "If I Could Turn Back Slime" (title via Cher's song hit "If I Could Turn Back Time"), "Blindfolded Musical Chairs," "Tuba Toothpaste," and "Mt. Saint Ellen."

Selena Walker, an audience member from 2019 who is also a hospital nutritionist, reminisced in a 2022 blog, "In my forties I can appreciate the fun and challenges of Ellen's game show. I enjoyed spectating . . . not sure I'd want to be up there doing it. . . . I also realize how game shows seem to have gotten, well, dumbed-down and how celebrities seem to be a prerequisite, along with heavy marketing."

But the games, all sorts, continue, and the last three years have seen more reboots and upcoming reboots than ever before.

The Wheel and the Pyramids

The parlor game Hangman inspired more than one game show. Among the earliest, *Down You Go* debuted in 1951 on the DuMont TV network. On prime time it ran through 1956 after airing on all four networks. On DuMont, CBS, and ABC its host was Northwestern University English professor Bergen Evans and, on NBC, Bill Cullen.

Down You Go's four celebrity panelists tried to guess common phrases, expressions, and song titles submitted by home viewers hoping for cash prizes if theirs was used, and more if it stumped the panel. After the game initiated with a clue, each panelist asked one question about the phrase and then it was time to guess which letters were part of the phrase.

In 1974, Merv Griffin Enterprises shot a pilot for the Hangman-inspired *Shopper's Bazaar*, hosted by Edd "Kookie" Byrnes from the TV series *77 Sunset Strip*. The retitled show bowed on NBC on January 6, 1975, as *Wheel of Fortune*, with a different handsome host, Chuck Woolery. Griffin had to persuade the reluctant singer-actor to give hosting a go. Ironically it was Griffin who let Woolery go in 1981 after a salary dispute, replacing him with local weatherman Pat Sajak.

Wheel was more involving than *Down You Go*. Three players (no sedate celebrities) in turn spun the big wheel that could bestow penalties or cash amounts that enabled guessing at a consonant that might fill in a blank of the first round's word puzzle. When necessary, a contestant could buy a vowel. The biggest money winner got to play a solo bonus round, added in 1981; assorted other changes have kept the show lively and fast-paced.

Susan Stafford was the original "letter turner," manually revealing each letter of the puzzle. She departed in October 1982, replaced successively by three women, the third of whom was Vanna White (a *Price Is Right* contestant in 1980) in December 1982. Because of the breakup of his second marriage and losing *Wheel of Fortune*, Chuck Woolery attempted suicide but was found by friends and taken to a nearby hospital.

In 1989 Sajak ceded *Wheel's* daytime edition to former footballer Rolf Benirschke, succeeded six months later by Bob Goen. Sajak hosted an eponymous late-night talk show that went up against Johnny Carson's *Tonight Show* and failed. Meanwhile Pat and Vanna's nighttime partnership was proving popular. Where Susan

Stafford's had been a womanly, fashionable presence, Vanna came off more like Sajak's kid sister who liked to play dress-up, favoring flashy eveningwear and assuming model-like poses. Her unique first name didn't hurt as she became famous through magazine publicity, the TV movie *Goddess of Love*, her memoir *Vanna Speaks*, and playing herself in the big-screen *Naked Gun 33 ⅓* (1994).

In 1992 *The Guinness Book of World Records* declared White the world's number one clapper, putting her hands together for *Wheel*'s players 140,000 times per season, an average of 720 times per episode. She weathered the 1996 scandal of being listed among "madam to the stars" Heidi Fleiss's celebrity clients, who were mostly males. Two of Heidi's "girls" penned *You'll Never Make Love in This Town Again*, recounting their alleged adventures with celebs from Warren Beatty to Vanna White.

Wheel's greatest success began late in 1983, thanks to King World's aggressive syndication, nighttime viewing with bigger prizes, and luck. Said Sajak in 1984, "It was a matter of timing and the general state of the syndicated market. . . . There isn't very much out there. And *M*A*S*H* is getting a little weary . . . we can all say the lines with the characters. I think we filled a nice void at the right time."

In 1984 *Wheel* replaced *Family Feud* as TV's top-rated syndicated series. In turn, *Wheel of Fortune* was dethroned in 2011 by *Judge Judy*. But the wheel spins on, and Pat and Vanna are signed through the 2023–2024 season.

(Dick Carson, *Wheel* director, was Johnny Carson's brother, and producer Nancy Jones was a chaperone on *The Dating Game*.)

The $10,000 Pyramid (1973) was another hit launched during the 1970s. It had little to do with pyramids (the show's were flat-topped anyway) and more than a little resembled *Password*. Bob Stewart, whose company produced the *Pyramid* series, had worked for *Password*'s Mark Goodson and Bill Todman. Both shows comprised two teams of a celebrity and contestant giving descriptive clues to try and elicit answers. A *Pyramid* team chose one of six categories and then tried to guess seven words to do with that category in 30 seconds. Clues on *Password* were limited to one word, but on *Pyramid* an entire sentence was acceptable.

After three rounds of two categories per round the team with the most points entered the Winner's Circle. The bonus game had the contestant guessing six categories on the board in 60 seconds from a list of brief clues given by the celebrity partner (e.g., a cloud, an airplane, and a radio broadcast might all be "things in the air"). Moving up the pyramid earned the winner $10,000. The fastest-ever celebrity to clear all six categories on the pyramid was Billy Crystal in 1978 in 26 seconds.

When *The $10,000 Pyramid* debuted on CBS hosted by Dick Clark, it fared moderately in the ratings. Clark ignored criticism of his low-energy style, insisting that the game was exciting enough. The show's popularity built, and when it transferred to ABC in 1974, ratings jumped. In 1976 it was retitled *The $20,000 Pyramid* (that's inflation!). It ran till 1980.

It was unrealistic to use a figure in the show's title because it kept changing. But the various *Pyramid*s' popularity kept it and Dick Clark as a game show host afloat for a long time. A syndicated *$25,000 Pyramid* (1974–1979) was hosted by veteran Bill Cullen, followed by Clark's syndicated *The $50,000 Pyramid* for a season in 1981, and then back to CBS with Dick from 1982 to 1988 for *The New $25,000 Pyramid*, partly concurrent with Clark's syndicated *$100,000 Pyramid* from 1985 to 1988, after which he stepped down. Whew.

Then came a two-season *$100,000 Pyramid* in 1991 hosted by handsome grinner John Davidson and a 2002 two-season merely titled *Pyramid* with Donny Osmond. *The Pyramid* in 2012 lasted one season with Mike Richards, the public revelation of whose bigoted comments cost him the coveted *Jeopardy!* hosting position after Alex Trebek (later, Richards also "was exited from his post as executive of both *Jeopardy!* and *Wheel of Fortune*"). Black former football star Michael Strahan became host of ABC's revived and ongoing *$100,000 Pyramid* in 2016.

In 1981 Dick Clark told the *Washington Post*, after confessing his short attention span and unenthusiasm for game shows, that *The $20,000 Pyramid* was the best game show ever. The series has had fervent fans. Patty Duke affirmed, "It's so challenging! I love being on it though my blood pressure soars." Guest player David Letterman felt, "Man, that is some show!" and game show icon Arlene Francis said, "My husband Martin enjoins me to keep silent while he watches, which I'm glad to do . . . I leave the room."

William Shatner got so upset after blowing a clue that cost the contestant the bonus round's big-money prize that he picked up his chair and hurled it outside the Winner's Circle. (What would Mr. Spock say?)

11

The Match Game

THE *MATCH GAME* DEBUTED DECEMBER 31, 1962, SUPPOSEDLY THE result of a Goodson-Todman producer named Frank Wayne asking coworkers to jot down one fact about elephants. The goal was to see how many answers matched.

Hosted by Gene Rayburn, the NBC show ran to 1969, returned several times, and is still running. The most successful version ran from 1973 to 1982, which was also hosted by Rayburn. However, the first version began sluggishly. Unlike the second, which pitted two contestants against each other and boasted six celebrities, the original had two teams, each comprising two contestants and a guest star. Rayburn would read an easy question like Name something you pour gravy over or a fill-in-the-blank phrase like (Blank) and gravy. The six people jotted their answers, results were compared, and the team with the most matching answers won. Exciting, no?

Mark Goodson had intended *Match Game* to be quietly cerebral, akin to *Password*. It didn't work out that way, owing to Gene Rayburn, who a year previously was declined as *Password* host in favor of Allen Ludden. Gene tried to up *Match Game*'s energy quotient by injecting jokes, imitations, and distractions like impromptu chats with people from offstage. Goodson fired off memos stating Rayburn's laughs were detracting from the show. Gene responded that there wasn't that much show to detract from.

In 1965 when the show's future was in doubt, question writer Dick DeBartolo, who also wrote for *Mad* magazine, started penning questions in a more risqué way. For instance: Mary likes to pour gravy on John's (blank). Gene heartily approved and (blanks) were in. Ratings rose, and *The Match Game* ran another four years. It became popular and was presented as a comedy show.

The Match Game returned on CBS as *Match Game '73* (its name would be updated annually). During the more freewheeling 1970s, the show became TV's top-rated daytime program; Mark Goodson once appeared on set to make the fact widely known. The show boasted more celebrities than any other besides *Hollywood Squares*, which had nine. One reason *Match Game* attracted so many was there were no wrong answers, and thus, celebs never looked dumb. Actor-director and acting coach Charles Nelson Reilly offered, "Many famous people aren't very bright, which if they went on *Jeopardy!* or *Password* would soon become obvious. But on *Match Game* your ability to produce laughter trumps your I.Q."

When the mid-1970s sitcom *Welcome Back, Kotter* starring comedian Gabe Kaplan and his four "sweathogs" became a hit, *Match Game* invited the cast to audition. Kaplan was tied up, but Robert Hegyes, Lawrence Hilton-Jacobs, Ron Palillo, and John Travolta showed up. Celebrity coordinator Kay Henley recalled, "We played the game with them. . . . Travolta was such an ass and every other word out of his mouth was (bleep). I realized he was just a kid, but still it was a disappointment. The more he acted up, the more the other boys did.

"But Ron and Bobby could play the game and we did use them—Ron more than once. And Bobby did *Tattletales* later on." (Hegyes and Palillo died prematurely.)

Match Game's celebrity panel counted three regulars. Orson Bean, who guest-hosted *The Tonight Show* more than 100 times when it was New York–based and then guested almost 100 times, wasn't one of them. Bean was a regular on *To Tell the Truth* "for six or seven years" before moving to Australia. "Mark Goodson never really forgave me for that. I came back a year and a half later and the producer wanted me to be a [*Match Game*] regular. They had an open seat . . . but Mark said, 'No, he can guest . . . but not a regular.'"

The regulars were Charles Nelson Reilly, Richard Dawson, and Brett Somers, wife of actor Jack Klugman. After he did various Goodson-Todman game shows Klugman requested the company to aid his marriage by inserting "my loudmouth wife" into one of its shows, as she was "desperate" to work. Somers became a lively but controversial *Match Game* fixture, a vocal buttinsky sometimes fueled by alcohol and often critical of other celebs. (The marriage didn't last.)

Late in 1977, CBS made a big mistake, switching *Match Game '77* from afternoons to mornings. Teenagers constituted a good percentage of the show's audience, watching after returning home from school. Ratings dropped. Three months later, the network returned it to afternoons, but by then, many stations had substituted local programming and viewers, especially teens, didn't resume the afternoon habit. The show held on until April 1979.

Dawson, whose *Family Feud* success swelled his ego, left *The Match Game* in 1978, two years after achieving his goal of hosting his own show. Many *Match Game* viewers had felt he was too domineering. Reilly offered, "Richard is a ham, like me. Unlike me, he felt being part of a celebrity lineup was beneath him. . . . He seemed to believe he was the show's cohost."

Dawson drew as much or more laughter as any other celeb and was the favorite of contestants when it came time for a winner to select one star in a bid for major money. Frequent guest Marcia Wallace from *The Bob Newhart Show* put it down to "Dickie being English, so average contestants thought he's the smartest one."

The Match Game board game, brought out in 1963 by Milton Bradley, proved a favorite with home players. The company purveyed classics like *Chutes and Ladders* (1943), *Candyland* (1949), and *Yahtzee* (1956), as well as myriad games based on quiz shows and sitcoms, from *Hollywood Squares* to *Laverne and Shirley*. The original *Match Game* board game featured some 100 cards with six questions per card, a scoreboard, and six crayons. Its object was matching a partner's answers.

Ultimately there were six editions, as well as pricier versions. The Fine Edition's cards were slick rather than cardboard, the Collector's Edition came in a leatherette case that buttoned closed, and the Briefcase Edition was housed in a hard plastic case with handle for chic transport.

With *Match Game*'s 1973 revival, the board game was reintroduced and updated; however, the questions were more kid-friendly than on TV, frequently in the manner of "Name a kind of store" or "Name a kind of muffin." Not too thrilling, yet the 1970s board game went through three editions. Milton Bradley also had hits with board games of the show's UK version, *Blankety Blank*, and its Aussie version, *Graham Kennedy's Blankety Blanks* (the well-agented host's name was part of the show's title).

Goodson-Todman employee Gil Fates, in charge of foreign productions, helped adapt overseas versions to local cultures while keeping an eye on ratings. Though the most popular international programs were in the UK and Australia, there were also foreign-language versions in Germany, Holland, Mexico, and francophone Canada.

In 1975 a weekly prime-time version, *Match Game PM*, was introduced. The syndicated series ran for six years. After the daytime Monday through Friday series was canceled in 1979, new daily episodes were shot for syndication until 1982. There was still life in the old (blank), and in 1983 *Match Game* resurfaced on NBC as half of *The Match Game/ Hollywood Squares Hour*. The block was a TV first, made possible by Mark Goodson Productions (Bill Todman had died) acquiring rights to *Squares* from the film company Orion, which held them at the time.

The initial idea was to combine *Match Game* with *Jeopardy!*, but one was a guessing game and the other a knowledge game, whereas *Match Game* and *Hollywood Squares* were both guessing games. Gene Rayburn was back, but Peter Marshall wasn't. Sha Na Na singer Jon "Bowzer" Bauman hosted the *Hollywood Squares* half. Each host was a panelist during the other host's half. During the second half, a third tier of three celebrity seats was added for the nine instead of six celebs. The "stars" mostly weren't as special as in the versions in the 1960s and 1970s, and by 1983 Paul Lynde, the cynosure of *Hollywood Squares*, was deceased.

"Mark Goodson made a mistake in hiring Jon Bauman," Gene Rayburn later opined. "He took him out and bought him a whole wardrobe for the show, then ended up spending an hour after each show telling him what he did right and [usually] what he did wrong."

Bauman had guested on the 1970s *Match Game* in *Grease*-type costume as "Bowzer," his naturally curly hair slicked back. Gene's daughter Lynne Rayburn pointed out, "Bauman had been 'Bowzer' to the public for years. He performed at Woodstock and was always in that character . . . [there was] no real familiarity with Jon Bauman outside that character. For the viewers, it was like a total stranger was hosting *Hollywood Squares*."

There were complaints about the modern but "cheesy" set, the age discrepancy between the hosts (who reputedly didn't get along), the fact that some contestants and celebrities played one game better than the other, and the energy level between the two halves sometimes varied. Charles Nelson Reilly, who guested on the *Hour*, felt, "*The Match Game*'s convivial party atmosphere was missing . . . so was the pizzazz and enthusiasm from *The Hollywood Squares*.

"I'm sorry, but just do one thing well. Don't try two things half-assed!"

Peter Marshall said, "I kind of hate to admit that I was happy when it didn't even last one season." (It lasted 39 weeks.)

Next it was Gene Rayburn's turn to get shafted. The youthful Gene was older (born 1917) than he looked. Though Mark Goodson was on the fence about rehiring him for a planned new *Match Game* edition on ABC, Rayburn was the leading contender. But as luck and ageist discrimination would have it, a 1989 episode of *Entertainment Tonight* wished Gene a happy birthday and stated his age: 72. Suddenly he was "too old" to host and no longer hirable.

The host hunt was on. Several dozen males were considered. Offbeat choices weren't out of the question. Rumor had it that Goodson offered the job to Jamie Farr of *M*A*S*H*. In 1986 he'd hosted the unsold pilot of *Oddball* and in 2006 narrated *The Real* Match Game *Story: Behind the Blank*, a one-hour documentary for the Game Show Network.

In the end an established host was chosen, Bert Convy, who was 16 years younger and a 1970s *Match Game* guest best known as host of *Tattletales*. Rayburn once hosted *Tattletales* while Convy sat in as a player. "I found out the producer was saying to him, 'Why don't you try doing this . . . the way Rayburn would do it?' It had to do with the way he moved his body when he was hosting. Convy told the producer, 'I can't do that. I would never turn my back on camera.' He wasn't loose. He was a tight guy."

Convy shot the pilot for the 1990 *Match Game* but was soon too ill to host. He died the following year from a brain tumor. Mild-mannered comedian and talk host Ross Shafer (Rayburn's junior by 37 years) was brought in to host. The new edition's set was markedly different, based on art deco (no more orange shag carpeting), and there was just one regular, the valiant Charles Nelson Reilly.

Ambidextrous ventriloquist Ronn Lucas was later added as a regular after an earlier ventriloquist was let go because he couldn't write answers (fill in the blank) with a different hand than the one he used to maneuver his dummy. Former regular Brett Somers guested briefly. "Without Gene it didn't work. . . . The boy left out the humor, he played it too straight. He didn't host with authority or the zip Gene Rayburn had. And *still* has!"

Ratings weren't as high as hoped, and critics perceived a diminished uniqueness among most of the celebs. Said Somers, "The word 'clone' is applicable. Not to sound like Norma Desmond, but we had personalities then." Shafer stated that ratings were "very good . . . but the continuing interruptions with the first Gulf War coverage lost millions for ABC. So they wanted to cut corners anywhere they could. When this happened . . . ABC [was offered] an extra half hour of *The Home Show* for free. It solved the network problem and we were bounced" in 1991.

Announcer Gene Wood admitted, "When Rayburn did it, he was in charge. I told Ross, 'You're one of the stars . . . you've got to get them to accede to your wishes.' But it was hard for him." Betty White, who appeared on the 1990–1991 version as well as prior *Match Games*, noted, "Ross was very nice. . . . But with six celebrity egos you can't be *too* nice . . . you need to be a bit of a lion tamer."

Elliot Feldman, who wrote for the 1970s and 1990–1991 *Match Game*, held that the latest iteration overemphasized the game and ignored the fun. "Ross left out the jokes, and that to me was a mistake. . . . People tuned in to the show not for the game, they tuned in for the interaction." Reilly had characterized the Rayburn *Match Game* editions with "This is not a job; it's a social engagement."

Die-hard fans felt the rules had been needlessly changed for the sake of change. "The classic *Match Game*," observed Marcia Wallace, "was less fussy . . . and easier to follow. It flowed better."

After *Match Game*, Shafer became a public speaking coach and author.

Like a boomerang, *Match Game* kept returning. Minus Mark Goodson Productions and also Mark Goodson, who died in 1992 (see chapter 4). In 1997, a pilot for yet another *Match Game* was shot, which was hosted by Charlene Tilton from *Dallas*. The new producers adjudged the result not "fun" enough—not that the prior show was either. Some insiders whispered sexism after a male host (who was 40 years younger than Rayburn) was hired: talk host and actor Michael Burger. He carped, "I got passed over for Charlene Tilton. . . . She shouldn't be hosting that any more than I should be the love interest on *Dallas*. It just didn't make any sense." Tilton remarked, "I have hosted a few things . . . [and] if it's the right thing it's fun."

The 1998 *Match Game* (a resurrected *Hollywood Squares* bowed the same year) carried over the art deco set but reduced the celebrity panel to five and dropped the previous version's choice of A or B questions for categories more suited to puns. The four regulars were George Hamilton, comedian-accordionist Judy Tenuta, Nell Carter, and Vicki Lawrence. The fifth celeb rotated on a weekly basis.

Michael Burger explained, "We [booked] some soap opera stars and whomever else we could get that wanted to play," for the fifth spot.

Some critics felt the show had been dumbed down. *Match Game* expert Ashley Hoff stated, "The questions were less dependent on clever double-entendre and often featured a more, shall we say 'obvious' sense of humor." Writer Elliot Feldman said where the Ross Shafer version skimped on humor, "The [Michael Burger] version was almost the opposite—too many jokes . . . it kind of bogged [the game] down." Burger admitted, "The angle we went with was to make the show very funny." It was canceled in 1999.

Burger, who idolized the 1970s *Match Game* and its host, attested, "We tried to make Gene Rayburn proud. I wanted that show to work more than anything." After *Match Game*, Burger was the warm-up comedian from 2010 to 2015 for live audiences watching the taping of *Hot in Cleveland*.

In 2006, *Match Game* was showcased as a DVD boxed set, *The Best of Match Game*, that featured the original 1960s pilot and a tribute to Gene Rayburn. A 2006 six-week charity *Game Show Marathon* hosted by

Ricki Lake included one week of *The Match Game*. The same year, *Match Game* reruns were the number one program on the Game Show Network, almost a quarter century after its final original episode.

After *Celebrity Family Feud* proved a summer success in 2016, ABC chose to revive *Match Game*. Movie actor Alec Baldwin was picked to host and made an executive producer. "Hosting a game show is certainly not the only thing I want to do in life," but he confessed the money was "very generous" and the work schedule light, also that the network was helping fund his charitable foundation.

The Hollywood Reporter approved Baldwin "carrying over Rayburn's love for in-character clue readings, [like] a dismal-but-terrific Mick Jagger impression." The show was racier than ever and besides trying to recreate the 1970s spirit provided spirits a-plenty. Executive producer Jennifer Mullin proclaimed, "We encourage a party spirit" (among celebrities and not contestants).

Guest celeb Wendy Malick: "They got us all in a room together for an hour, hanging out and having cocktails." Chris Colfer: "I wasn't expecting to have a full bar when I walked in!" Writer Chancellor Agard reported after a taping, "Each time the show paused for a commercial break, a man dressed in all black would walk on stage carrying a tray of drinks for the celebrity panelists."

Ana Gasteyer cooed, "It's a gorgeous bar, and a good-looking bartender." Malick added, "They have pretty much anything you want and they encourage you to drink, heavily. That's the secret to this show's success." Cheryl Hines informed *Entertainment Weekly*, "I've been here since 8:30 in the morning and I have been drinking since then. It's like college days." But not like the best of *Match Game*. Nonetheless as of this writing the show continues.

"Mark Goodson's original idea," summed up Virginia Heffernan in the *New York Times*, "was for a kind of guess-what-I'm-thinking show. . . . That soon became boring, and matches were not frequent enough. Someone suggested turning to bluer material, or at least hinting at blueness, and the rest is history."

Game Show Network and Buzzr

Viewer demand for reruns of classic game shows—often more interesting and distinctive, likewise their hosts—helped popularize the Game Show Network (GSN). It began with a 91-word letter from broadcasting business consultant Dick Block to a friend at Sony (owners of Columbia Pictures), asking if Sony would be interested in helping start a game show channel.

Block had learned that dozens of thousands of hours of game show videotapes lay dormant in company vaults. It would be easy to provide programming for such a channel if the companies agreed. GSN launched in 1994, its success perhaps more of a surprise to insiders than the public.

"I was completely mystified by the success of Game Show Network," said longtime Bob Stewart Productions employee Francine Bergman. "To my way of thinking, we were just cranking these shows out and once they were played, they were done, no looking back."

Game shows, usually low man on TV's totem pole, hadn't automatically been considered for reruns. But recent decades' overall decline in creativity and memorable guest-star and hosting personalities boosted GSN's ratings, as did tougher times and nostalgia.

GSN was soon creating original programming about game shows—interviews and documentaries—and devising new game shows and then rebooting some older ones.

Growing demand led to Buzzr in 2015. Owned by Fremantle (a division of the German Bertelsmann Group), it started as a YouTube channel and went on to amass a library of 154 game show series, roughly 40,000 episodes. The first show it broadcast was the pilot for *Let's Make a Deal*.

Buzzr used to broadcast three hours a week of educational children's programming, as mandated by the Federal Communications Commission, but under the Trump administration, that was diminished to one hour. Not as prolific as GSN, Buzzr airs some paid programming and "infomercials" during lower viewership hours.

The success of GSN and Buzzr inspired networks and cable channels to devote more time to game shows. Betty White remarked early in 2021, "Too much escapism may not be healthy, but if watching a few game shows a day makes someone feel happier, I say go for it!"

12

Host with the Most: Gene Rayburn

SOME CALLED HIM THE HOST WITH THE MOST, POSSIBLY THE BEST game show host of all. Born in 1917 to Croatian parents—his father died while he was a baby—Eugen Peter Jeljenic grew up in Chicago. Fond of stepfather Milan Rubesah, Gene took his surname, modifying it to Rubessa. A would-be opera singer and lifelong music lover, Gene moved to New York after a year of college.

Singing lessons in Manhattan proved too costly, so Gene sought theatrical work. He was nearly broke when a friend helped him land a job as a pageboy at NBC Radio in Rockefeller Center in 1936 (future *Hollywood Squares* host Peter Marshall was also a pageboy there). "Gene Rayburn" took announcing lessons at night in the same class as future *Today Show* host Dave Garroway.

In 1940 Gene wed Helen Ticknor, his wife for 56 years. In 1942 they had their only child, Lynne. Rayburn had become a radio announcer but during World War II enlisted in the Air Force, where he manned B-17s as a bombardier-navigator. In 1946 he became half of radio's first two-person morning team, on WNEW's *The Jack and Gene Show*. When Jack Lescoulie left after six months, it was retitled *Rayburn and Finch*. For the next seven years Gene and (male) Dee Finch hosted what became New York City radio's most popular program.

NBC planned to move the show to television in 1953, but Finch declined, and Rayburn was on his own. In 1954 he became the first announcer for *The Tonight Show*, starring Steve Allen. Gene also acted on TV dramas. From 1958 to 1960, his was the voice of Pontiac in their radio and TV ads. For one of the latter, he appeared in a dream sequence, talking to himself. Because it was live, a double was used, wearing a toupee with a fake nose and fake Slavic cheekbones like Gene's. The double was Peter Marshall.

In 1960 Rayburn starred on Broadway in the hit musical *Bye Bye Birdie* after Dick Van Dyke left the show to try his wings on prime-time TV. Gene's understudy was Charles Nelson Reilly. In 1961, Gene became one of the rotating hosts of NBC's radio series *Monitor*. He stayed with the show for a dozen years. After *Birdie*, Rayburn toured in the musical comedy *Come Blow Your Horn* and appeared in 1962's *Aqua Carnival*. He relished acting but as a game show host was offered few opportunities. From 1961 to 1965, he hosted the Miss Universe Pageant before turning it over to Bob Barker.

Rayburn had made his game show hosting debut in 1955 via Mark Goodson-Bill Todman Productions' *Make the Connection*, an NBC summer replacement in which four celebrity panelists—one was Betty White—tried to guess the connection between two or more contestants (inspired partly by *What's My Line?*). It lasted less than three months; original host Jim McKay had departed after four weeks.

Rayburn's next hosting gig lasted fewer than three months: a 1956 Goodson-Todman all-kiddie game show inspired by *Beat the Clock* titled *Choose Up Sides*, featuring two teams of four children each (what fun).

Before *Match Game*, Gene Rayburn had less success hosting than guesting on shows like *The Name's the Same* from 1954 to 1955. In 1956 he was a substitute host for Jack Barry on *Tic Tac Dough*, but in 1958 hosted his own game show, the music-themed *Dough Re Mi*, which ran through 1960. "I didn't start out to be a game show host," he later declared. "I would say to anybody starting out, don't stick to one thing . . . vary your interests as a performer. Do different things. It'll make you a better 'whole' entertainer."

In 1962 Rayburn took over *Play Your Hunch*, another Goodson-Todman show, which had been running for four years. Its original host was former singer Merv Griffin. After his departure, ratings fell. Five weeks in, NBC dismissed a stunned Gene. (Announcer Johnny Olson got a chance to host on two separate days during Griffin's absence. *Play*

Your Hunch was Olson's first Goodson-Todman show. He went on to announce more than 15 of their series during a 27-year period. It's rather a mystery why he never became a regular host.)

Serendipitously, Rayburn being out of a job left him available for Goodson-Todman's upcoming *The Match Game*. Producer-director Ira Skutch "persuaded the management to give Gene a chance and not penalize him for NBC's precipitous decision. It proved ideal for 16 years in its two separate runs."

While not hosting, Rayburn kept busy on the stage. In the mid-1960s, he, his wife, and daughter costarred in the generation-gap comedy *The Impossible Years*. Gene wished to move to the West Coast where *Match Game* was filmed but Helen didn't, so he flew to Los Angeles every two weeks and taped 12 shows over one weekend. He later regretted not making the move. "Except for stage, L.A. is where it's at for TV comedy, for drama, game shows, also motion pictures. . . . Hosts almost never get hired for movies but you know, you can't play if you're not at the table."

Flying back and forth, Gene's needlepoint helped pass the time. Other hobbies numbered gardening, gourmet cooking, and woodworking. To keep fit, he bicycled, skated, played tennis and croquet, and rode his Honda motorcycle.

Match Game guest Orson Bean noted, "He was the least robotic game show host. . . . When *Match Game* began, the powers that be wanted him behind a podium or at any rate standing still. No way! Gene was all over the place. He'd lie down, get down on one knee, he'd come up behind you and tickle or kiss you. He flirted with everybody, he had no fear. He was puckish and a classy clown.

"His motto was: Whatever happens, keep the camera rolling. Mistakes are human, audiences enjoy them."

The fun Rayburn created on his show drew other game show hosts as guests, among them Steve Allen, Bob Barker, Bill Cullen, Bob Eubanks, Art Fleming, Art James, Tom Kennedy, Allen Ludden, Peter Marshall, and Dick Martin. In 1967 *Tonight Show* host Johnny Carson paid an impromptu visit to humorously harass sidekick Ed McMahon, who was guesting for a week. The following year, McMahon hosted *Match Game* for a week while Gene Rayburn sat in as a celebrity panelist.

Sports stars who might have avoided *Jeopardy!* and *Password* gladly guested on *The Match Game*. In 2003 Mickey Mantle's *Match Game* contract from 1966 fetched $2,500 on eBay. Included was a letter thanking the baseball star for guesting and stating that a check was enclosed for $649.10 (after taxes) for the episodes airing on May 30 and 31 and June 1, 2, and 3.

Like Paul Lynde on *Hollywood Squares*, Gene had some stellar fans. Fred Astaire thoroughly enjoyed his characterizations as Old Man Periwinkle, who figured in many *Match Game* questions. Gene received several letters and phone calls from the legendary former dancer. Lauren Bacall appeared on the show more than once because she was a big fan of the show and its host.

But Gene's life wasn't all sunshine and (blanks). Peter Marshall offered, "Goodson-Todman never paid him well. For as big a star as he was, he was vastly underpaid. I was kind of the first guy to make a lot of money because I kept saying, 'I don't want to do this,' and I would quit, so they'd pay me all this money."

In 1970, a car accident briefly landed Rayburn in the hospital (he'd broken his leg skiing in 1957). In 1972, his new home near Cape Cod burned down. He invested in a skating rink that Marshall said also burned down. However, Gene co-owned a profitable Cape Cod factory that manufactured plastic brick facing for interior and exterior house use.

In 1972–1973, he was a semi-regular panelist on a syndicated revival of *I've Got a Secret*, which was hosted by Steve Allen. He hosted a failed pilot for *Celebrity Match Mates*, which later proved a success as *Tattletales* hosted by Bert Convy. *Match Game '73* then "saved his life," said guest Debralee Scott. "He said . . . those were the nine most hectic but happiest years of his life."

Following the unpopular *The Match Game/Hollywood Squares Hour*, Rayburn hosted a revival of *Break the Bank* in September 1985. When the producers didn't get *Match Game*–type ratings they let Gene go in December. He was replaced with a younger man, Joe Farago (later an infomercials host), but the show left the air the next September. Gene's final show was *The Movie Masters* for the American Movie Classics cable channel, involving movie trivia. It aired now and then during 1989–1990.

Peter Marshall had starred in the national company of the hit gay-themed stage musical *La Cage Aux Folles* and late in the 1980s Gene visited him for a week. "He wanted to do that show so badly. I said, 'Go after it!' So he finally did," returning to acting in 1991 at the famed Bucks County Playhouse in New Hope, Pennsylvania.

When the Game Show Network started airing 1970s *Match Game* episodes in 1994, they brought the host a new generation of fans as the show became its top-rated offering.

In 1996, Gene's wife Helen died. Insiders said he was lost without her, and his health began deteriorating. In 1998, he moved to Los Angeles, reportedly to be closer to his game show colleagues. But heart trouble caused a move back East. In 1999, he moved in with daughter Lynne in Gloucester, Massachusetts, for the final months of his life. In October that year he was finally recognized with a Lifetime Achievement Award by the National Academy of Television Arts and Sciences. In November 1999, Gene Rayburn died of congestive heart failure at 81.

Like most people, TV producer Howard Felsher liked Gene "a great deal" but felt "he didn't become the big star he wanted to be. . . . He wanted to be a star like Marlon Brando. Not like a he-man, but he wanted to walk down the street and everybody recognize him."

Game and talk show producer Burt Dubrow said, "I don't think he died knowing how good he was," and revealed, "The moment that camera went on, he turned on. . . . Off camera he was quieter. I would call him a bit of an intellect. He knew a little about everything and he was fairly serious. On camera, he was just up and high as a kite."

According to California State University professor of media psychology Stuart Fischoff, "The best example of a TV game show being raised to a rare level by its host, with format and host ideally complementing each other, is *The Match Game* and Gene Rayburn."

Behind That Voice

Number one game show announcer Johnny Olson (1910–1985) was the youngest of 11 children born to Norwegian parents living on an 85-acre dairy farm in Minnesota. (Wonder if he knew Betty White's Rose Nyland?) Whereas Briton Noel Coward developed his distinctive clipped speaking voice due to his mother's hearing handicap, Olson developed his vocal style due to his mother's problems with English. "Because of her interests and demands I amplified an average baritone voice into one that is loud and clear."

By 14, Johnny was working part-time in a jewelry shop. After high school he got a radio job in Poynette, Wisconsin, at "The Friendly Farmer Station" before becoming, at 18, the youngest station manager in the US at KGDA in South Dakota. By 1938 he was performing with a five-piece jazz band, the Rhythm Rascals. He continued in radio, announcing and hosting umpteen shows—more than 20 half-hour shows a week, including quiz shows, in 1949 alone.

When television came along, he was in the thick of it, hosting the first daytime network TV program to come out of New York, *Johnny Olson's Rumpus Room*, a variety show airing daily on the DuMont network from 1949 to 1952. When game shows became popular, Olson announced *I've Got a Secret*, *To Tell the Truth*, and *What's My Line?*, among others. Later, *The Match Game* and *The Price Is Right*. Johnny opened the 1970s version of the former with "Get ready to match the stars!" and, on the latter, after a contestant's name was read, shouted the invitation, "Come on down!"

"I never realized how good [Johnny] was until I tried to do a show without him," said Gene Rayburn. *Match Game* producer-director Ira Skutch noted, "He was not only the best at what he did, he was the most even-tempered person I have ever known, always pleasant, cooperative, and helpful."

In no particular order, eight of the most famous game show catchphrases follow

"Come on down!" *(The Price Is Right)*

"I'd like to buy a vowel." *(Wheel of Fortune)*

"Will the real [John Doe] please stand up." *(To Tell the Truth)*

"Is that your final answer?" *(Who Wants to Be a Millionaire?)*

"Enter and sign in, please!" *(What's My Line?)*

"Say the secret word." *(You Bet Your Life)*

"I'll take door number [two]!" *(Let's Make a Deal)*

"You are the weakest link—goodbye!" *(The Weakest Link)*

13

They Get Dumb Ideas

Confetti-loving comedian Rip Taylor recalled asking "a [game show] producer how their companies come up with great ideas? He said that first they get dumb ideas. . . . But some of those get made into shows too, you know." Taylor hosted *The $1.98 Beauty Show*, which actually ran two seasons.

"It's hard to predict what'll have legs"—that is, what will last— explained producer and TV personality Dick Clark. "Some concepts sound lame, but lots of lame pilots get picked up. A few do very well." He cited a 1956 show about pricing items of merchandise that became the long-long-running *The Price Is Right*. "Lame or not, it's the audience that determines success or oblivion."

Producer Ira Skutch noted that networks and syndicators often green-light dubious projects because "They're afraid to miss out on the next big thing. . . . No one has a crystal ball, and a well-thought-out or logical or likeable game idea may or may not yield a big viewership."

What Are the Odds? (1958) was meant to impress with big facts of life and seriousness. Presented as a syndicated game show, it mostly delivered random facts and figures (e.g., reassuring viewers that "The odds are 100,000 to one against your being in a train wreck"). Back when there were three channels and the two alternatives might have been a wrestling match and yet another western, that may have been entertaining enough—for one season anyway.

Sometimes a concept wasn't bad, but its execution wasn't good enough. Walter Kiernan and later Mike Wallace hosted *Who's the Boss?*, which aired on ABC prime time for six months in 1954. It used the then-popular format of four celebrity panelists to try and ferret out who a secretary contestant's famous boss was. The boss in question might be a performer, a big-city mayor, or hotelier Conrad Hilton. Most famous people have a secretary, and public curiosity about working for such a one is understandable, though learning how smoothly the relationship ran and what the employer's personality was like was unlikely.

"I tuned into that show," said psychologist Dr. Joyce Brothers. "Even at the time, I found it somewhat cutesy and sexist. The tone of the questions was sometimes grating. . . . The secretaries were definitely condescended to."

Too, there were celebrity panels and celebrity panels. Some panelists were nationally known, like radio comedian Fred Allen and columnist Dorothy Kilgallen, both on *What's My Line?* The *Who's the Boss?* panelists were actress Polly Rowles, actor Dick Kollmar, *Saturday Review* travel editor Horace Sutton, and Sylvia Lyons, married to *New York Post* columnist Leonard Lyons. Not being famous didn't mean personality, zest, and charm were lacking; nor did it necessarily make one interesting.

In 1959, the show was revived as an NBC prime-time summer replacement, which was hosted by Mike Wallace. The title changed to the monetarily more interesting *Who Pays?* The panel was reduced to three: Oscar-winning actress Celeste Holm, actor Sir Cedric Hardwick, and actor/disc jockey Gene Klavin. Contestants could also be a famous person's cook, butler, hairdresser, tailor, and so on. The boss, employing an assumed voice, could issue comments from an offstage booth. The debut's stars were Oscar-winning actor Red Buttons and Broadway star Carol Channing.

Nonetheless *Who Pays?* ended with the summer. So did Mike Wallace's 10-year hosting career. He began narrating *Biography* in 1961, joined the CBS news department in 1963, and was part of the original *60 Minutes* team in 1968, remaining with the show until 2008.

More than one show that didn't work was later brought back with new hopes and a new title. The syndicated *Oh My Word* was hosted by Jim Lange of *The Dating Game* in 1966. It was the brainchild of San

Francisco State College professor Arthur Hough, debuting locally (only) in 1965. Two celebrity guests tried to decide which one (only) of four panelists was giving the correct definition of an unusual word. Despite Lange's easygoing presence, *Oh My Word* ran only a season. Too many critics thought the concept and execution stuffy or "overly academic."

Its true-or-false concept was similar to *Liars Club*, which debuted in 1969, hosted by *The Twilight Zone*'s Rod Serling, and ran one season. Four contestants tried guessing which of four celebrity panelists was correctly describing the function of an unusual object. The syndicated show returned in 1976, which was hosted by Bill Armstrong and, ironically, Allen Ludden from 1977 to 1979. Ironic because Ludden hosted the most famous word game show of all, *Password*. Few quiz shows have zeroed in on words, and fewer have been hits.

Liars Club was more visual and comic, dealing with bizarre objects and not words. In 1988 it returned for another syndicated season, with host Eric Boardman. Perhaps it wasn't a coincidence that the program's most successful run, in the 1970s, included "celebrity liars" like David Letterman, Betty White, Dick Gautier of *Get Smart*, and comedian Larry Hovis of *Hogan's Heroes*. Guest panelists also included game show hosts Bill Cullen, Peter Marshall, Tom Kennedy, and Bob Eubanks.

The word-oriented *Oh My Word* returned in 1982 as *Take My Word for It*, again syndicated, again hosted by Jim Lange, and again lasting one season. There was an audience for such shows but not big enough, and the words were usually too obscure to relate to or remember. One, nowhere near the longest, was "piddock," defined by the *Oxford Dictionary* as "a bivalve mollusk which bores into soft rock or other firm surfaces." It was too dull for too many viewers.

Of the many shows hosted by Jim Lange he deemed *Oh My Word* his favorite. A longtime disc jockey and sports announcer, he felt more at home on radio than TV. "I've worked here, worked there . . . have done this and that . . . but most people only remember me from *The Dating Game*." He admitted that precious few remembered him for his two word shows or had even heard of them.

Surprisingly—or not, in view of the success of their *Password* (1961)—Mark Goodson and Bill Todman produced the 1965 NBC daytime show *Call My Bluff*. Hosted by Bill Leyden, its two teams of two contestants and one celebrity tried to deliver the correct definition of an obscure word. Though the company recruited hosts Gene Rayburn, Bill Cullen, and Art James as guests, the program began in March and ended in September.

Also word-related was the syndicated September-to-December 1967 flop *It's Your Move* (with host Jim Perry). Two players battled two players by bidding how much or how little time it would take to mime particular words to their partner. What were the producers thinking?

Contrasting with *Oh My Word*, whose reboot, 16 years later, went practically unaltered, was *On Your Way*, a September 1953 prime-time DuMont offering. It was sponsored by Welch's (Welch's Grape Juice was originally advertised as "Dr. Welch's Unfermented Wine"). *On Your Way* ran seven months, total. Hosted by Bud Collyer, it was a Q and A show where a contestant chose a destination, and each correct answer got them one-fourth of the way to said destination. The contestant ending up with the most correct answers won a trip to the destination. Proving the program had heart, it sometimes awarded a runner-up a trip to the hoped-for destination if their story was sad enough.

On Your Way had a clever enough concept but perhaps not enough time to find its audience. A number of long-running shows took time to become popular. In January 1954, the show switched to ABC. Its new hosts were John Reed King and Kathy Godfrey, sister of TV star Arthur Godfrey. In February, its original premise was abandoned, and *On Your Way* (now to what?) became a talent show with its audience deciding who won. In April the show was on its way—to oblivion.

Besides (just) word games, another game show category that usually fared poorly was joke-telling. In olden, less well-funded days, what could be cheaper than a show, especially on radio, of comedians eagerly telling jokes? But a format of joke after joke after joke palled, and according to "closet game show fan" Robin Williams, "The aggression . . . and desperation of the average stand-up [comic] plying his trade in a nakedly competitive format can be hard-going for civilians."

One such show, *Stop Me If You've Heard This One*, bowed in 1948 on NBC with a three-comedian panel that included Morey Amsterdam (future game show host and *Dick Van Dyke Show* fixture). Viewers mailed in jokes that the host (Roger Bower and then Leon Janney) read aloud. If a panelist recognized the joke, they stopped the host and told the rest of it. If the comic didn't supply the correct ending, the home viewer received a gift. Coproduced by Irving Mansfield, husband of future novelist Jacqueline Susann, the show stopped after little more than a year.

Tag the Gag, another NBC prime-time show, also had a comedic panel. They competed in trying to guess the punch lines to jokes acted out by a group of performers. The panel again included the gleeful Mr. Amsterdam. *Tag the Gag* lasted two weeks in 1951.

Draw Me a Laugh was a four-week 1949 ABC prime-time production that didn't use jokes but supplied a gag line. A cartoonist did sketches based on ideas supplied by home viewers. A studio contestant was simultaneously given the gag line but not the cartoon idea and within two minutes had to draw a sketch. A quartet of audience members decreed which of the two cartoons was funnier.

Another let's-laugh entry was *Draw to Win* (CBS prime time, April to June 1952). The show found four panelists guessing the caption of a cartoon based on a home viewer's idea. Ideas used gained viewers $5 each—more, if the caption was not guessed. A cartoon example was a man being drawn out of the water by a Southern belle. Its caption: "Saved by the bell." Audiences back then were more easily satisfied.

"In a movie, the script is everything," said actor-director George Clooney's father Nick, who hosted *The Moneymaze* on ABC daytime from December 1974 to July 1975. "In a game show, it's the formatting." *Moneymaze*'s sizeable maze, with one spouse (from on high) guiding the other through it toward the prize, was ridiculed as too gimmicky, diverting attention from the Q and A game element. The handsome, personable Clooney had the potential to be a popular game show host but . . . saddled with an inevitable flop like that?

Host and former baseball star Joe Garagiola (*Joe Garagiola's Memory Game*, among others) believed, "Celebrities bring in audiences. If the concept's okay, a famous face can make the difference in getting renewed. At least for the second season."

As the years wore on and ratings grew more important, many shows tried to up the ante with celebrities (e.g., *Jackpot Bowling* in 1959–1960 and separately 1960–1961). Because bowling is a sport, the first host was baseball eminence Leo Durocher. He lasted two weeks and was succeeded by assorted sports figures. (The two bowlers competed for a $1,000 weekly payoff.) When the NBC prime-time show returned in 1960, its host was the network's biggest star, Milton Berle, who was not a sportsman. The version not hosted by a celebrity lasted five months, and Milton's six months. Star power didn't prove potent.

Don McNeil was better known as host of ABC Radio's *The Breakfast Club* (1933–1969) than the ABC Sunday afternoon game show *Take Two* (1963). Four celebrity guests were shown four photos on a screen—say, a politician, an actress, a dog, and an actress. They had to figure out what two of the four had in common; in this theoretical case, two were both actresses. Tough, huh? The format was weak, and after a few weeks, the celebrities were cut down to two. The producers realized a weak concept couldn't be much enhanced by celebrity presence. Three months and it was over.

Sometimes a concept sounds okay, even cute, but audience disinterest and critical reaction finally and fatally underline its flaws. *Double Up* lasted seven weeks on NBC in 1992 and featured a real-life brother and sister trying to pick "an ideal date" for each other and simultaneously match the studio audience's choice. Reviewers founded it "forced and intrusive" and even "semi incestuous," which it was not.

Proving that even winners can't predict a likely negative outcome (or they imagine that past success might neutralize it), *Let's Make a Deal* host and coproducer Monty Hall hosted and coproduced the 1977 NBC three-month flop, *It's Anybody's Guess*. Two competing contestants tried to guess whether five audience members would give a predetermined answer to a question (e.g., Name a frequent guest on *The Tonight Show*; the selected answer was Don Rickles). If a contestant thought one person out of five would give that answer he could play for a point, if one person out of three then two points, and so on, with the first competitor to achieve five points winning the game. But who really cared?

Sometimes a snazzy title hid the thinness of a concept, as in 1996 with *Secrets of the Cryptkeeper's Haunted House*, which was more puerile than juvenile. Someone at CBS with a green light must have liked the title. Or a titular concept was enough to sell a show, as with *The Guinness Game*, a one-season syndicated 1979 show that went through two hosts and was based on *The Guinness Book of World Records*. Three contestants guessed whether a particular record-breaking feat could be accomplished on the show or accomplished, period. Each individual was given $1,000 and could bet as much as 90 percent of it. After three rounds, or feats, the player with the most money left was the winner. Hip, hip, hooray?

In 1958 former kiddie show host Dick Van Dyke hosted *Mother's Day* on ABC daytime. It lasted less than three months and, despite good intentions, was sexist even then because it judged three women on their "homemaking skills," such as being able to choose a hard-boiled egg from four eggs or select a four-pound steak from six steaks (for hubby, no doubt). The winning contestant was pronounced Mother of the Day, and the grand prize among her merchandise was a mink coat—no comment! From a "golden age" extreme of limitations and pigeonholing to an age of no limits to bad taste. . . . In 2008 the G4 cable channel presented the one-season low titled *Hurl*. The show, created, produced, and perpetrated by Tom Crehan and Dale Roy Robinson, had no host and no director. Its winner was simply the last contestant to puke (or not puke).

14

Let's Make Deals!

CANADIAN GAME SHOW HOST AND PRODUCER MONTY HALL HAD A SIGN in his office that read "You can learn more about America by watching a half hour of *Let's Make a Deal* than you can from watching Walter Cronkite for an entire month." What that said about America is open to interpretation.

Sometimes a game show becomes distinctive minus creative input or planning. *Let's Make a Deal* didn't start out with audience members wearing kooky costumes. That began in 1964, less than a year after the show, via Stefan Hatos-Monty Hall Productions, debuted in 1963. Dozens of audience members were selected before the show as that episode's possible traders. To catch the host's attention, eventually a few arrived in attention-getting getups.

Soon they became the show's trademark; that, plus potential and actual contestants excitedly jumping up and down. No other game show's audience boasted "Indian" braves, brides, convicts, Santas, devils, scarecrows, doctors, clowns, and people dressed as dice.

The program dealt in trading: Contestants swapping items they'd brought along and also pricing and guessing games for prizes hidden in outsized boxes or behind doors that could be worth plenty or might be "zonks," prizes almost nobody would want or couldn't take home, like an elephant, although one runner-up did insist on taking delivery of a llama.

Hall would deal with one, two, or three people on a given swap, heightening the tension by offering them varied options. The finale was two contestants given the choice of trading again for the Big Deal of the Day, which lay behind door number 1, door number 2, or door number 3.

Quietly perky announcer Jay Stewart was also Monty's sidekick, often bringing in trays of merchandise or participating in zonks (e.g., inside a giant box was Jay, dressed as a toddler and licking an oversized lollipop).

Unlike, say, *The Price Is Right* with its revolving roster of models ominously known as Barker's Beauties, *Let's Make a Deal*'s model Carol Merrill remained on the show for its entire network run, 1963–1976 (it also ran in syndication from 1971 to 1977).

Boldly, gleefully lowbrow, *Let's Make a Deal* quickly became the butt of jokes and was roundly dissed in the media. Despite its excellent ratings success in daytime on NBC, it wasn't considered for a nighttime version until 1967 as a summer series. Naysayers chortled when it was scheduled against *The Ed Sullivan Show* on Sundays. The surprise was that *Let's Make a Deal* became the first program to compete successfully with that long-running hit show.

When *Let's Make a Deal* left NBC's daytime schedule in 1968 for ABC, the former lost millions in revenue, and ABC became the number one daytime network. To publicize the move to ABC, Monty Hall did surprise walk-ons on *The Dating Game*, *The Newlywed Game*, and *Dream House*.

In 1972 he guest-hosted *Password* when host Allen Ludden played against wife Betty White. Hall guested on among others *The Tonight Show*, *The Hollywood Palace*, *Phil Donahue*, *Geraldo*—for a game show legend tribute—and *The Rosie O'Donnell Show*. A sometime actor, he appeared on *That Girl* (as a dentist), *The Odd Couple* (twice), and *The Wonder Years*. He executive-produced *The McLean Stevenson Show* (1976–1977) and played General Sam Brewster in the telefilm *The Courage and the Passion*, a 1978 pilot for an NBC drama series that didn't eventuate. The same year, Monty toured cross-country in the musical comedy *High Button Shoes*.

But mostly, besides *Let's Make a Deal*, Monty Hall did benefits and fundraisers. He was the most charity-oriented game show host ever.

To backtrack, he was born Monte Halparin in Winnipeg, Canada, in 1921, as the older of two sons. His father ran a meat market. Once asked if he were "a proverbial Jewish child prodigy" Monty replied,

"I'm not sure I was ever a child." A serious scalding accident was followed by double pneumonia during an era when prescribed drugs were intermittently effective, and pneumonia wasn't "just" something that killed off seniors. "It was very touch and go," remembered Hall, who was forced to miss a year of school.

Parents Rose and Maurice tutored him at home. Once the lad returned to classes, he kept skipping grades until he graduated high school at 14. The Halparins didn't have enough money for Monte to attend college, and he was too young to get a job, so his father hired him as a delivery boy. By 1938 he'd saved enough to enter the University of Manitoba but only for one year. He returned in 1940 and earned a bachelor's in science in chemistry.

In his memoir *Emcee Monty Hall*, he admitted he'd volunteered to join the Canadian army but was rejected, though he'd been in the Canadian Officers Training Corps (similar to the US's ROTC). Hall was also rejected three times when he applied to medical school. During college, he was a disc jockey. After graduating, he relocated to Toronto and radio station CHUM, where his boss urged him to legally change his name. In 1947 Monty married actress Marilyn Plottel, whom he'd met at university. They had two daughters and a son.

On CHUM, Hall hosted a radio quiz show titled *The Auctioneer*, the prototype for *Let's Make a Deal* almost two decades later. In 1949, Monty started his own production company and devised a quiz show, *Who Am I?* (which famous person?), that he tried in vain to sell to the Canadian Broadcasting Corporation (CBC). Eventually it was syndicated and lasted more than a decade. Hall debuted on Canadian TV in 1953 with *Matinee Party* but, by 1955, was only hosting *Who Am I?*, which paid modestly. That year he moved to Manhattan looking for work.

When Gene Rayburn departed the local quiz show *The Sky's the Limit*, Hall replaced him. The show folded the following year, which saw Hall introducing oaters on *Cowboy Theater*, which soon folded. In 1958, he hosted a local but pioneering interactive show, *Bingo-at-Home*, that had no studio audience because the players were at home. Later that year, he hosted *Keep Talking* on CBS for three months; its poor ratings were nothing new to the emcee.

In 1958 he hosted four weeks' worth of *Twenty-One* on NBC while host Jack Barry did a nightclub tour. That suddenly ended when a contestant contacted the district attorney to charge that the show was fixed (see chapter 8). Hall then did three months with a local New York TV show and some sports announcing. In 1960 he was tagged to replace Jack Narz as emcee of *Video Village*, a popular CBS daytime game show based on a Milton Bradley board game. Its two players were "pieces" who walked the village's three streets. Finally, Hall had a hit show. When it moved from NYC to LA, he moved his family to Beverly Hills. *Video Village* closed shop in 1962.

The same year, Hall produced his first game show, *Your First Impression*, for NBC with Bill Leyden hosting. Also in 1962, Hall teamed with producer Stefan Hatos to form Hatos-Hall Productions, which in 1963 sold their concept *Let's Make a Deal* to NBC. For almost 30 years, Monty Hall would host his own show. Despite its enormous success, NBC declined to schedule it regularly in prime time, so in 1968 Monty and company decamped to ABC, where the show crushed the NBC competition and became the year's top-rated daytime program.

Let's Make a Deal remained popular through the early 1970s. Hall only missed hosting 30 or 40 episodes out of some 4,700, due mostly to injuries or flu. He later informed TV historian David Baber that the show was sometimes hazardous to his health. "People with football helmets jumped up to kiss me and the face guard would give me a smack in the head. Others wearing boxes put together rapidly at home with pins sticking out would scratch me or people jumped up and knocked me down the aisle."

By 1976 *Let's Make a Deal*'s ratings were sagging, so the syndicated version moved to the Las Vegas Hilton for one more season. Hall had already branched out into acting and also did a mildly popular Vegas nightclub act. From 1969 to 1979, he served as Hollywood's honorary mayor.

In 1972, Hatos-Hall sold *Split Second* to ABC, which was hosted by veteran Tom Kennedy. The easygoing Hall clashed with the show's producer Stu Billet. "I used to come into the office and say, 'Don't be so hard on these people.' The difference between Stu and myself was that if someone asked a question and the answer was 'Marie Antoinette' and the contestant answered 'Maria Antoinette' Stu ruled them wrong. I was furious. I said, 'This is not life or death. This is a quiz show.'

"We used to have fights about that. Even on *Jeopardy!* today they rule people out if they get a syllable wrong . . . they shouldn't be that way."

(Actress Markie Post was a staff researcher on *Split Second* and later worked on *Double Dare* for Mark Goodson Productions.)

After *Let's Make a Deal* left the air, temporarily, Hall hosted a CBS revival of the often inane *Beat the Clock* in 1979. *The All New Beat the Clock* lasted one season. "I hated it with all my heart. The people were asked to do stupid stunts. . . . I'm so glad it wasn't successful."

A new syndicated *Let's Make a Deal*, a season's worth, filmed in Vancouver, Canada, debuted in 1980. In 1984, Hall was back with *The All New Let's Make a Deal*, which was done in Los Angeles; it lasted two seasons. *Split Second* returned in 1986, was taped in Canada, and was emceed by Monty Hall, who after its one-season revival announced his retirement from hosting.

But he wasn't done yet. In 1990 NBC resurrected *Let's Make a Deal*. By then, its iconic host wasn't interested in emceeing—4,700 episodes were enough. He helped find a new host, auditioning people in person and on tape. After three months game show announcer Bob Hilton was selected. The show taped at Disney World in Florida, where a big studio was built specifically for the show. Sadly, the show and new host (or vice versa) drew minimal interest.

NBC informed Hall that if he didn't take over as host, the show would be terminated. "It was a very, very sad blow to Bob and . . . I didn't want to do the show again. But to save the show I went down to Orlando and did the next three months." Monty wasn't too disappointed when after a single season the show was canceled in 1991. He was able to give up hosting at age 69.

In Toronto in 1947 Monty Hall had joined Variety Clubs International (VCI), which helps underprivileged children around the world, raising money "to build hospital wards for the sick and camps for the disabled." An especially active member, during and after *Let's Make a Deal*, Hall annually made 60 unpaid cross-country appearances to host telethons, auctions, and other fundraisers.

"We are very scrupulous about the money and how it's raised and the cost of raising it. Everybody is a volunteer and our international board pays their own expenses to attend meetings. I love this charity because all the money goes to the kids."

Hall earned more than 500 humanitarian awards and raised more than $1 billion to benefit VCI's children's charities. In 1975 he became its international president, in 1977 its chairman of the board, and in 1981 was named international chairman for life. The game show host and producer rated his TV work third in importance, after his close-knit family and his charity work. "It was my television stardom that enabled me to help raise the money for Variety Clubs International."

His wife Marilyn became an award-winning producer of movies for television, among them the pioneering Alzheimer's-themed *Do You Remember Love?* Daughter Joanna Gleason appeared on TV and in movies and won a Tony Award. TV director Sharon Hall, his other daughter, produced *Let's Make a Deal*'s 2003 edition (her husband coproduced the TV series *The Practice*). His son Richard won awards as a documentarian and television producer.

Monty's retirement from TV hosting wasn't static. He continued fundraising, performed speaking engagements, and hosted *Let's Make a Deal* for conventions and organizations. Sadly, his wife Marilyn predeceased him by four months. Monty Hall died in Beverly Hills of heart failure in 2017 at age 96.

A dozen years after Monty Hall last hosted it, he agreed *Let's Make a Deal* should be brought back, somewhat ironically via NBC. "They knew it was too popular to keep buried," said previous *Let's Make a Deal* director Joe Behar. "But then greed and bad taste interfered. . . . The caliber of network executives seems to decline every generation or so."

The 2003 version, hosted by Billy Bush of the Texas political family, was protested by more than a few loyal viewers. "They must have wondered why a fun, tried and tested format was trying to become blatantly sexy," observed Behar. "I'm also surprised they didn't rename it *Who Wants to Make a Million Dollar Deal?*"

The first episode's first deal presented three males, one dressed in a kilt, one in a grass skirt, and one in a toga. Three female contestants were given the choice of reaching up between a man's legs to grab hold of the prize he had hidden in his nether garment or accepting a $500 payoff.

Monty explained, "I turned down about 19 out of 20 suggestions. I let that one go through. I was not happy with it, I was disgusted with it. But you should have seen the stuff they tried to put past me."

Five such episodes were filmed. Three aired, and then the reboot was booted off. Asked if NBC would ever air the other two episodes, Hall exclaimed, "I don't care! I don't want to do a *Deal* like that ever again!"

Six years later, CBS learned from NBC's mistake and revived the show without tampering with it. Probably the biggest change was host Wayne Brady, who was born in 1972 in Georgia of West Indian parents. Raised in Florida by his grandmother, he graduated from the University of Miami and, by 2009, was known to TV viewers for various projects. He'd been a regular on the comedy improv show *Whose Line Is It Anyway?*, which was hosted by Drew Carey and then Aisha Tyler, and had his own eponymous talk show. He acted on *How I Met Your Mother* and other series.

With more than a passing interest in music, Brady was the original host of the game show *Don't Forget the Lyrics!* and appeared on Broadway during the 2015–2016 season in the musical hit *Kinky Boots* (music and lyrics by Cyndi Lauper) as Simon, who's also Lola, a drag queen. Wayne was Grammy-nominated for his cover of Sam Cooke's song "A Change Is Gonna Come" and, after winning on *The Masked Singer* as "Fox" in 2019, was a guest panelist on that show.

As a child, Wayne stuttered and was often bullied. The recurring anxiety that caused lasted a long time. Like Drew Carey, who replaced Bob Barker on *The Price Is Right* in 2007, Brady has suffered from—in his case clinical—depression and, in 2014, had a mental breakdown on his 42nd birthday. He's married twice and has one daughter.

Monty Hall made appearances on *Let's Make a Deal* in 2010 and 2013 and did promotional publicity photos with Brady early in 2017. Until his death, Hall was credited as "Creative Consultant" on the show.

"Monty was proud of his show's continuing success," affirmed Joe Behar. "When he passed, the latest *Let's Make a Deal* had been on some eight years, and now [in late 2019] a decade. . . . Few shows can match that record."

In 2022 the program continues with Brady. "In my humble opinion *Let's Make a Deal* succeeds today because not only are we one of the best straight game shows, but we have fun and don't take ourselves seriously."

- TV game shows involving shopping, swapping, bartering, and marketing made their mark early on. CBS Radio had a hit (1941–1951) called *Missus Goes-a-Shopping* that it brought to television in NYC only in 1944. It was partly stunt-oriented (e.g., competing female shoppers raced through a supermarket balancing several soaps in one hand). In 1948 it was retitled *This Is the Missus* and included even more stunts (e.g., women blowing up balloons until they exploded and a blindfolded man kissing three women before selecting the one who was his wife). That all ended in January 1949 (shopping is serious business!).

  It's in the Bag (not to be confused with one of *The Price Is Right*'s pricing games), on NBC in 1952, was one of the first daytime game shows. Its set resembled a grocery store, and when a contestant entered, a bell rang. The host, or seeming store manager, asked the questions. Each player's shopping bag filled up via correct answers. The first right answer earned 6 cans of food, the second was worth 12, and third, 24. A fourth correct answer yielded an appliance. Straightforward but possibly not too exciting, *It's in the Bag* lasted a month and a half.

- The first nationally televised shopping show, *Cash and Carry*, premiered on June 20, 1946, on the DuMont network. Its host was pioneering Dennis James (born Demie James Sposa, but in those days hosts and actors weren't supposed to be Italian, only singers and gangsters—see *492 Great Things about Being Italian*, also by this author). James's career spanned nearly 60 years. He appeared on the first television commercial and the first show recorded on videotape.

  The show aired Thursdays at 9 p.m. James made a different entrance each week, sitting in a barber's chair or a bathtub, and so on (as Alfred Hitchcock later did on his series). The show's set looked like a grocery store—not that any real grocery store would only stock Libby's products, but the program sponsor was Libby's Foods. Each product had a question attached to it, worth $5, $10, or $15.

Besides answering questions, *Cash and Carry* incorporated the then-popular home viewer element that weekly allowed someone to call in and guess what was beneath a big barrel. Plus, like the popular *Truth or Consequences*, it included stunts on the order of a blindfolded wife feeding her husband ice cream and a man imitating a woman undressing before taking a bath.

The show originated in the converted Wanamaker's department store on Ninth Avenue and Broadway in Manhattan and lasted one season.

("Cash and Cary" was the media nickname for Woolworth heiress Barbara Hutton and movie star Cary Grant during their brief marriage. Their divorce got even more publicity because the tightfisted but deeply closeted actor was Hutton's only husband who didn't demand alimony.)

• The difference between the sedate *Cash and Carry* and *Supermarket Sweep* 19 years later was telling. "Greed runs amuck!" headlined one review of the ABC show that ran from December 1965 to July 1967. Hosted by Bill Malone, the sweepers were three husband-and-wife teams running amok in actual East Coast supermarkets, scooping up as many groceries as possible in their assigned time. The 90 seconds allotted each pair was expanded if the wife priced items correctly or closest. Each pricing game involved four items.

When the round ended, the husband ran through the market with a shopping cart gathering up to five items of one kind. There were also bonus items to be discovered in the store that were worth extra money. The pair with the biggest total won and returned to compete with two new teams.

In April 1967, *Supermarket Sweep* started taping exclusively in Miami. In July it was canceled in favor of a spin-off, or one could say it transitioned into, *Honeymoon Race*, filmed at the Hollywood Mall in Hollywood, Florida. Bill Malone emceed, and the three opposite-sex couples were on their honeymoons, participating in a scavenger hunt for five items in the mall's stores.

The wives drove the electric golf carts that transported the duos from venue to venue. The couple that found the most items in the scheduled time won, but then the producers chose to restyle (or de-style) *Honeymoon Race* into a stunt show, as if there hadn't been enough of those. The honeymoon was over after 4½ months.

More successful than either was the 1990–1998 *Supermarket Sweep* hosted by David Ruprecht for the Lifetime cable network. Twenty-three years on, the three pairs weren't necessarily marrieds or boy-girl and the supermarket, singular, was built on a Los Angeles set. Again, the base time was 90 seconds. Pricing games could add 10 seconds to a pair's "shopping" time. A tricky bonus round allowed the winning twosome a chance at $5,000 cash.

The show resurfaced in 2020 on ABC, hosted by comedian Leslie Jones from SNL and the the 2016 female reboot of the movie *Ghostbusters*. (Ruprecht went on to host the live version of *The Price Is Right* at Bally's in Las Vegas.)

• *Sale of the Century* opened with Q and A and then lured contestants into accepting various "instant bargains" that could be bought with a contestant's accumulated cash total. The most cash determined the winner, who got to shop at the Sale of the Century where a high-end item could be had more or less for peanuts—like a new car for $250. *Sale of the Century* aired on NBC daytime from 1969 to 1974 and was hosted by actor Jack Kelly (from TV's *Maverick*) and from 1971 by former baseball catcher Joe Garagiola. Its original three contestants were changed in 1973 to two couples. The change didn't help.

The show had a longer run when revived in 1983 (to 1989), again on NBC daytime, and was hosted by Jim Perry, who'd been a straight man to comic Sid Caesar. Perry also emceed the Canadian game shows *Definitions*, *Eye Bet*, and *Fractured Phrases*. The new *Sale of the Century* was back to three contestants, each given a bankroll of $20, adding $5 for answering a question correctly and deducting $5 for a wrong answer. A new element was called the Fame Game, requiring a solution to Who Am I?

Over the years, the game show made changes to retain viewer interest. Unusually, the pilot was shot in Los Angeles, but the show taped in Manhattan. In the 1980s some game show sets were bigger or gaudier, and that of *Sale of the Century* was so large it couldn't fit in the lift in New York, so it had to be sawed in half before taking its place at NBC in Rockefeller Center.

Most shopping shows are daytime. *Sale of the Century* made it to nighttime in reruns. A 2007 syndicated version hosted by Ross Morreale was retitled *Temptation: The New Sale of the Century*. Not tempting enough though, because it lasted one season.

- *Shop 'Til You Drop* featured knowledge of shopping, slogans, and merchandise but also required each of two teams of two people to perform a stunt. (*Truth or Consequences* and *Beat the Clock* had a lot to answer for.) The series ran intermittently for 10 seasons between 1991 and 2005, first on Lifetime cable, then Family Channel, and finally on Pax. The first three editions were hosted by Pat Finn and the final one by JD Roberto. The show took place in a mall-like set. Points accrued if questions were answered correctly and stunts completed within the time limit.

  In the bonus round the winning team had to open each of six gift boxes within 90 seconds and choose to keep the prizes or swap them for others in the mall. If so, one team member ran to another store and picked a replacement box. The object was to amass prizes totaling more than $2,500 to be able to win a bonus vacation.

- Family Channel also aired the two-season *Shopping Spree*, which began in 1996. TV critic David Sheehan called it "foolish and cheap." Regarding the latter, one aspect of the show was seven different "celebrity" guests—not in person but in drawings. The former referred to contestants having to second-guess the merchandise that a stranger would choose. As with other shopping shows, this involved running to a store to choose the item the contestant thinks their team member had selected based on clues attached to their clothes.

Winning on *Spree* was determined not by cash totals or points but how long it took a team member to correctly guess which one of four gifts from six different stores their teammate chose. (One runner-up claimed a nervous breakdown after appearing on the show.)

You Bet Your Life was more a platform for Groucho Marx's trademark wit and sarcasm than a challenging game show. It enjoyed a successful run from 1950 to 1961.
NBC/Photofest

Columbia professor Charles Van Doren (left) and Army veteram Herb Stempel competing on the quiz show *Twenty-One* in August 1958. They were at the center of a rigging scandal that tarnished the reputation of game shows for years. The scandal was the subject of the 1994 film *Quiz Show* starring Ralph Fiennes and John Turturro and directed by Robert Redford. *NBC/Photofest*

On the set of *The Price Is Right* in the 1990s, with two icons of game show history, Johnny Olson and Bob Barker, seated in front of some of the women known as "Barker's Beauties." *CBS/Photofest*

Let's Make a Deal (1963–1977) chose its contestants from the studio audience, so in order to get attention people started wearing costumes and other gimmicks. Here famed host Monty Hall apparently makes a deal with the devil. *NBC/Photofest*

An episode of the network comedy *The Odd Couple* had Oscar (Jack Klugman) and Felix (Tony Randall) appearing as contestants on *Password*. Allen Ludden presides while real-life wife Betty White sits to his right. *ABC/Photofest*

The all-star panel of *I've Got a Secret* in 1959. From left to right: Bill Cullen, Jayne Meadows, Garry Moore, Henry Morgan, and Betsy Palmer. *CBS/Photofest*

Gene Rayburn, the longtime host of *The Match Game. CBS/Photofest*

Hollywood Squares featured celebrity tic-tac-toe and pre-written one-liners that were occasionally laced with sexual innuendo, especially from comedian Paul Lynde (center square). *NBC/Photofest*

The late Alex Trebek and contestants on *Jeopardy!*, one of television's most admired and longest-running game shows. *King World Productions/Photofest*

Host and matchmaker Jim Lange presided over *The Dating Game* from 1965 to 1973. *ABC/Photofest*

The original *Newlywed Game* hosted by Bob Eubanks exposed couples' intimate moments and even led to some divorces. *ABC/Photofest*

Regis Philbin was the first host of *Who Wants to Be a Millionaire?*, a show that was adapted from a program of the same name in Great Britain. *ABC/Photofest*

15

Before Stardom and After

EARLY IN THE 1950S IN MANHATTAN A YOUNG MAN FROM INDIANA WAS hired as a *Beat the Clock* stunt stand-in. On Thursdays, 15 stand-ins, mostly unemployed actors, were assigned to test the crazy stunts devised by the show's staff, which included future playwright Neil Simon. Stunts always involved ordinary household items but ranged from stacking cups and saucers atop a beach ball to trying to scoop a ping pong ball out of a vat of Jell-O with one's mouth. *Beat the Clock* was Mark Goodson-Bill Todman Productions' "answer" to the successful *Truth or Consequences.*

If a given stunt proved too difficult or impossible, it was dropped. The stunts that worked or mostly worked were tried out on 15 different stand-ins the following Saturday. One Thursday stand-in was a standout. He succeeded at every stunt and for that reason was fired. The producers realized he was much too skillful to represent an average contestant. His name was James Dean.

During the 1950s political witch hunts myriad liberals, gays, and Jews lost their jobs via the excuse of Communist Party membership or supposed pro-Communist sympathies. Attacking Hollywood was an easy way for power-hungry Senator Joseph McCarthy (R-WI) to gain publicity. The Red Scare scared television networks and Hollywood studios into falling in line with the pro-fascist leader; many celebrities were accused of having been "prematurely anti-fascist" by opposing Adolf Hitler and Benito Mussolini before the US entered World War II.

One stagehand for *I've Got a Secret* was terminated by CBS for "Communist leanings." Like James Dean, Joseph Papp went on to better things. New York theater, less cowardly than the mass media, was nowhere as rigid about blacklisting people and ruining their careers. A future three-time Tony winner, Papp founded the Public Theater and launched Shakespeare in the Park, which in time spread from Manhattan to local audiences nationwide.

In a later era, a job offer might also be problematic. "The agonizing thing about show business," said Phil Hartman, "is you never know what a job may lead to. Will it move you up? Or pigeonhole you into career stagnation? . . . I didn't want to stay an announcer, or in game shows. But when I got offered a job announcing a new music game show [*The Pop 'N Rocker Game*, syndicated, 1983] I jumped at it.

"Today I'd say I was lucky it went just one season." The show was hosted by Jon Bauman, formerly of Sha Na Na, also a *Match Game* panelist and later cohost of *The Match Game/Hollywood Squares Hour*. In 1986, Hartman moved ahead to *Saturday Night Live* and, by 1998, was starring in the sitcom *NewsRadio* when he was fatally shot by his drug-addicted wife.

Meghan Markle significantly boosted her status when she became the wife of Britain's Prince Harry and, thus, the Duchess of Sussex. But in 2006, she was an aspiring actress who got a job as Briefcase Model number 24 on the second season of *Deal or No Deal*.

The show boasting the most contestants before they became famous was *The Dating Game*, especially late in the 1960s and early in the 1970s. A big percentage were aspiring actors. John Ritter, son of cowboy star Tex Ritter, was 19 when he bested his two competitors for a date. "That's when I realized I was a good enough actor. I was a nervous wreck inside, my lip twitched . . . but when I saw it on TV later I just seemed mildly nervous. . . . The camera never lies? Bull!"

Steve Martin was on twice and twice won a date. Bob Saget won one out of two times but didn't get the holiday in Guatemala because of problems there. Suzanne Somers did get to enjoy her romantic trip to the Bahamas. Host Jim Lange described contestant Jennifer Granholm as "cute and curvaceous." Later governor of Michigan, she became Secretary of Energy under President Joe Biden. At the conclusion of Farrah Fawcett's April Fool's Day segment, she and the audience were aghast when the three bachelors got into a big angry fight. It was soon revealed the trio were stuntmen.

After bodybuilder Arnold Schwarzenegger described his Mr. Olympia measurements he asked one "bachelorette," "Vat do ve haf in common?" She answered, "You get smaller as you go down." When the laughter died down, he remarked, "By ze vay, zis is not true." (A subsequent nude photo in *Spy* magazine appeared to contradict him.)

In 1986 director Judd Apatow won a date and a trip to Acapulco. As bachelor number 1, he'd proclaimed, "I'm tanned, blonde, and blue-eyed, baby!" In 2015, he recalled that he got so sunburned on the Mexican Riviera that he had to spend two days in his hotel room. In 1994 Jon Hamm (*Mad Men*) lost despite promising "some fabulous food, a little fabulous conversation, and . . . a fabulous foot massage for an evening of total fabulosity." Maybe the young woman was overwhelmed. She chose a stuntman.

The Dating Game showcased some already celebrities whose TV fame was basically over (e.g., Butch Patrick, who played Eddie on *The Munsters*—one "bachelorette" accidentally called him Bitch—and Jerry Mathers, the once-cute title character in the sitcom *Leave It to Beaver*).

Interesting how many gay, lesbian, and bisexual celebrities and celebs-to-be appeared on what was strictly a heterosexual dating game (for that matter, umpteen early game shows specified husband-and-wife contestants and TV's heter-only bias still predominates). Zany comedian Rip Taylor appeared on *The Dating Game* twice. "I didn't take it seriously. . . . You might have seen Snow White interviewing three very short men." Despite his longtime male partner, Rip remained closeted.

UK singer Dusty Springfield was urged by her US publicist to appear on *Dating Game* to gain "straight creditability." A more puzzling star turn was big-screen character actress turned small-screen witch, Agnes Moorehead (Endora on *Bewitched*). Why would the crusty 60-plus thespian deign to appear on the show? Perhaps like several 40-plus stars she wished to inject her image with youth.

Paul Lynde, who played Samantha's Uncle Arthur on *Bewitched*, deemed Moorehead "classy as hell but one of the all-time Hollywood dykes." His *Dating Game* participation was motivated by his campy image. On two TV sitcoms, he starred as a husband and dad. Both flopped. Not that all the "dates" were carried out. As announcer Johnny Jacobs stated, "Dates with celebrities are subject to their availability." Some were permanently unavailable but always ready for publicity.

Ann B. Davis, who played housekeeper Alice on *The Brady Bunch*, opined, "Going out for dinner with someone isn't necessarily anything more than a nice meal and conversation, which is pleasant, right?"

Paul Reubens did three turns on the show, including as his alter ego Pee-wee Herman. Other "alternative" daters included frequent *Match Game* guest Fannie Flagg, a teenaged Michael Jackson, a former TV sitcom child star, half of a famed sister-brother act, an older horror star, a deeply closeted far-right future TV star, a bi protégé of Sal Mineo turned TV star, and an almost openly bisexual movie superstar.

John Glenn, a Marine pilot in 1957, knew enough about music to win $25,000 on *Name That Tune* (the money went toward his two children's college education). In 1962 he became the first American to orbit the Earth and later served as a senator from Ohio.

During the big-money game shows of the mid- to late 1950s some stars did appear on game shows. For instance Edward G. Robinson and Vincent Price tied ($32,000 each) on *The $64,000 Challenge* in 1956. The chosen quiz field of each was art; both men were serious collectors. In 1958 Price, who'd spent most of his film career in supporting roles (later becoming a horror movie star), hosted ABC's prime-time *E.S.P.* Its two contestants were isolated in separate booths while experiments tested their extrasensory perception. (How well could one expect that to go?)

After three weeks, it was no longer a game show, though its remaining three weeks did stick to the psychic subject.

One 1950s game show regularly featured stars—in disguise. *Masquerade Party* ran from 1952 to 1960, shifting between the three networks, usually airing during summer, and was emceed by six separate hosts. Guests wore costumes, wigs, heavy makeup, latex, prosthetics, fake facial hair . . . whatever it took to hide their identities (not dissimilar to the current *The Masked Singer*, minus melody). The panel could each ask up to five questions of the guest or guests, and guests could win up to $300 each for their chosen charity. Gloria Swanson appeared as a silent-era Keystone Kop. The Gabor sisters were *Macbeth*'s Three Weird Sisters, and in 1959, the Three Stooges caused a laugh riot disguised as Magda, Zsa Zsa, and Eva Gabor.

Monty Hall's company acquired the rights to *Masquerade Party* and brought it back, syndicated, in 1974 and hosted by Richard Dawson. It lasted one season.

A rare appearance was that of legendary artist Salvador Dalí on the 1950s show *The Name's the Same*. The eccentric Spaniard expressed the wish that "All men wear a mustache like mine." He proceeded to paint a thin, flowing mustache on host Dennis James, who invited Dalí to sign the work and thus increase James's "face value." (*Name's the Same* was a gimmicky yet four-season show that featured ordinary people with famous names, like Abraham Lincoln, Albert Einstein; for that matter, actor-director Albert Brooks's real name is Albert Einstein).

Of course, game shows in the 1950s were also a recourse for dimmed stars who'd shone during Hollywood's golden age. Their guest appearances or hosting a program was publicity and profitable. Melvyn Douglas had been a 1930s and 1940s male lead opposite Greta Garbo (thrice!), Marlene Dietrich, Joan Crawford, and so on. But in 1953 he hosted the short-lived *Your Big Moment*. Happily, in his senior years he won two supporting Academy Awards. His stage actress wife Helen Gahagan's first movie was her last, the costly, intriguing 1935 flop *She*. Gahagan then became a congresswoman but when she ran for the Senate was defeated by Richard Nixon, who used smear tactics. Helen was reportedly the first to nickname him Tricky Dick.

Nixon, running in vain for California governor in 1962, made an appearance on *Your First Impression* (and later appeared on *Rowan & Martin's Laugh-In*, which was not a game show, prior to becoming president). *First Impression* was about guessing the identity of a famous guest temporarily sequestered behind the celebrity panel in a soundproof room. It lasted two years and its theme song was "Three Blind Mice," which was also that of The Three Stooges.

Needless to say, few "talents" on *The Gong Show* went on to bigger and better. Two exceptions were 12-year-old Andrea McArdle in 1976, who soon won the lead in the Broadway musical hit *Annie*. Her rendition of its anthem "Tomorrow" remains definitive. The following year, Steve Martin strummed a mean banjo—with a fake arrow piercing his head.

Lisa Cardellini made her TV debut on *The Price Is Right* in 1994. At 19, she was five years away from *Freaks and Geeks* but won a new fireplace she says she still prizes. Aaron Paul appeared on *The Price Is Right* with shaved head and glasses before he appeared in *Breaking Bad.* He screamed at Bob Barker, "You're the man, Bob! You're my idol!" Paul's manic behavior, he later confessed, was fueled by "six cans of Red Bull. Which is very dangerous, by the way." After getting to the Showcase Showdown, Paul's disappointment was huge when he overbid a mere $132 on a prize sports car worth $26,500.

Stefani Germanotta, the future Lady Gaga, also blew it, on *Boiling Points* in 2005. The MTV show required contestants to stay cool and calm—but they didn't know it—when their restaurant meal was taken away and then returned with trash on it. Losing her cool and using profanity cost the young lady the $100 reward (big spenders, MTV).

When someone has tasted fame they'll do almost anything to hang on to it. Nick Adams pushed hard to get small roles in hit movies before starring in the TV series *The Rebel*. His high point was *Twilight of Honor* (1963, starring then-boyfriend Richard Chamberlain), for which Adams was nominated for a Best Supporting Oscar. He spent a then-serious $10,000 campaigning for the prize but didn't win. His career slid downhill, and he wound up doing monster movies in Japan.

"One of the saddest meetings I've had was with Nick," said writer Robert Synes, who later cocreated and executive produced *The $1,000,000 Chance of a Lifetime*. "We had some mutual friends, so . . . long story short, he wanted me to get him on a quiz show. Any quiz show.

"Nick assumed he would win . . . and thought being on a quiz show would give him an audience of millions and restore his celebrity. . . . He also said he'd been on a quiz show early in the 1960s as a celebrity panelist.

"I was unable to help and, to not raise his hopes, I was a little brusque. I wish I hadn't been, in light of his dying not long after that." He died in 1968 at age 37, a possible suicide but possibly a murder victim.

"I've been offered my share of game show hosting duties," boasted Adam West, a red-hot TV star in the mid-1960s via the twice-weekly prime-time hit *Batman*. West claimed he was offered the role of James Bond (a Yank 007?) and declined it. His biggest disappointment was not being asked to reprise the caped crusader when Batman was revived for the first of several big-budget movies.

West turned down "hosting duties" but occasionally appeared on game shows. "Sooner or later every star guests on a game show. It's not a come-down, it's part of being famous. . . . They need you to enhance the contestants and host. It's a long time since those long-ago shows that had no stars.

"The downside is when people tune in to see how you've aged . . . but I have aged pretty well, if I may say so."

After his hit 1970s variety series, comedian Flip Wilson hosted *People Are Funny* on NBC prime time from March 24 to July 21, 1984. The stunt-oriented program began on radio in the 1940s, moved to TV in 1954, and ran until 1961. Most of the reboot's action occurred on the streets of Los Angeles. Sample stunts included two men trying to lure a passing pedestrian to join them in "fishing" at a manhole and a child pleading with a restaurant patron to eat up her veggies before her mommy returned from the powder room.

Wilson's participation in such a show was limited, and the low-rated experience was a career setback. "Like they think I'm so funny I can turn anything into laughs and big [ratings] numbers. But anyone coulda done *this* . . . and they didn't do a good job getting it ready for everyone to watch." As to future hosting, "No way, man. Forget it!"

A handsome, debonair Brit, Brian Aherne was a Hollywood leading man opposite stars like Marlene Dietrich, Joan Crawford, Katharine Hepburn, and Rita Hayworth. By the 1950s, still slim and good-looking, he was nonetheless old hat. Early that decade he was a substitute host for *The Name's the Same*. "One might call it pitiable," he told a UK interviewer. "But there's no cure for the common birthday. . . . There comes a time either one doesn't work, hopefully having saved enough money, or one accepts what is proffered and wears a smiling public face."

Or they switch fields, as did Ronald Reagan, to politics. The B movie actor was ripe for game show hosting but had rich, influential contacts in California politics. "I think Reagan would have accepted a game show," opined producer Bob Stewart. "I'd have offered him a job. You don't have to share someone's opinions to hire them."

Stewart noted the similar career trajectories of Reagan and John Cameron Swayze, who did host a game show, the short-lived *Chance for Romance*, in 1958. Swayze began as an actor but became a news commentator and hosted a TV drama series, a travel program, and was a substitute host for *To Tell the Truth*. A longtime spokesman for Timex watches, he also did ads for Studebaker cars and other products. Reagan hosted *G.E. Theater* on television and did ads for everything from shirts, cigarettes, Royal Crown Cola and V-8 vegetable-blend juice to Wildroot hair tonic. His film career practically over, he switched tracks by playing a villain in a 1964 remake of the 1946 classic *The Killers*. The flop was his final movie.

"Some former stars are mortified at the thought of hosting a game show," said Stewart. "Others appreciate that it's part-time, pays quite well, and can bring audiences a lot of enjoyment."

Some big names simply enjoy playing games. And have the time to do so between projects or during their golden years like Charades enthusiast Lucille Ball on CBS's *Body Language* (1984–1986), hosted by Tom Kennedy. "We got physical comedy at its best whenever Lucy guested on our show," said Kennedy. "She was always up for fun . . . and very limber for a lady in her seventies . . . youthful and un-self-conscious."

Burt Reynolds appeared on various game shows after attaining movie superstardom. "I've been advised it's wrong, it's dumb, it's demeaning to guest on a game show. Being on one's going to get my box-office record revoked? . . . It's not only a hoot, it's me paying recognition that game shows—being seen on them—helped get me into movies. It opened up those opportunities for me. . . . I love game shows! I even became a mini Merv Griffin," via his and Bert Convy's Burt and Bert Productions.

Game shows, then, are a way to have fun and regain the spotlight. Former president Bill Clinton did both when he went on NPR's quiz show *Wait, Wait . . . Don't Tell Me* in 2012 and correctly answered three questions about the TV show *My Little Pony: Friendship Is Magic*.

Pride of Hosts

"Truly, what could be more fun than playing games and getting paid for it?" asked Bill Cullen, who was known as the Dean of Game Show Hosts.

The sunny-dispositioned Cullen wasn't touchy, like some. Numerous hosts have stressed they didn't start out to be hosts or avoided it for a long time. Some hosts avoided interviews and having to discuss their work before they became hosts because it might be like admitting they hadn't succeeded as actors, singers, and so on.

Said faded golden-age movie actor Don Ameche, "I thought long and hard before saying yes" to hosting the 1950 NBC game show *Take a Chance*. It lasted less than three months. "It's a gamble, and I lost big." Later in the 1950s Ameche agreed to substitute host on the established hit *Strike It Rich* (other substitutes included Monty Hall and actor Robert Alda).

But "show" is an unpredictable business and in 1985 Ameche was part of the elderly ensemble cast of *Cocoon*, a surprise hit directed by Ron Howard (he also costarred in its sequel). It resulted in a Best Supporting Actor Academy Award. Ameche thereafter expunged his TV hosting experiences from his resumé and on at least one LA talk show denied involvement with "any radio or TV game shows . . . not my 'thing,' as they say."

Actress Patti Deutsch possessed an incongruously splendid mane of red hair and a nasal but flexible voice that placed her in demand for voiceover work, especially cartoon characters. A frequent panelist on *The Match Game* during the 1970s, she confessed that when she couldn't think of something to fill in a blank she usually wrote down "Richard Nixon" (timely, due to Watergate) or "Monty Hall," which made little sense but typically drew laughs.

Why Monty Hall? While on *The Tonight Show* after moving west to work on *Rowan & Martin's Laugh-In*, Deutsch chatted about the differences between the two coasts' lifestyles. She joked that people in LA were not only more apt to list themselves in the phonebook but also to offer their name, address, phone number, and credits. "For instance Carl Reiner," she recalled, "and I gave an address and telephone number and I went 'Writer, producer, actor' . . . a whole list.

"Then I did somebody else and a whole list and then I went, 'And Monty Hall.' *Pause.* Well, when you're new you don't think anybody's really watching. Apparently he was, and he got pissed off.

"And he said to somebody, 'Just have her up here to do run-throughs and never hire her!'

"I thought that was so funny, getting so angry about something so silly and inconsequential. So it was my prerogative to get back at him for getting back at me. I never went up there for any reason because I had heard what he was doing.

"So that's where 'Monty Hall' came from."

16

What Is *Jeopardy!*?

THE SHOW'S TITLE WAS GOING TO BE *WHAT'S THE ANSWER?* THE STORY goes that Merv Griffin's then-wife Julann asked him why should quiz show contestants always have to answer a question? Why couldn't they supply a question to an answer? At first Merv thought it impractical or, worse, borderline illegal—not dissimilar to what caused the 1958 game shows scandals.

(Another version held that when Griffin didn't "get" Julann's concept she simply stated, "79 Wistful Vista." To which Merv replied, "What's the address of Fibber McGee and Molly?" a popular radio show pair.)

When Griffin held a demonstration of the proposed show for NBC executives they were expecting a comedy quiz show. Talk show hosts Steve Allen and Johnny Carson had done recurring skits as the Question Man and Carnac the Magnificent, respectively, in which an answer was supplied before a humor-making question was uttered. But *Jeopardy!* was tough, not comedic, and after the demonstration NBC chief Mort Werner exclaimed exasperatedly, "I didn't get *one* right!"

Fortunately the gathering included Grant Tinker, one of the developers of *G.E. College Bowl*, another tough knowledge program that was nonetheless popular and long running. He urged Werner to buy *Jeopardy!* Werner finally assented but warned Tinker he'd be liable if the show flopped.

(The network wanted to eliminate the term Daily Double, afraid antigambling viewers would connect it with horse racing and make protests. But alliteration and Merv's persistence won the day.)

Jeopardy!'s premise and method have remained basically the same, with three contestants, including a returning champion, selecting from a grid board of six knowledge categories with five answers each. Incorrect answers (that is, questions) result in the value of that particular question (that is, answer) being deducted from the contestant's dollar total.

Any selection could disclose a Daily Double, allowing a contestant to wager anything or all on their ability to question the subsequent answer. Some "answers" are visual, for example during this writer's 1998 turn, a still photo of Henry Fonda, Jane Darwell, and other actors in a movie. I was to identify the name of that family. I hadn't seen the film but recognized the Depression-era classic *The Grapes of Wrath* and stated, "What is the Joad family?" (I was ready to spell the surname but wasn't asked.)

Two rounds of play—"question" values in Double Jeopardy! are doubled—precede Final Jeopardy!, where contestants wager any amount of their winnings toward the revealed, unchosen concluding category.

From *Jeopardy!*'s 1964 inception to 1975 and 1978–1979 Art Fleming hosted the show that became a bulwark of NBC's daytime schedule. It made him and announcer Don Pardo famous. A navy veteran, Fleming was an assistant on the quiz show *Dr. I.Q.* in 1954 and acted in the 1958 TV western *The Californians*, the 1959 series *International Detective*, and did commercials. He took emceeing seriously, hosting daytime and from 1974 to 1975 *Jeopardy!*'s syndicated nighttime edition, never missing one of its 2,753 episodes before its 1975 demise.

Don Pardo, who only missed one show, had announced NBC's first daytime game show, *Remember This Date*, in 1950. On November 22, 1963, he was the first to read NBC's bulletin that President Kennedy had been shot in Dallas. Pardo became *Saturday Night Live*'s announcer on its debut in 1975 and, in 1987, enacted a radio game show host in Woody Allen's *Radio Days*.

Jeopardy!'s first champion, Jane Eubanks (no relation to Bob), won $345. (After the five-day limit was abolished during the 2003–2004 season, ratings could rise when a returning champion kept returning, as did Ken Jennings with 74 wins in a row.) In 1972, the show observed its 2,000th show with comedian Mel Brooks as the 2,000-Year-Old Man. A 1984 song parody by Weird Al Yankovic was titled "I Lost on *Jeopardy!*"

In October 1978, NBC brought back *Jeopardy!* in daytime, relocating it from New York to Los Angeles, but it only lasted five months. Still, the show had proven its popularity and outwitted network execs who kept urging Griffin to decrease its level of difficulty, holding up "seventh grade" as their preferred level of intellect. Merv ignored the requests—which were requests, not demands, due to high ratings—but admitted he usually found the "questions" too personally difficult. So what made *Jeopardy!* such a hit?

USC professor Dick Block cited "the tremendous change in American education in the 1960s, in that college was now considered mandatory." In movies up to and even into the 1950s, college student characters were often held in contempt by older (often jealous) characters. Dr. Block pointed out that people watching *Jeopardy!* "were seeing other people being rewarded for having a higher education."

So why did the show peter out late in the 1970s? One theory was it had become too familiar. Few game shows last decade after decade after decade, as *Jeopardy!* has done since its 1984 comeback. What accounts for *that*? Psychologist Dr. Betty Berzon felt, "Now that college isn't a rarity and self-improvement, both physical and mental, is more than a trend, a show that's pretty challenging is more readily accepted. Even if you miss a question, you can learn something.

"Less traditionalist generations aren't as easily threatened . . . they've learned that knowledge can be fun."

In 1984 Art Fleming declined Merv Griffin's invitation to come back for *Jeopardy!*'s reboot. Fleming felt the show had been dumbed down (!); he disliked the new computerized game board and disapproved that now only the day's champion got to keep their winnings. So the hunt was on for a new host and eventually the mantle settled on Canadian Alex Trebek, who in time would become virtually synonymous with *Jeopardy!*

But first, a word about our producer. (What's the longest word in the English language? "And now a word from our sponsor. . . . " The longest sentence: "I do.")

Merv Griffin was born in 1925 in San Mateo, California (where this writer lived for eight years). He sang in the church choir and, at nine, started singing on radio in nearby San Francisco. He earned money as a church organist. Come World War II he was classified 4F, reportedly for health reasons. A singer whose sole hit was "I've Got a Lovely Bunch of Coconuts" in 1950, he was discovered by Doris Day. She arranged a screen test for him, but it didn't yield an offer.

Day's music-producer son Terry Melcher told the *San Mateo Times's* Barbara Bladen, "Merv didn't have looks, voice, or charisma. But he was smart. Instead of being a star, he interviewed them . . . for many years. And his company came up with game shows, a couple of them extra successful."

Griffin settled into TV cohosting and then emceeing the game show *Play Your Hunch*. He approved its temporary hiring of a handsome young artist turned unemployed actor named Robert Redford for $75 (the future director of *Quiz Show* about the 1958 game show scandals). In 1958 Merv married. The twosome, officially together until 1976, had one child, a son. Griffin left *Play Your Hunch* (1958–1963) in 1962 to host a daytime talk show for six months. In 1963 he founded Milbarn Productions, whose first game show *Word for Word* on NBC (1963–1964) he got to host. In 1964 he changed the company name to Merv Griffin Enterprises.

His second talk show ran from 1965 to 1986. His second game show was *Jeopardy!* Its original run ended January 3, 1975, but on January 6 Griffin's other long-running show, previously titled *Shopper's Bazaar*, premiered as *Wheel of Fortune*. None of his company's other game shows came near *Jeopardy!*'s and *Wheel*'s success, but he coproduced the music program *Dance Fever* (1979–1987), hosted by Deney Terrio, who'd taught John Travolta to disco dance for *Saturday Night Fever*. In 1991, Terrio sued his former boss for sexual harassment. The suit was dismissed, but by then, a salacious saw about male talk show guests had long been making the rounds: "To get on *Merv*, you have to get on Merv."

In 1986, the year his talk show career ended, Merv Griffin Enterprises was sold to Coca-Cola for $250 million. At the time, Coke owned Columbia Pictures. When Japan's Sony bought Columbia, Merv's former company was absorbed into Sony's television arm. For a while Griffin was semiretired if not inactive. He'd long been interested in real estate and eventually bought several hotels (including the Beverly Hilton) and casinos. He became a prime competitor to Donald Trump and, in 1988, wrested control of Resorts International from him.

Trump's private but widely circulated comments about Griffin's sexuality were said to have prompted his using Eva Gabor as a constant beard, though he genuinely enjoyed her company. Eva and her *Green Acres* costar Eddie Albert were lasting friends. This author met Albert, whose wife was Mexican actress Margo, at a Latinx conference at the Los Angeles Airport Hilton that I cohosted because of my book *Hispanic Hollywood*. The actor, born Edward Albert Heimberger, during a backstage conversation brought up the topic of Merv and Eva being "entirely platonic dates" and that Albert had previously employed a recent boyfriend of Griffin's.

In 1991 Griffin's longtime employee—not the one referred to by Eddie Albert—Brent Plott, age 37, who served as driver, bodyguard, and horse trainer, filed a palimony suit against Merv, age 66. Plott claimed they'd been lovers and shared the same bed (unlike Merv and Eva's separate bedrooms while traveling). The suit was later dismissed, but it's noteworthy that until recently, results of lawsuits involving homosexuality often ignored the truth (e.g., three times Liberace sued for being [accurately] described as gay, and three times he won). Also, it's no longer against the law to call (or "call") someone gay or lesbian.

Merv Griffin Entertainment was formed in 1996 and did game show reboots and a few new ones like *Merv Griffin's Crosswords*. Also small-screen efforts like *Inside the Osmonds* in 2001, two feature films, and a movie coproduction (*Shade*, 2003) that cost $10 million and earned less than half a million. No matter, the failed singer and failed actor was by then one of the richest men in showbiz.

Griffin's gayness was an open secret in Hollywood. Game show producer Bob Stewart theorized, "He could have been honest without repercussions [because] he wasn't a leading man or sex symbol . . . he let himself get heavy. He was his own boss. . . . Could be his Catholic background, his Republican persuasion . . . and his generation, which internalized shame and guilt."

Stewart said the four prominent game show announcers who worked for Griffin also worked for Bob Stewart Productions. "Two of them did mention his double life . . . Merv was in the closet but couldn't entirely hide his attraction when dealing with good-looking younger men. . . . Don Pardo once saw Merv in a dimly lit restaurant, not a celebrity hang-out, with a thirty-ish guy in a booth, very close together, clearly flirting."

There was speculation from on-set witnesses that Griffin soured on handsome host Peter Tomarken while preparing *Monopoly* (1990) partly because Tomarken felt he'd crossed the line and become overly physical—apart from disagreements over the show. Tomarken wasn't merely let go, Merv seemed to get back at him by replacing Peter not with another professional host but a contestant who'd been on *Jeopardy!* and the *Monopoly* pilot. (Calling to mind Columbia chief Harry Cohn's anger over Rita Hayworth rebuffing him by giving a deliberate star buildup to "Miss Deepfreeze of 1953," starlet Kim Novak.)

When the *Japan Times* asked two necessarily anonymous *Jeopardy!* staffers why Merv Griffin didn't come out, one replied, "I think he might if he weren't a father." The closest he came was a 2005 quote in the *New York Times*: "I tell everybody that I'm a quart-sexual. I'll do anything with anybody for a quarter."

Griffin died of prostate cancer at age 82 in 2007. In the *Hollywood Reporter* talent coordinator and segment producer Ray Richmond wrote about his late boss, "Merv Griffin was gay. Why should that be so uncomfortable to read? Why are we still so jittery even about raising the [subject]. . . . The mainstream media somehow remains trapped in the Dark Ages when it comes to labeling a person as gay.

"What a powerful message Griffin might have sent had he squired his male companions around town rather than Eva Gabor. . . . Imagine the amount of good Merv could have done as an uncloseted gay man in embodying a positive image."

When *Jeopardy!* returned in 1984, it had a new host in Alex Trebek and a new announcer, Johnny Gilbert. It was syndicated by King World, a minor outfit specializing in rerun packages of 1930s *Our Gang* short subjects. That is, until 1983 when it was granted syndication of *Wheel of Fortune* and helped make that show more successful than before. Naturally, cash amounts on *Jeopardy!*'s new version were increased. During its first decade, the one-day record win was $34,000, while the low was $1, won by an Air Force colonel who however returned the following day and earned $13,402.

In summer 1990 *Super Jeopardy!* pitted former winners against each other for a $250,000 jackpot. In 1992 *Celebrity Jeopardy!* bowed as an annual event. Its contestants would include Ed Asner, Carol Burnett,

Kelsey Grammer, Bill Maher, Cheech Marin, Rosie O'Donnell, Luke Perry, Emma Samms, and Jay Thomas.

When he'd moved to the US in 1973 George Alexander Trebek (1940–2020) was already a Canadian TV celebrity. Born in Sudbury, Ontario, Alex's father was a chef who immigrated from the Ukraine. His mother was French Canadian. Late in his teens Alex got a US job as a garbage collector. "My mother was working in Cincinnati for a family and I came down to spend a summer with her." During college, he got a job as a radio announcer to help defray expenses. The station, CBO-AM, was affiliated with the Canadian Broadcasting Corporation (CBC), which was patterned on Britain's BBC.

That job led to doing weather, sports, and news on radio and television. After graduation Alex was broadcasting full-time. In 1963 he hosted the CBC TV show *Music Hop* and, in 1966, lucked out with *Reach for the Top*, a difficult quiz program featuring two high school teams. He emceed that *Jeopardy!*-esque show for seven years and also its spin-off *Trans-World Top Team* for two seasons, from 1968. In 1969 Trebek hosted *Strategy*, a Q and A game show that played out around a giant dartboard (darts being more popular in the UK and Canada than the US).

Fellow Canadian TV celebrity Alan Thicke had already emigrated to the US. A writer for the game show *The Wizard of Odds*, in 1973 he suggested Alex come audition for its hosting spot. Alex came and got hired but didn't want to rent, let alone buy, a house in Los Angeles yet. He knew how often American game shows got canceled. For three months, he stayed at Thicke's home, but when NBC renewed the show for six months, he bought a house. In 1974 Trebek married Elaine Callei, a former *Playboy* Bunny who had a daughter. The marriage lasted until 1981.

Wizard, which involved answering questions based on the law of averages, got canceled in 1974. It was the first US step in Alex's professional journey toward the career grand prize of hosting *Jeopardy!* for 37 years. At times it was lonely and financially dubious, but he persevered and kept busy during trying times with hobbies like gourmet cooking, carpentry, practicing his French (Canada being officially bilingual), and reading.

The Wizard of Odds was followed by *High Rollers*, also in 1974. Though it involved dice, it was keyed to answering questions. It ran until 1976 when its format altered and contestants guessed the identity of a celebrity photo; the syndicator supposedly dumbed the show down to attract more viewers . . . the opposite happened. In 1978 NBC aired *The New High Rollers* for two years, with Trebek again hosting (when it returned in 1987 for one season, the host was Wink Martindale).

Meanwhile in 1976 Alex hosted CBS's *Double Dare*, which used the by-then anachronistic isolation booths that highlighted some 1950s game shows, including rigged ones. Contestants had to guess names of things, places, and people. Most of Trebek's shows would be knowledge-oriented (could one imagine him hosting *The Gong Show*?).

In 1977 he hosted *The $128,000 Question*, based on the notorious 1950s hit *The $64,000 Question*. The syndicated show commenced in 1976 in New York City with host Mike Darrow; Trebek hosted in Toronto for its final season. Not only were the questions hard but also one wrong answer lost a player all their winnings. A security guard in charge of questions was employed to reassure viewers and authorities there was no hanky-panky.

In 1980 Trebek was unemployed, later allowing that the situation further diminished the quality of his marriage. For one week while Chuck Woolery was sick, Trebek hosted *Wheel of Fortune*. Not until late in 1981 did Alex find work—two jobs, in fact. *Pitfall* was a syndicated Q and A game show out of Vancouver. The production company went broke in 1982.

"*Pitfall* was not a pleasant experience. They bounced my payment check. It came at a bad time because my father had died and my marriage had dissolved. . . . I could have used the money." Alex later framed the bounced $49,000 check and hung it on a wall.

His other new job in 1981 was emcee of NBC's *Battlestars*, which he dubbed "the son of *Hollywood Squares*." Instead of squares it had triangles. Celebrities answered the host's questions and then contestants had to judge the replies true or false. The show lasted 26 weeks.

In 1982 Alex hosted a pilot for *Starcade*, a video arcade game show for NBC that the network rejected. WTBS Superstation and then a syndicator took it up, minus Trebek. In 1983 he hosted *The New Battlestars*, but it petered out after three months. Then he hosted *Malcolm*—an odd name for a game show—an NBC pilot that didn't go to series.

Frustrated and lonely, dwelling in a barely furnished Hollywood apartment, he expanded his carpentry talents and built most of a 10-room house by himself in the Hollywood Hills. Late in 1983, Robert Murphy, vice president of Merv Griffin Enterprises, telephoned Trebek, inviting him to host the pilot for a new edition of *Jeopardy!* The drawback was the poor salary.

"They weren't going to pay me very much. So I asked them, 'Can I produce it also?' and they said okay. So for the first three years I produced and that way I was able to earn as much money as I had hosting my previous shows."

It took time for the new *Jeopardy!* to reconnect with audiences. Perhaps uncertain of his new show's future (who could guess it would eventually be headed for 40 more years?), Trebek did three more failed game show pilots in the mid-1980s.

In 1987 he became host of NBC's *Classic Concentration*. When he wasn't taping the two shows, he was on the road doing promotion and contestant auditioning for *Jeopardy!* Since 1981 he'd remained single, dating occasionally. In 1988, he met 25-year-old Jean Currivan, but they didn't keep in touch until several months later. They dated for a year and wed in 1990. In 1991, Alex became the father of a son and, two years later, of a daughter.

Also in 1991 he took over hosting the revived *To Tell the Truth* on NBC for its last three months. *Classic Concentration* was canceled in 1991. Henceforth, Trebek hosted *Jeopardy!*, period. In 1996, he became a US citizen and was summoned two weeks later for jury duty.

The years rolled on, and *Jeopardy!* and Trebek became an institution. Then in 2019 he revealed he had terminal pancreatic cancer. Alex died at age 80 in 2020 and was not replaced by a single host. Rather, a parade of hosts and potential hosts ensued. But the show, so firmly established and revered by many, continues supplying answers that must be responded to in the form of a question and keeps entertaining and enlightening new generations of viewers.

Inside *Jeopardy!*

Before I ever thought about being on *Jeopardy!* I wondered, in view of its name, who's in jeopardy? No risk involved, beyond possibly looking "dumb." Frankly, when the long-anticipated day arrived and I was on the set at Sony Studios (formerly MGM) in Culver City, lined up beside the other two contestants with Alex Trebek across from us and the cameras ready to roll, I reproached myself *why* was I doing this? What if I came in third? Even second, but especially *third*.

And "consolation prizes"—what an inevitably sad phrase.

But then the show commenced and zoom!—no commercials, no breaks, no chance to get nervous—it was Final Jeopardy! time. The category: Financial History. A mixed blessing for me. History, though not particularly US history, I'm a whiz at (not because my professor father taught it, though he did). But *financial* . . . ironic because my life partner of 22 years (now 47) was a banker. I knew plenty about economics, but the category's combination was daunting. How specific was this going to be?

And though I'm good at math (in school I didn't think so because I was better at the other subjects), my brain froze trying to figure out a formula for how much to bet on the outcome and still retain a few dollars if I guessed wrong.

The returning champion and I were about neck and neck, the third-place contestant was way behind but could conceivably win the game if we two males bet big but answered wrong. Happily, she, very nice, more than the pompous-seeming returning champ (maybe he was secretly nice) came in second. I was the only one with the correct answer.

To backtrack, I'd sometimes watched *Jeopardy!* while living in northern California. After moving south I tried out for it in 1986. I tried out annually 10 or 11 times and got on in 1998. Two strikes against me were geographical. The show seeks a diversity of contestants, so even if, say, half the people trying out were from southern California, preference usually went to those who passed the test and were from, say, Kalamazoo or Islin, New Jersey. Besides, I wasn't only from Los Angeles, I was from Beverly Hills. If, say, three of us from LA County passed, the two not from the hills of Beverly would likely get preference.

A frustrating thing about all those tests is you were never informed how many questions you must answer correctly to pass. And you were never given the answers. Afterward, you tried to remember as many questions out of the dozens you answered or guessed and looked up the answer.

After all the tests were completed and handed in, you waited long enough to watch at least one complete episode of *Jeopardy!* on a big screen. Then a talent coordinator, a movie-star handsome young man with a Jewish surname, came back in and read off the names of those who "passed," by whatever criteria, and could stay. The rest of us were free to go—in my, or our, case, to a nearby Famous Amos on Sunset Boulevard for a consolation mini binge of chocolate chip cookies and coffee.

I have to admit that being gay, I began to wonder after the fourth or fifth or eighth time I tried out whether I'd been perceived as gay and was possibly being discounted for that reason? Impossible to know the answer.

At one point I took a year or so off from trying out, somewhat discouraged and appalled. But eventually I figured I'll shame them into putting me on. I'm qualified, so I'll keep trying out year after year, decade after decade. If it reached that point, I could write an article for the *New Times*, the *LA Weekly*, or (less likely to be published in, then) the *Los Angeles Times*, on having tried out 20 times and, for some questionable reason, being denied contestantship on a game show devised (originally by his former wife) by Merv Griffin, a closeted gay man.

I don't recall what the nice gal in third place—ended up in second place—bet, but the returning champ and I each had more than $8,000 and each bet nearly all of it. We knew not to bet every single dollar. I won because before Ron and I travel—more than 60 countries, to date—I always read up on where we're going, on its history, culture, customs, sometimes its language (Istanbul is a favorite city, so I know about 200 Turkish words). Most of my knowledge has come since getting a master's degree, from frequent and voluntary reading, by far mostly nonfiction.

My birthday that year was in Vancouver, so I read up about Canada's fur-trapping early history and how animal pelts were used as *money*: yes, *financial history*! I won $16,400.

Lessons learned? Books, mostly nonfiction, keep making you smarter. And: *Persist!*

17

The Laughs Factory and Chuck Barris

CHUCK BARRIS WAS A WALKING CONTRADICTION. SEEMINGLY MODEST, he crowned himself the Game Show King (no doubt Mark Goodson was not amused). Yet he admitted he didn't like most game shows. Mild-mannered, he eventually came out in print as a purported hit man for the CIA; his memoir *Confessions of a Dangerous Mind* became a movie, the first directed by George Clooney. Fun-loving and casual, he was an ambitious media presence who at one time had five game shows on network daytime TV, Monday to Friday, and two at night.

Barris indulged his gourmet tastes and spent years living in France. Yet his TV creations were often tasteless, sometimes too much so to get on the air. Surprisingly, at one point he'd worked at ABC's Standards and Practices—its rules and censorship division (after getting hired as an NBC page thanks to a fake résumé offering several NBC execs as references; nobody checked.)

Of course, small-screen taste is in the eye and ear of the beholder. One of Chuck's hits was *The Newlywed Game*. Howard Hughes, who'd placed a bid to purchase ABC-TV, tuned in to the network's afternoon programming and then contacted his chief of staff: "Cancel my bid on ABC. I would never buy anything that played crap like *The Newlywed Game*."

Though Chuck Barris Productions was the most fun TV company to work at and Chuck enjoyed devising game show concepts with his well-treated staff, he said his goal was producing movies. Soon as he could, he made a movie—a resounding flop—after becoming a TV star by hosting *The Gong Show*. That first and final film was the self-directed starring vehicle *The Gong Show Movie* (1980).

Chuck Hirsch Barris was born in 1929 into a Philadelphia Jewish family. His father was a dentist, and his uncle singer-songwriter Harry Barris. Chuck played the guitar, wrote for the school paper, and graduated from the Drexel Institute of Technology. During his spare time at ABC he composed the song "Palisades Park" and sold it to the network's *American Bandstand*'s guest singer Freddy Cannon. ABC was shocked, fearing conflict of interest and bad publicity in the wake of the payola scandals.

Even so, Barris got promoted to ABC vice president in charge of daytime programming. His mission was choosing new game shows. After finding that the shows pitched to him were too boring or derivative, he departed ABC to found his own production company and create better and "hipper" show ideas.

Back he went to ABC where he pitched a winner. It was inspired by *Where the Action Is*, a youth-oriented program that helped Chuck conceive a show where a young woman talked to a few young men to choose one for a date. She asked her questions of unseen males behind a wall. In 1965 the notion of a young woman or "girl" choosing whom to date (rather than waiting to be asked) and disappointing two men was semi-radical. However, the gamble drew a sizeable female audience.

Comedian Rip Taylor, who later hosted Barris's *The $1.98 Beauty Show*, explained, "The word 'game' in *The Dating Game* didn't refer to a game show, though it was one. People used to call a profession or activity a 'game'... 'I'm in the insurance game' or that musical *The Pajama Game*. So this show was for people curious about the dating game." It premiered December 20, 1965.

Barris intended his maiden production (he'd already done an unsold pilot) to stand out. It featured a live rock band and dancers. The show's burgeoning popularity and fast pace didn't require either. Both were gone within a few months. What it required more of, five times a week, were contestants: "bachelorette" (occasionally bachelor) interviewers, plus three guys to be questioned, twice per show, thus 40 contestants a week.

The questions and answers were staff-designed to be risqué. Because how the answers were delivered was crucial, contestants were more apt to be trained actors than ordinary people.

To ensure a steady stream of contestants, Barris paid them. Typical game show players participate in hopes of winning money or prizes. On *The Dating Game* they were paid the hundreds of dollars mandated by the American Federation of Television and Radio Artists (AFTRA) as minimum payment for pros. The fact that mostly these weren't contestants like on other shows and the answers were often obviously rehearsed didn't bother most viewers, who enjoyed the humor, sex appeal, good-lookers, gaudy floral set, upbeat music, and suspense of who would the woman choose.

(The show's so-1960s theme music was "Spanish Flea," performed by Herb Alpert and the Tijuana Brass. A supposed reason for the choice was its resemblance to Spanish Fly, an alleged aphrodisiac actually made of dried beetle dung.)

Some viewers and a few critics carped about the prefab verbal exchanges but in vain because the resulting dates were genuine. Another potential liability was that Barris encouraged actors to become repeat contestants by employing a new look and a new name. Future "Pee-wee Herman" Paul Reubens appeared on *The Dating Game* three times (and 14 on *The Gong Show*). If the practice wasn't quite aboveboard, neither was the show rigged, and no one knew who would win a date.

The show announced itself, "From Hollywood, the Dating Capital of the World!" Its free 'n easy feel was fostered by host Jim Lange, a popular San Francisco disc jockey and sportscaster. Cheerful, easygoing, not handsome enough to compete with the bachelors, and an older-brother figure, he closed each show with trademark kiss-blowing to the audience from himself and the winning couples.

Lange called *The Dating Game* "probably the first reality show" because it didn't flow as predictably as a Q and A program. His job, he said, was to keep up the pace, "pull something out of the bachelors" if need be, and avoid or settle any confrontation.

After a prime-time edition of *The Dating Game* was added in 1966, the person interviewing the three opposite-sex contestants could be a celebrity. One was stripper Gypsy Rose Lee, who didn't really strip and was by then middle-aged though svelte. The ensuing confrontation was one Lange couldn't do anything about. The 6' 4" gent who won the date with Lee wasn't quite a gent. After placing his arm around her he touched her where he shouldn't and she slapped him hard.

"The camera was not on them when she hit him. I was telling them where they were going on their date. . . . While they were taking beauty shots of Europe to cover my voice-over she whacked him. I just kept going.

"When they came back they took a shot and he was still smiling but he had a little blood coming down his mouth. That was on camera. I'm sure the people at home thought, 'What the heck is happening?'"

(Chuck Barris later claimed that his chaperoning *Dating Game* winners on overseas dates allowed him to perform the murders assigned by the CIA.)

The nighttime *Dating Game* lasted until 1970. In 1973, ABC canceled the daytime version. It resumed two months later in weekly syndication but was gone after one season. It returned in syndication in 1978 for three seasons (Jim Lange hosted) and then from 1986 to 1989, hosted by Elaine Joyce as *The New Dating Game* and Jeff McGregory as *The All-New Dating Game*.

From 1996 to 1999, it was hosted by Brad Sherwood and then Chuck Woolery. It resumed in mid-2021 (eight episodes) as *The Celebrity Dating Game*, hosted by actress Zooey Deschanel and singer Michael Bolton. Only, the winners didn't get to go on dates with the celebrities.

ABC, for a long time the third-ranked network, was delighted with *The Dating Game* and Chuck Barris. So when a producing duo that included the creator of *Howdy Doody* contacted ABC about a simple game show premise jotted down on a napkin, the network presented it to Barris and later paid the two men royalties. The idea was trying to get matching answers from both halves of various pairs of newlyweds. As with *The Dating Game*, *The Newlywed Game* in 1966 proved a virtually instant, and long-running, hit. (For more on the show, see chapter 21.)

Chuck Barris Productions had a staff of six late in 1965; a year later, 60. In 1967 the average age of Chuck Barris Production employees was

24 (Barris was 38 years old). Not only was there no dress code, but if a newcomer came to work in a suit, he was smilingly ordered to go home and get casual after his necktie was ritually scissored. Music lover Chuck encouraged staffers to bring in musical instruments so they could enjoy jam sessions. A tradition emerged regarding the sale of a new game show: Chuck's entire team would surround him and then he announced the latest success while pouring beer over his head. The youthful boss frequently wore funny hats to induce laughter and often ran up to workers and hugged them. Football games in the office weren't unusual.

"It sounds like goofing off . . . but everybody got their jobs done," said Shelley Herman, who had friends among Barris's employees. "Everybody got their questions written for *The Newlywed Game* and did the screenings for *Dating Game* contestants and got all the prizes coordinated. Everybody had a job and worked very hard at it.

"I think the secret was the amount of fun you had working for Chuck. If your boss encourages jam sessions and parties and football games you fall in love with that job so much that you dread the idea of working anywhere else. So in a way everybody worked hard so they could keep goofing off."

Wink Martindale recalled, "I hosted two shows for Chuck and neither lasted very long but it left a lasting impression. He had a really fun staff. In my entire career I never saw a company that had more fun knocking out TV shows than Chuck's staff. It was such a great environment."

Yet as mentioned, Barris had greater ambitions. In 1968 he confessed, "The real purpose of our group is to produce motion pictures. . . . We have used the game shows as a base so we can get into other things . . . I constantly live in fear of being called a 'game show producer.'" He optioned several novels for filming but none went before the cameras.

Dating Game and *Newlywed Game* were the company's mainstays. Subsequent shows and concepts didn't match their success. Some were fortunately short-lived (see chapter 26), and some were nixed before they hit the air, including *The Divorcée*—remember that 1960s sitcoms avoided divorced characters, especially if they were women.

In 1967 Barris debuted three new game shows, and none was a winner. Two were *Dream Girl of '67* and *How's Your Mother-in-Law?* (see chapter 26). The other was *The Family Game*, involving three sets of parents with two of their kids, ages 6 to 11. Hopes were high because the program was inspired by *The Newlywed Game*. But it wasn't a very happy set because host Bob Barker didn't get along with Chuck's staff.

Newlywed host Bob Eubanks revealed that at one point Barker refused to say the words "belly button" and sequestered himself in his dressing room until the question was rewritten. Chuck gained admission to the dressing room but came out looking grim. "'Belly button' is out," he softly informed an employee. *The Family Game* lasted half a year and Barker and Barris didn't cross paths again.

It was probably unrealistic to expect *The Family Game* to match *The Newlywed Game*'s popularity minus the latter's risqué, often adults-only humor.

Barris ventured outside the game show format to produce *Operation: Entertainment*, a 1968 ABC variety show. Each week it originated from a different military base and had a different host but flaunted the Operation: Entertainment Girls. The in-person audience was servicemen. Four were selected to go on stage, ogle, and flirt with the girls. Musical and comedic celebrity guests performed numbers. It lasted a season.

Chuck Barris Productions' first show to go directly into syndication—his product was increasingly less popular—rather than air on ABC was 1969's *The Game Game*. It was advertised as the show that revealed a little more about your favorite celebrities and yourself. (Barris often said he was more interested in learning about shows' personalities than in "clues, questions, or arbitrary game rules.") *The Game Game*'s participants were three celebs and a contestant representing "yourself." Each episode centered on a question like How romantic are you? or How shy are you? All four participants took a five-question quiz "validated" by the Southern California Institute of Psychology. The noncelebrity could win money by correctly guessing whether their score at show's end would be lower or higher than the celebrities'. Hosted by newcomer Jim McKrell, the program endured one season.

McKrell had shown up at *The Game Game* auditions to try for announcer, but Chuck Barris thought the tall blond Texan was auditioning for host and hired him as such. Jim later explained, "Chuck taught me a lot about hosting. Chuck told me that the host is a traffic cop. My main job was to keep things moving. And he really hammered home the point that I'm not the star of the show. The game is the star.

"Chuck could be a little goofy sometimes but I liked him because I could see how he treated his staff. Chuck, even as the boss, showed loyalty to the people who worked for him."

Barris's 1960s show *The Family Game* hadn't worked out, but in 1972 his game show factory produced *The Parent Game*. Forgoing children, it featured parents and USC psychologist Dorothy Thompson. Radio host Clark Race was tapped to host. Three wedded couples each answered five questions about raising kids. The questions had multiple-choice answers and varying point values. The child psychologist weighed in with opinions, and at show's end the points were added up to determine a winning couple; it lasted one syndicated season.

In 1973, Barris played it safer by acquiring the rights to *Treasure Hunt*, which had aired on ABC prime time and then NBC prime time and daytime between 1956 and 1959. Where the original had two contestants answering questions and 30 treasure chests on stage to choose from, the new syndicated weekly version had three contestants and 30 boxes. Chests/boxes contained anything from a head of lettuce to money (in the 1970s a check for $25,000).

The New Treasure Hunt ran four years and then returned in 1981 as *Treasure Hunt*, which was syndicated daily. Both versions were hosted by Geoff Edwards. "It was a unique experience," said the understated Edwards, who once got a pie in the face while on air from Barris for laughs. "Chuck can be somewhat extreme in his personality and debatably unethical in his professional intentions" (see chapter 24). Although the 1981 *Treasure Hunt* boasted 66 boxes and upped the grand prize to $50,000, it ran just a year. The show is said to have been an inspiration for *Deal or No Deal* in 2005.

In 1976, Chuck Barris became a national figure through the everybody's-talking-about-it *The Gong Show*. He hadn't intended becoming a host but constraints of time, budget, and pro hosts' reluctance resulted in his emceeing the daytime NBC version, whereas *Laugh-In* announcer and renowned disc jockey Gary Owens hosted the nighttime edition.

A merciless spoof of amateur talent shows, *Gong Show* acts were rated by a three-part celebrity panel on a scale of 1 to 10, unless one or more judges decided an act was too awful to continue and got up and gonged it. An episode's highest scorer won $516.32 ($712.05 during prime time; when the show returned in 1988 its top prize was $701.).

The Gong Show ran four years and spawned both a noncompetitive prime-time hour titled *The Chuck Barris Rah-Rah Show* (February to April 1978) and its own basically awful 1980 movie. By then Chuck's laughs factory was irretrievably sliding downhill. A significant factor was his 1979–1980 show *Three's a Crowd* (see chapter 26), which revolved around men with wives and secretaries and reportedly caused three divorces. The sexist show drew criticism from both feminists and morality watchdogs. It was accused of encouraging adultery and exploiting it for entertainment. At the predawn of the Reagan era, the protests caused many stations to drop the program.

Concern that *The Newlywed Game* had become too prurient caused it to lose Ford and Procter & Gamble as sponsors. The show was filmed at KTLA, whose conservative owner (and former movie cowboy) Gene Autry and wife were ready to evict it, but its syndicator canceled it first. *The Dating Game* and *The Gong Show* were also canceled in 1980 despite their successful runs in syndication.

"Media coverage, sometimes exaggerated, of the not very widespread protests resulted in [Chuck Barris's] reputation quickly turning unsavory," said publicist Andrea Jaffe. "Not just low-brow, but almost smutty. . . . Stations were backtracking . . . all of a sudden more afraid of nervous advertisers and 'community standards' groups that were specifically targeting the Barris shows. Whether anti-Semitism was a part of that, I'm not sure."

Chuck tried a mini comeback in 1980 with the noncontroversial and uninteresting *Camouflage*, based on a same-name 1961 ABC show. Its object was to locate an object—a dragon, a toaster, and so on—hidden in a cartoonish drawing. It aired from February to April. By late 1980, for the first time, Chuck Barris Productions didn't have a single show in production. He exited the game world for a year and then renamed his company Chuck Barris Industries and revived *Treasure Hunt* which lasted the one season. Again he left.

In 1984 he returned from France and did a week's trial run of a less risqué *Newlywed Game*, which was hosted by Jim Lange. That led to a 1985 syndicated *The New Newlywed Game* hosted by Bob Eubanks. It ran until 1989; in 1988 comedian Paul Rodriguez took over as host.

Chuck Barris was also an author. His 1974 first novel was inspired by the breakup of his first marriage to the niece of a CBS cofounder. A decade later, he published his first supposedly nonfiction book, *Confessions of a Dangerous Mind: An Unauthorized Autobiography*. It didn't sell particularly well despite its "unauthorized" author's claim of having been a CIA assassin. Reviewers were skeptical. One Canadian critic opined, "This book is the desperate bid for unceasing attention by the emcee whose manic, erratic hosting of *The Gong Show* thoroughly proved his descent into egomania."

Book sales took off after the 2002 movie version in which he killed 33 people. The CIA vehemently denied that Barris had ever worked for them (but then, they would). Professor of media psychology Stuart Fischoff noted, "Mr. Barris has made known his resentment at being vilified for both his successful and unsuccessful small-screen entertainments . . . to the extent that in disgust he abandoned career and country, albeit temporarily.

"His boast of having been a serial killer may be recompense for his low public standing . . . a twisted attempt at heroism and power."

Barris wasn't called on to explain or excuse the immorality of killing CIA-defined "enemies." Rather, media focus was on whether or not he'd lied, even though in 1984 he stated on *The Today Show*, "No, I was never a CIA hit man. I never did those things." He said he'd once applied to the CIA but was then offered a TV job. On the heels of the movie, Barris published a memoir sequel that continued his assassinations claim and in 2010 replied during a Television Academy Foundation interview, "I'll never say, one way or the other."

Barris wrote several more books, including novels, *The Game Show King* and *Della*, a memoir of his drug-addicted only child who died at 36.

Although 1986 saw a return of the syndicated *Dating Game*—hosted, as noted, by a woman—in 1987 Barris sold his shares in his company and moved back to France. The following year a *Gong Show* revival (one season) was hosted by "True" Don Bleu. In 2000 the Game Show Network produced *Extreme Gong*, and in 2008 it returned as *The Gong Show with Dave Attell*; it resurfaced in 2017 with host "Tommy Maitland" played by chameleon Mike Myers.

Chuck Barris's company changed hands and names before merging into Sony, which in 1996 (to 1999) brought back his two biggest hits as *The Dating/Newlywed Hour*. His name may not be part of the credits of the reboots of his more popular shows but reruns of the shows he brought to television and the one hit he hosted live on electronically. In the 1990s, Barris contracted lung cancer but lived until March 21, 2017. He died of natural causes in Palisades, New York, at age 87.

18

Hollywood Squares and Peter Marshall

FOR 25 YEARS BERT PARKS (NÉ BERTRAM JACOBSON IN 1914) HOSTED the Miss America Pageant and was nationally known and spoofed for crooning "There she is, Miss America. . . ." He hosted one of the first long-running TV game shows, *Break the Bank* (1948–1957) before becoming Mr. Miss America in 1955. By the 1960s he was sometimes criticized for his emotive hosting style, responding heatedly that television personalities had become too bland. In 1965 Parks hosted the pilot for a new game show as "The Master of the Hollywood Squares."

Its packager, Merrill Heatter-Bob Quigley Productions, pitched the pilot to all three networks. It was later theorized that their quick refusals were due to Parks's age and also his "schmaltzy, old-fashioned appeal," per Canadian actor-host Alan Thicke. Heatter and Quigley, confident in their basic yet fun, celebrity-studded concept, substituted Peter Marshall, Parks's junior by 12 years and more laid-back. The show's host wasn't intended to "compete" with its nine celebrities the way ebullient Gene Rayburn did with his stars on *The Match Game*.

Peter, whose primary interests were music and the stage, had briefly hosted a Los Angeles game show and originally declined emceeing the new pilot. Hosting wasn't his goal. He'd recently been seen on Broadway in *Skyscraper* (1965–1966), a rare Julie Harris musical, and was considering a musical stage version of Truman Capote's novella *Breakfast at Tiffany's* (which when it hit the boards with Mary Tyler Moore and Richard Chamberlain was a resounding flop).

What prompted Marshall to take the gig was hearing that if he said no, the producers would pick Dan Rowan to host. Peter, who avowed he disliked practically nobody, much disliked Rowan, later famous for *Rowan & Martin's Laugh-In*. In the 1950s, Marshall had teamed with Tommy Noonan (best known as Marilyn Monroe's bespectacled fiancé in *Gentlemen Prefer Blondes*) in a successful comedy act. Rowan blatantly stole material from their act. By hosting the pilot Peter got to "screw Dan Rowan out of a job," even though he figured the pilot might not sell or if it did it would last 13 weeks or at best one season.

Larry White was an out-of-work TV director when Heatter and Quigley hired him to helm their pilot. By the time they pitched it to NBC a second time White was head of the network's daytime programming and greenlit *Hollywood Squares*, which was inspired by tic-tac-toe. Dan Rowan never had a similar solo success as Peter Marshall, who hosted the show for 15 years and more than 5,000 episodes.

It debuted in October 1966 and became a phenomenon, eventually airing in daytime, nighttime, and syndication. For a while there was also a Saturday-morning kiddie version, *Storybook Squares*, in which celebrities appeared costumed as nursery rhyme or fairy tale characters.

Hollywood Squares didn't have to scramble for celebs to fill its nine squares; they clamored to guest on the program or become regulars. The most memorable regular was Paul Lynde, the sassy-mouthed center square (he joined the show in 1968), who wound up receiving more fan mail than Peter Marshall, who graciously credited Lynde with the show's ongoing success. Long-retired legend (back when that word meant something) Greta Garbo was so devoted to *Hollywood Squares* that she wrote Lynde a widely publicized fan letter. By 1970 *Hollywood Squares* was daytime's top-rated TV show.

Marshall felt another key to the program's success was its simplicity. The two contestants had merely to agree or disagree with a given celebrity's response to the host's question. The actual answer usually followed a laugh-getting reply. For instance Peter asked TV fixture George Gobel, "True or false: A pea can last as long as 5,000 years?" The middle-aged Gobel half-joked, "Boy, it sure seems that way sometimes." Then he rendered a "true" or "false," and the contestant who'd picked him agreed or disagreed, winning or losing that square while trying to achieve three squares in a row—"across, up and down, or diagonally" (Marshall reeled off the rules at the start of each program).

Although the show's jokes were prepared, not ad-libbed, there was no conflict of interest or potential scandal because the contestants and celebs weren't given the questions in advance. Nor did Peter know ahead of time what the gags would be. Under his podium were nine slots, one per star. When a contestant chose a particular star, Marshall pulled out a question from that particular slot. The selected star, if memory didn't serve, could unobtrusively view the corresponding gag answer and deliver the apparently spontaneous punchline.

A few insiders deplored the planning, whether for ethical reasons—despite the funny lines not affecting the game's outcome—or jealousy. Game show titan Mark Goodson accused *Hollywood Squares* of practicing "actionable fraud." The Federal Communications Commission, concerned about the funny lines, investigated but didn't ask the show to stop the mirth. Rather, Peter Marshall's rules spiel now concluded: "And remember, although the stars are briefed in advance to help them with their bluffs, they're hearing the actual questions for the first time."

Besides the zingers, another attraction was seeing so many famous people not playing roles but appearing as themselves. Said Merrill Heatter in 1967, "People enjoy seeing celebrities test their intelligence on the air. It brings the star down to the audience's level . . . putting them in a vulnerable spot where they might come up with a wrong answer."

Over the years *Hollywood Squares* attracted some stars who didn't usually do game shows, from former superstar Betty Grable to stage icon Helen Hayes and movie stars Walter Matthau and George C. Scott. Burt Reynolds often returned because he felt the show had launched his career. A booker for *The Tonight Show* saw him on *Squares* and booked him onto the country's number one talk show, hosted by Johnny Carson, which led to Reynolds landing his star-making role in the film *Deliverance*.

The *Hollywood Squares* staff intermittently had to deal with up-acting stellar egos. One Gabor sister was known for occasional temper tantrums if her hair wasn't styled just so. Michael Landon was at times rude to autograph seekers during breaks. A few celebs had to be kept from drinking too much alcohol during meal breaks. Once in a while, a celebrity failed to show up for a taping.

One time two celebs canceled at the last moment. A crisis was averted when guest and impressionist Rich Little was assigned two extra celebrity squares bearing names of stars whom Little imitated. When a contestant chose one of them, Little would move into that box and answer as the selected star, be it James Stewart or Carol Channing.

When an earthquake took place during a taping, eight celebrities rushed down and away from the three-level tic-tac-toe set. Only Paul Lynde remained static in his center square until the shaking was over.

Peter Marshall was born Ralph Pierre (Peter in French) LaCock in West Virginia in 1926. Though would-be celebrities often changed their names, few took their stage name from a sister, as Marshall did. After his father's suicide in 1937 Peter's mother and older sister Letitia LaCock moved to Manhattan, where the teen was signed by modeling agent John Robert Powers and renamed Joanne Marshall. (She later changed it to Joanne Dru and acted in the films *Red River*, *All the King's Men*, and *She Wore a Yellow Ribbon*.) Earning good money, the model was able to bring her brother to New York to live with her and their mother.

At 14, Peter was working as an usher at the famed Paramount Theater. Soon he was a page at NBC Radio and singing with the Bob Chester Band. However, he returned to West Virginia at 17 to complete high school before getting drafted and shipped to Italy. There, he reconnected with a radio personality from NBC and spent a year and a half spinning records as a disc jockey in Naples.

In 1946, Marshall relocated to Florida, where he sang regularly on a radio station and in Miami bars and wed the following year. He and Nadine Teaford had two daughters and two sons. But Peter wasn't going to set the world on fire as a singer and, by 1949, was in Los Angeles, where his sister's then-husband, actor John Ireland, had a brother, Tommy Noonan, who was aiming for comedy stardom. (His other most famous role was in the 1954 *A Star Is Born* with Judy Garland.) Noonan and Marshall became a comedy duo in the mold of Dean Martin and Jerry Lewis because Peter needed to earn enough money to pay a $78 dental bill.

Although their act got hired for radio, television, stage, and a handful of movies—with Marshall as the straight man—they didn't go far, for two reasons. They continued working individually and often weren't jointly available when opportunity knocked. Too, they didn't possess significant star quality, together or individually. By 1962 they'd broken up for good after splitting in 1954 and then reteaming four years later. Noonan died in 1968 at age 46 of a brain tumor.

Peter's goal of stage stardom looked possible in 1961 when he appeared on Broadway in *How to Make a Man*. But it ran from February 2 to February 11 and Broadway didn't soon beckon again so he found further and farther stage work in Las Vegas and London (as *Bye Bye Birdie*'s male lead, the role played by Dick Van Dyke on Broadway and in the film version) before supporting Julie Harris in *Skyscraper*.

Once *Hollywood Squares* came along, Marshall kept busy year-round. He acted in summer stock and guested on TV programs, mostly sitcoms. With a *Squares* producer, he formed a company, Marshall-Armstrong Productions, to create game shows, but none materialized. In 1976 he got to star on TV in *The Peter Marshall Variety Show*, but it lasted 19 weeks.

After *Hollywood Squares* ended in 1981, he returned in 1982 as cohost of *Fantasy*, an hour-long series that made chosen individuals' nonmonetary "fantasies" come true. It lasted a season. In 1984 Marshall was back on stage as a replacement for one of two male leads in the gay-themed Broadway musical *La Cage aux Folles*. It toured the country for two years before returning to the Great White Way.

While touring, Peter hosted a new ABC game show, *All-Star Blitz*. It featured two contestants and four celebrities. Marshall asked a star a question, often eliciting a funny response prior to a realistic answer, with the contestant who picked the celeb either agreeing or disagreeing. It was reminiscent of *Hollywood Squares*, but instead of playing tic-tac-toe, correct answers (or guesses) yielded a portion of a word puzzle whose solution won the game. The show was canceled that December.

While appearing in Atlantic City in the musical *42nd Street*, Peter signed to host *Yahtzee*, a game show based on the popular game that used five dice—giant dice in the TV version. It debuted in January 1988 with two teams of three players each replying to questions and attempting to match answers with a panel of five stars. The higher-scoring team got to roll the great big dice. The goal was to roll five of the same number, called a "yahtzee." Marshall deemed it "a really good show," but the syndicated program experienced financial problems and was soon off the air.

In 1988 Peter was asked to host a new show titled *3rd Degree*, via Burt & Bert Productions, formed by Burt Reynolds and Bert Convy. Marshall wasn't enthusiastic but Convy talked him into it. Peter taped the pilot, and then Bert was let go as host of *Win, Lose or Draw*, which he owned with Reynolds. The show's syndicator wanted a younger host to draw a younger audience. Convy decided to take over hosting *3rd Degree* himself, and in 1989, Burt & Bert dropped Peter Marshall as host. He filed a lawsuit charging Burt & Bert with breaking their contract.

"If [Bert] wanted to do the show, he should have called me and said, 'Hey, Pete, can I have lunch with you? Look, they just fired me from my own show. I want to do *3rd Degree*. I'll tell you what we'll do. We'll make a deal with you.'

"I would have said, 'Go ahead and do it, that's fine.' I didn't want to do it in the first place. I didn't think it was that good of a show, but they made me such a deal that it was almost impossible to turn it down.

"That's all [Bert] had to do, was be straight with me. But he wasn't."

Convy hosted *3rd Degree* during 1989–1990, but it wasn't renewed for a second season. In 1990, Peter scratched his lawsuit because of the brain tumor that would take Bert's life in 1991 at age 57. "I didn't want to have to sue his children and I didn't want to sue the estate."

Early in the 1990s Marshall did more stage work and developed a one-man singing-and-dancing show he peripatetically performed in nightclubs. In 1994 he rotated as host of *The $25,000 Game Show* with Bob Eubanks and Dennis James. The untelevised for-tourists live show was performed in Branson, Missouri. Peter departed after a few months. "I didn't want to stay in Branson."

He returned to hosting on TV in 1998 with *Reel to Reel* for the new cable channel Pax. Drawn from the board game *The Reel to Reel Picture Show*, it involved two teams comprised of a celebrity and a contestant and movie-trivia knowledge. Based in Orlando, Florida, the show did well for Pax and was about to transfer to Los Angeles for easier star access when the production company went belly up after 13 weeks. Marshall recalled, "They owe me a ton of money. I never got paid and none of my stars were paid." It was Peter's final game show.

After game shows the music lover kept busy doing concerts nationwide and hosting a syndicated daily radio program, *The Music of Your Life*.

"I've been doing it for over 15 years . . . I get to play my records and talk about the music of the 1930s and '40s. . . . I was part of the Big Band era." Peter also released music CDs, including *Boy Singer*. In 1987 he humbly apprised the *Los Angeles Daily News* that his 15 years with *Hollywood Squares* made the rest of his career possible and that without the game show he would be "an unknown."

Marshall's first marriage lasted from 1947 to 1973, his second from 1977 to 1983. In 1989 he remarried. Early in 2021, he and Laurie were diagnosed with COVID-19. She recovered handily, but Peter was hospitalized, then got 24/7 home care and recovered, and soon after caught pneumonia. His son David died from the virus in August 2021 in Hawaii at age 68. On announcing David's death to the media, Peter Marshall urged everyone to get vaccinated, for their own sake and that of their loved ones.

Son Peter LaCock, born in 1952, was a Major League baseball player with the Chicago Cubs and the Kansas City Royals.

In 2006 Marshall was bestowed the Bill Cullen Award for Lifetime Achievement by the Game Show Congress. In 2007 he was one of the first inductees into the American TV Game Show Hall of Fame in Las Vegas. In 2013 he was inducted into the West Virginia Music Hall of Fame and was introduced by journalist, TV host, and friend Nick Clooney (brother of late singer Rosemary Clooney and father of actor George).

The next year Peter returned to West Virginia to tape four games of *West Virginia Squares* as part of Charleston's FestivALL. The shows featured the state's music and history and were broadcast on local public TV and made available to schools there. In 2017 he narrated the documentary *Wait for Your Laugh*, about Rose Marie, a child star later best known for *The Dick Van Dyke Show* and as a longtime *Hollywood Squares* regular.

Hollywood Squares aired three seasons in syndication when it returned in 1986, hosted by John Davidson with Joan Rivers in the center square. It was also syndicated from 1998 to 2004, hosted by Tom Bergeron with Whoopi Goldberg in the middle until she left prematurely. But it was never again as popular as with Peter Marshall and Paul Lynde.

In 2002, after 21 years, he returned to the show for one week as the center square and as host. The author of the memoir *Hollywood Square* explained, "They asked me if I'd like to do the show. I had a book out and said, 'If you'll plug the book every day and let me host it one day, I'll do the show.' And they said, 'Sure.'"

Shockingly, most of the original *Hollywood Squares* shows were never rerun because NBC had erased the tapes for use in taping newer shows. Fortunately, Filmways, the production entity, made copies before the network blanked out the masters. Some 3,000 tape copies lay forgotten in a warehouse in "beautiful downtown Burbank" until TV executive Jim Pierson started tracking down episodes of the gothic soap opera *Dark Shadows* and happened on the *Squares* episodes. Ownership had passed from Filmways to Orion to MGM; Pierson informed the Game Show Network, and *Hollywood Squares* experienced another new lease on life starting in April 2002.

King of the Zingers

At a time when US TV censors prevented Mick Jagger (in 1967) from singing the words "Let's spend the night together" on Ed Sullivan's variety show, comic actor Paul Lynde (1926–1982) was getting away with zingers like the following.

P.M.: Diamonds should not be kept with your family jewels. Why?

P.L.: They're so cold!

P.M.: What did the Lone Ranger always leave behind when he left town?

P.L.: A masked baby.

P.M.: Nathan Hale, one of the heroes of the American Revolution, was hung. Why?

P.L.: Heredity.

P.M.: What is a good reason for pounding meat?

P.L.: Loneliness!

P.M.: Who was known as Old Blood and Guts?

P.L.: Barbara Stanwyck.

P.M.: In television, who lives in Doodyville?

P.L.: The Ty-D-Bowl Man.

P.M.: True or false: Many people sleep better in their street clothes than they do in their pajamas?

P.L.: Yes. We call them winos.

P.M.: From what animal do you get silk blouses?

P.L.: An animal to you, Peter, but kind and generous to me.

P.M.: You're the world's most popular fruit. What are you?

P.L.: Humble.

P.M.: If the right part comes along, will George C. Scott do a nude scene?

P.L.: You mean he doesn't have the right part?

P.M.: In the Shakespeare play King Lear, King Lear had three of them—Goneril, Cordelia, and Regan. Who were they?

P.L.: King Lear had Goneril?

P.M.: At the end of the movie *Planet of the Apes* what does Charlton Heston see that makes him realize he is actually in New York?

P.L.: A Puerto Rican.

P.M.: Is it possible to drink too much water?

P.L.: Yes, it's called drowning.

P.M.: Paul, did the recently deceased Smokey the Bear leave a widow?

P.L.: Let's just say at the services they had to sedate Ranger Bob.

P.M.: Does (multi-Olympic gold medalist) Mark Spitz believe it's easier to swim nude?

P.L.: Well, it's easier to steer.

P.M.: In Alice in Wonderland who kept crying, "I'm late, I'm late"?

P.L.: Alice—and her mother is sick about it.

Tic Tac Dough

Hollywood Squares wasn't the first game show based on tic-tac-toe—just the most star-studded and witty. *Tic Tac Dough* debuted in 1956, initially hosted by coproducer Jack Barry. In 1957 it added a nighttime version that ran 15 months. The daytime version ceased in 1959.

It returned in 1978, airing for 45 network episodes but 1,560 syndicated episodes until 1986. Its longest-running host was Wink Martindale, from 1978 to 1985. Making the new program more distinctive was its mascot, a colorful dragon with big nostrils featured during the Beat the Dragon bonus round. Martindale gave away dragon T-shirts, and from 1979 on, each of the show's Fridays became Hat Day, when Wink got to show off unusual hats sent in by viewers.

Tic Tac Dough was revived in 1990 for syndication—65 episodes—hosted by actor Patrick Wayne, son of John. The revival's theme music was the last that multi-Grammy winner Henry Mancini composed for television.

Based on a basic international game, *Tic Tac Dough* spawned several foreign versions and was popular in Australia, Germany, and Honduras, besides Britain, where it was titled *Criss Cross Quiz*, Spain (*XO Da Dinero*, meaning XO Gives Money), and Indonesia (*Tak Tik BOOM*).

In 2021, NBC greenlit a pilot for a new *Tic Tac Dough*, hosted by Tom Bergeron.

19

She Hosts, Too!

IN 1983 BETTY WHITE BECAME THE FIRST FEMALE GAME SHOW HOST to win an Emmy Award for the short-lived *Just Men!* In 1949 Arlene Francis pioneered by hosting TV's *Blind Date,* following up with three more 1950s shows, all four which were short-lived. TV star Arthur Godfrey's sister Kathy Godfrey briefly hosted in 1954, but not until the women's rights movement in the 1970s did female hosts become more common.

Why did it take so long? Betty recalled that in 1964 Mark Goodson-Bill Todman Productions chose her to host the new game show *Get the Message,* but ABC vetoed her. "They didn't want a woman . . . they were afraid people wouldn't tune in to see a woman in charge. I think the network underrated its viewers."

The networks underrated women, period. "They were adjuncts to the men, to the hosts," said future Columbia Pictures president Dawn Steel. "Like with a magician's pretty and anonymous assistant. . . . They were models. . . . They were 'demonstrators' who did nothing but stand next to a product or prize and smile at it. It was pathetic and demeaning."

The Big Surprise (1955–1957), hosted by Jack Barry and then Mike Wallace, had two categories of questions. The easy questions were carried in by Sue Oakland, credited as Easy Question Girl, and hard ones by Mary Gardner, the Hard Question Girl. Change, when it occurred, was slow. In 1974 bottle-blonde Ruta Lee stood next to *High Rollers* host

Alex Trebek. Sometimes costumed in polka dots or with a bow on her dress, the talented actress was there to roll the contestants' dice.

In later decades, the women were sometimes billed as "assistants" but, added Steel, "You never saw a woman over forty or somewhat overweight. . . . Under whatever title or pretext, they were objects of display, to be looked at. Their self-limiting job was to enhance the hosts and please the male viewers."

Though game show hosts don't have near the control and input that, say, movie directors do, they're the symbol or mascot of a given show as well as its authority figure. Rose Marie, former child star and *Dick Van Dyke Show* costar, called it a Catch-22. "It's like for new actors. They can't get a job without a union card but they can't get a card without a job.

"The guys in charge said audiences weren't used to seeing a lady hostess but that's because the guys hardly ever gave them the chance." When they did, the woman typically emceed a show built around stereotypical interests like looks, makeup, cooking, housewifery, and . . . men.

Kathy Godfrey hosted numerous shows over the years plus the game show *On Your Way*. She offered a reason game shows were usually closed to female hosts. "They're about prizes and money. Money was serious, a masculine domain. It was business. . . . There weren't businesswomen, that word didn't exist."

Women on game shows had one of two functions: decoration or comedy. Rose Marie did *Hollywood Squares* for 14 years. "Yeah, a few times I did think about being an em-shee. But not seriously. Who'd hire me? . . . What they might've thought was me hosting a talk show. They didn't mind women talking . . . gabbing.

"But that wasn't my thing. I was happy on *Squares*. It was only lots later I realized no matter how smart or talented a gal was, she was only there to entertain. Not to help run things."

During the 1970s and 1980s, cracks appeared in the white-male-only monopoly of game show hosting. Black singer Adam Wade broke the color bar hosting *Musical Chairs* in 1975. It lasted less than five months. Comedian Nipsey Russell, a frequent *Match Game* panelist during the 1970s, also pioneered, hosting *Your Number's Up* in 1985. It lasted three months. "I was proud to be a host. Only, it's a whole different ball game. You don't really get to be funny having to smile so much and remembering all your lines and all the rules."

Men of any background were still more likely to be hired to host. Arlene Francis, one of the longest-serving game show panelists, admitted late in life that the failure of the shows she hosted relegated her to guest and panelist. "When those programs didn't last, the gentlemen in charge didn't question how good the programs were or weren't, they just decided a lady host wasn't a good idea."

Francis was born Arline Kazanjian via an Armenian father. Not until early in the twentieth century were Armenians, who are Caucasian but derive from western Asia, legally declared white. The conformist century discouraged diversity of any kind. Jewish hosts from Hal March and Monty Hall to Bert Parks and Jack Barry typically had to change their names. The standard was male and Anglo (ergo "Dennis James" dropped his Italian surname, Sposa).

Celebrity guest Marcia Wallace (*Match Game*, *Password*) acknowledged, "I wouldn't at all mind [hosting]. . . . In this business I'm tagged as 'zany' . . . yet I prefer it to being some anonymous pretty lady.

"A lot of shows have one male, the host, but a gaggle of females—the models, the assistants, the girls who mostly just smile. That gives them less individual importance . . . it makes them more anonymous and replaceable. Also, subconsciously—doesn't it?—it equates to one man being worth three or four women."

Los Angeles TV news anchor Chris Burrous asked in 2006, "I wonder what women really think of the 26 models hired mainly for their legs on *Deal or No Deal*? They hang around like eager clones holding 26 briefcases while [host] Howie Mandel schmoozes with the contestant. . . . It's a cheesy way to make a living or get noticed." One of the "Briefcase Girls" was Meghan Markle, later the wife of Britain's Prince Harry.

Traditional perceptions of women's roles and abilities persisted. The boys' club didn't want to share. When Barbara Walters became the first news anchor to earn a million dollars in 1976, ironically via ABC, most of her male colleagues and the public were appalled. A majority of people polled didn't want to hear TV or radio news delivered by a female voice. Dr. Joyce Brothers pinpointed the double standard within the double standard: "If a woman's voice is too deep or 'rough,' she's not a fit host or announcer. If her voice is too high-pitched or 'feminine,' she's not fit either."

Betty White stated, "All those barriers lasted a long time. . . . I probably wouldn't have gotten [to host] *Just Men!* if I hadn't already been on practically every game show there ever was and if I hadn't been married to a host," *Password*'s Allen Ludden. Talk host Virginia Graham commented in 1994, "It's healthy to see a greater variety of faces on the small screen now. But I tell you, people who are wives and mothers are the last to be given lucrative public positions. I *know*."

An early influence in terms of behind-the-scenes power was Lin Bolen, age 31, hired in 1972 to oversee NBC's daytime programming. Brash and outspoken, she was the rumored prototype for Faye Dunaway's character in the Oscar-winning film *Network* (1976). Bolen sought to increase viewership for her network by appealing more aggressively to its primary demographic, women. How? By hiring more of what she semi-humorously called "my studs."

She not only sought younger, better-looking male hosts, she wanted to modernize the hosting image, making it "less uptight and in-uniform . . . more cool." She moved to get the men out of their suits and ties into more casual and revealing "leisure wear." Older, established hosts didn't wish to be left out or seem like fuddy-duddies, so several changed their wardrobes significantly. Dennis James even took to wearing artificial sideburns on *Name That Tune*. (The new look suited some hosts more than others, no pun intended.)

Bolen, whose eponymous production company produced the game show *Stumpers* in 1976, also initiated the glitzy look of daytime game shows. Sande Stewart, son of producer Bob Stewart, recalled, "It was 1974 and that's when game shows started to look like Las Vegas. We put as many blinking light bulbs on the set [of *Jackpot*] as possible to appease Lin Bolen, who loved visible light bulbs. And that's what every game show looked like from that point forward."

Bolen's innovations didn't further the cause of female hosts. Their chance to emcee, particularly a popular or serious show, would come much later. Sometimes through the side door of replacing an originating male host, as with Meredith Vieira, who succeeded prime-time host Regis Philbin in 2002. *The View*'s original moderator, later a cohost of NBC's *Today*, she was a contestant on *Who Wants to Be a Millionaire?* during its third Regis season and won $250,000 for charity.

After Philbin's run ended, the show's daytime syndicators wanted a different kind of host, "someone who would love the contestants and be willing to root for them." Also someone less perfunctory and smarter than Regis (which Vieira's sizeable win indicated). The position was offered to Rosie O'Donnell, who passed. A decade or more before, her voice and manner would have denied her the offer. Twenty-two years after Betty White, Vieira became the second female game show host to win an Emmy in 2005 (she won another in 2009). She is also, to date, the longest-serving female host, with more than 1,800 episodes of *Who Wants to Be a Millionaire?* during her 2002–2013 tenure. From 2005 until 2013, she served as executive producer of the show.

After *Who Wants to Be a Millionaire?*, Meredith had a mildly successful eponymous talk show and later returned as emcee of the daytime game show *25 Words or Less*, which was based on the board game.

The UK, which has had three female heads of state to the US's none, pioneered a negative in the way of female hosts, namely, Anne Robinson, named by one British magazine "The Rudest Woman on Television." The bespectacled host of *The Weakest Link* from 2000 to 2012 was dry, charmless, and quick to ridicule contestants. "In a nation where good manners are more prevalent than ours," said Los Angeles-based TV critic David Sheehan, "Robinson would be a bigger shock had [Prime Minister] Margaret Thatcher not paved the way."

In real life Robinson lost custody of her only child in 1973 and was an admitted alcoholic until 1978. She's drawn censure for an array of bigoted comments and supports fox hunting. Her signature line to losing contestants, "You are the weakest link—goodbye!" seemed chillingly sincere. In 2001 Robinson came to the US to host *Weakest Link* (no *The*) for NBC. It ran one season.

"I think the show went over better here than Anne herself did," offered Cal State University professor of media psychology Stuart

Fischoff. "We're used to women hosting. We're not used to hosts of either sex, but especially women, being that abrasive." Back in Blighty, where she's one of telly's most recognized personalities, Robinson took over the long-running (since 1982) game show *Countdown* from a male host in 2021.

The US wasn't ready for an American version of Anne when it came time for a *Weakest Link* reboot in 2020. Likeable and versatile gay actress Jane Lynch, who played fearsome Sue Sylvester on the cult-hit series *Glee*, was selected by NBC to host and executive produce *Weakest Link*. As Australian journalist Kerry Low noted, "We don't think of [game show] hosts as actors. But they are acting. It is a role. Maybe we underestimate their talent."

When a cable-TV executive inquired into Joan Rivers's interest in hosting a future game show she quickly declined, citing her desire to retain her own boisterous personality. She mentioned the example of a network expecting Peter Tomarken, best known for hosting *Press Your Luck*, to rein in his exuberance as a condition for emceeing an upcoming game show.

Of course since Arlene, Betty, Meredith, Anne, and Jane the doors have opened for Jane Krakowski (*Name That Tune*), Brooke Burns (*Master Minds*), Leslie Jones (*Supermarket Sweep*), Elizabeth Banks (*Press Your Luck*), and others. It's noticeable that a disproportionate percentage of female hosts are young, slim, and blonde. The same could be said of actresses past and present. That particular hair color, more often than not artificial, is judged (by men) as more decorative and sexier.

Prior to becoming the current *Let's Make a Deal*'s "prize model," Tiffany Coyle—tall, blonde, and lithe—was a professional dancer. In 2021 she explained, "The position of Game Show Model has definitely evolved. I love modeling the prizes . . . [and] there are a few games that I get to host, which is always really fun! One time Wayne [host Wayne Brady] and I switched jobs and I hosted a segment while he modeled the prizes. In heels!"

Things are evolving, in large part because they finally must. "For ages, it was received wisdom that women watching daytime TV definitely preferred male hosts," said psychologist Dr. Betty Berzon. "Preferred them, allegedly, as either secret sex symbols or father figures. . . . We don't know if the supposed preference was true. But it doesn't and shouldn't matter.

"Fairness has to come first. If some audiences prefer to see only one gender or one race or one sexual orientation, that's just too bad. Everyone has a right to be represented . . . that's what finally is starting—and I do mean starting—to happen," in 2005.

Lin Bolen, asked the biggest difference between game show hosts in 2016 and the 1970s, replied, "*Women* . . . But don't try and put me on the spot! I was hiring at a time when female hosts weren't under consideration. . . . Daytime was mostly women and teens, also college kids, watching.

"Nighttime was, if possible, even more male-dominated. . . . I think it's great, women coming into their own. And about time. . . . If women had spoken up more then, I'd have listened. The networks might have listened. But it took women a long time to find their collective voice."

Betty White once admitted that with game shows the format's the thing, more than the host. "*Password* remained a very entertaining show even without Allen. . . . You might tune in to a show for the host so long as it's not a dud show. . . . But I remember when hosts, who were practically all fellas, were instructed not to distract from the show itself.

"Producers didn't like it if a host was too colorful or personable. Which I always suspected was another reason they didn't want women hosting. Now, fortunately, the men are more colorful, less straitjacketed, and women are viable, be they colorful, personable, or what-have-you!"

Dr. Joyce Brothers

Psychologist Dr. Joyce Brothers became an overnight celebrity in 1955 on becoming the first female winner on *The $64,000 Question*. Her chosen quiz subject was boxing. Her husband, Dr. Milton Brothers, was a boxing fan.

Née Bauer, Joyce was the daughter of Jewish lawyers. On being accepted at Columbia University for her PhD, the dean of her department commended her outstanding credentials while regretting that she would be taking the position of a man who would use the degree . . . so he urged that she give up her position. She did not.

In 1955, Joyce Brothers was 28 years old and the mother of 3-year-old Lisa, a future ophthalmologist. Milton was an internist earning $50 a month. His wife, who had a photographic memory, aimed to get on *The $64,000 Question*. "The loser got a new Cadillac," she later explained. The car's sale would bring enough money to improve the family's far-from-affluent living conditions.

Each contestant had to choose a field of knowledge unrelated to what they did for a living. Joyce wasn't crazy about boxing but realized that unlike, say, art or music it was a finite subject. On being accepted for the program she had six weeks to study up. She set to work reading everything available on the subject of boxing including old boxing journals and viewed movie reels about boxing.

Once on the show, she progressed easily to the $16,000 level. It was then she realized she had an unseen enemy, ironically a Jewish one: Charles Revson, creator and head of Revlon, the cosmetics company he would run for half a century until his death in 1975. As the show's sponsor Revlon kept a tight rein on *The $64,000 Question*. Charles and his brother Martin insisted that producers control the questions so as to retain the high ratings that sold their products.

Revson "wanted me to wear makeup on the air. But I didn't wear makeup. I didn't want to wear makeup. So when I got to $16,000 Revson told the producers, 'Get that bitch off the show.'

"Suddenly the questions got a lot harder. Everything was aimed at getting rid of me. At one point instead of asking me about boxers they asked me a question about referees. And I got it right.

"Then they called some sports writers and asked each of them to come up with six questions that no one could answer. The actual $64,000 question had 16 parts. The show ran over its scheduled time. . . . But I won."

After her triumph, Joyce was made to wait to receive her prize money, "which made me very nervous." The show hadn't counted on her winning and didn't have the money on hand. Eventually the check was presented—publicly, amid corporate smiles—along with a camera-friendly oversized facsimile check "that I gave to my mother. She kept it on the wall above her bed till the day she died."

The $64,000 Challenge was the first TV game show spin-off. Winners from the mother program were invited back, and in 1957, Dr. Joyce Brothers won another $64,000 (against seven competitors). The $128,000 was the 2021 equivalent of $1.3 million and enabled her husband to set up his own practice. After winning on Challenge, the psychologist became cohost of WATV's Sports Showcase and, in 1958, hosted The Dr. Joyce Brothers Show on NBC, a nationally syndicated hit.

In 1963 she began a monthly column for Good Housekeeping magazine. She also did a daily column eventually carried by more than 350 newspapers. Dr. Brothers authored several bestselling books, guested on The Tonight Show more than 90 times, and made celebrity guest appearances on game shows including The Match Game and Hollywood Squares. She remained a TV and other media presence until her death in 2013 at age 85.

In 1960, Martin Revson sued his former boss—his brother—who blithely admitted, "I'm a bastard."

20

The Price Is Still Right

In November 1956, a TV game show debuted in which four contestants guessed the price of a store item, trying to come as close as possible to its manufacturer's suggested retail price, without going above it. *The Price Is Right*, hosted by Bill Cullen, proved popular enough to add a prime-time edition the following September. Cullen hosted until the program's demise in 1965.

The Price Is Right revived in 1972 with 48-year-old host Bob Barker, who'd emceed *Truth or Consequences* for 19 years. He stayed on until 2007. Comedian Drew Carey has since hosted the popular show.

When Goodson-Todman decided to bring back *The Price Is Right*, Mark Goodson planned it as a syndicated nighttime show. CBS expressed interest in a daytime show. The flattering interest of "the Tiffany network" (the show had aired on NBC and then third-place ABC in the 1950s and 1960s) determined Goodson to ensure that his *Price* would endure. After a run-through of the original game, he realized it was too slow for 1970s audiences.

CBS gave Goodson carte blanche and waited until he and his staff restructured the show, adding speed and variety by incorporating rotating mini games that still stuck to the central pricing premise. It debuted with Barker hosting the daily network version and Dennis James emceeing weekly nighttime syndication. The show's four contestants, chosen from the studio audience, were famously invited by announcer Johnny Olson to "Come on down!"

The show ran half an hour during its first three years and then doubled to 60 minutes and six pricing games per show. The busy Barker also hosted *Truth or Consequences* from 1972 to 1975 and replaced Dennis James on the prime-time *Price*'s final seasons (through 1979) after James left in 1977.

It's often forgotten that there were other *Price Is Right* hosts: Tom Kennedy emceed the revived syndicated series in 1985; it lasted a season. Doug Davidson, formerly of *The Young and the Restless*, hosted another one-season syndicated revival in 1994. The team of substitute hosts for Bill Cullen included Merv Griffin, actor Sam Levenson, announcers Johnny Gilbert and Don Pardo, and Arlene Francis.

But the person most associated with the show, in reruns and memory, is Bob Barker.

Robert William Barker was born in 1923. His father, a power-line foreman, died in 1930 after falling off a pole. Bob's mother was a teacher at the Rosebud Indian Reservation in Mission, South Dakota. Bob, one-eighth Sioux, later said he grew up among cowboys and "Indians" and dogs—lots of dogs. An animal lover from early on, he and his mother lived in a hotel in Mission, its sole two-story structure. When Matilda needed to locate her son, she would scan the area from the hotel roof and look for a pack of dogs.

Bob received a basketball college scholarship, but his higher education was interrupted by World War II and his training as a fighter pilot. In 1945 he married Dorothy Jo Gideon. She died of cancer at age 57 in 1981 and inspired the posthumous creation of Barker's animal-protection foundation named after Dorothy and his mother. His wife's influence changed him from animal lover to animal activist.

Like many classic game show hosts, Bob began in radio. After Bob and Dorothy, who'd taught school, moved to Los Angeles in 1950 he found the competition for announcing jobs stiff. So the pair devised *The Bob Barker Show*, which she produced. The local radio program, based in Burbank, featured audience participation and modest games for modest prizes. After Southern California Edison became its sponsor, the production moved around the state's southern half for several years.

Barker went national in 1956 when producer Ralph Edwards picked him to emcee NBC's daytime edition of *Truth or Consequences*. Edwards had hosted it on radio and TV from 1940 to 1951, with Jack Bailey (better known for *Queen for a Day*) hosting a prime-time revival from 1954 to 1956. Bailey didn't care to downgrade to daytime TV, so a new host was sought. NBC favored an established name, but Edwards had liked Barker's radio personality and then been impressed by his looks. He insisted on Barker and the network reluctantly agreed.

In 1966 Bob started hosting the Miss USA and Miss Universe pageants. Three years later, he began two decades of hosting the annual Tournament of Roses Parade as well as the Pillsbury Bakeoff. He also hosted the annual Indianapolis 500 Parade. In 1979 he became a vegetarian, like Dorothy. He encouraged people to adopt pets from animal shelters—rather than puppy mills and other for-profit outlets—where they would otherwise probably be destroyed. Each episode of *The Price Is Right* closed with, "Help control the pet population. Have your pets spayed or neutered." It became Barker's signature sign-off until his retirement in 2007.

Bob's support of animal rights involved him in occasional controversy. In 1989 he and associate Nancy Burnet, founder of United Activists for Animal Rights, were sued by the American Humane Association, which they accused of not protecting animals hired for motion pictures. Late in the 1990s Barker and Burnet charged that the TV series *Dr. Quinn, Medicine Woman* mistreated horses.

Bob was half of the *Ken and Bob Saturday Special* radio show in Los Angeles on KABC-AM. Over a year into the show, KABC asked Barker to modify his rigid animal-rights stance. He refused and was fired in 1983. Close to one hundred people marched outside the station in the rain to protest his dismissal.

By 1987 Bob had hosted Miss USA for 21 years when he protested its use of fur coats. He threatened to quit unless they were discontinued. The producers substituted faux fur but in 1988 brought back animal skins. Barker resigned from Miss USA and Miss Universe. That cost Miss USA close to 30 percent of its audience the following year. Over the decades Bob declined substantial offers to advertise fast-food chains and cosmetics companies that abuse animals by testing their products on lab animals.

Bob Barker's dedication to animals and animal charities was unquestionable. Not so his feud with fellow animal activist Betty White. The two clashed or, rather, he did in 2009 over the fate of Billy, an elephant who outgrew his living quarters at the Los Angeles Zoo, an institution White was more closely involved with than Barker. Billy's future drew media attention once celebrities became involved. Betty favored moving him to larger quarters in the zoo, while Barker—also Cher and Lily Tomlin—wanted Billy relocated to an animal sanctuary in San Andreas, California.

The Betty White faction prevailed and Billy moved to a new multimillion-dollar facility. The Los Angeles Zoo is publicized as one of the most animal-friendly in the country. Insiders said Barker was upset by the zoo's decision. It was reported that he'd declared White to be his "sworn enemy." Game Show Forum was unable to corroborate the quoted epithet. Another source said it originated in a tabloid, a print genre seldom known for veracity. However, Barker apparently didn't deny the words and lent credence to the one-sided feud when he threatened to boycott the first Game Show Network Awards in 2009 if Betty White showed up.

Barker was to receive a lifetime achievement award, while Betty was to present a tribute to Mark Goodson, who'd died in 1992. Rather than prevent Bob from receiving his award, Betty recorded her remarks on tape for the ceremonies. The host who'd retired two years previously gained no new fans by his behavior.

What seemed to have minimal effect on his popularity, back during his tenure, were the sexual harassment lawsuits filed by several *Price Is Right* models, known as Barker's Beauties (see chapter 24). Times hadn't changed that much since the 1940s when movie star Errol Flynn's popularity actually increased after his rape trial involving two female minors. (Predictably, he was acquitted.)

In 1987 *The Price Is Right* became American TV's longest-running daytime game show (it had been *Concentration*). Also, Barker let his hair go white because frequent dyeing had turned it pink. After executive producer Frank Wayne died in 1987 Bob took over the position, exercising yet greater control over the show—excessive control, some employees and former employees later claimed.

In 1990 *The Price Is Right* became the longest-running game show, period, surpassing the 18-year prime-time run of *What's My Line?*

Six years later Bob played himself in the Adam Sandler movie *Happy Gilmore*, whose highlight was a golf tournament. When Barker and the much younger Sandler's character get into a fight, the elder wins, using karate (Barker had taken lessons and earned a black belt). He also appeared in episodes of the TV sitcom *Something So Right* during the 1996–1997 season.

From then on until 2007, it was *The Price Is Right* and assorted specials marking one milestone after another. For instance a 1996 prime-time special heralding the start of the show's 25th year on television. Another celebrated its 30th anniversary. On one special Bob celebrated his 80th birthday. In March 2004 the show aired its 6,000th episode. Another marker was the announcement that since 1972 the show had given away more than $300 million in cash and prizes.

"I find it interesting," commented *Press Your Luck* host Peter Tomarken, "that *Price Is Right* consistently dates its start to 1972, never mind that it dates to the mid-1950s. . . . I've been told Mr. Barker likes getting the credit."

Asked what he liked best about his show, Bob replied, "The money, of course!" For each year *Price* remains on the air the former host and executive producer receives a generous bonus. He admits he seldom watches the show, on which he last appeared in 2015 in an April Fool's episode.

A two-hour prime-time special occasioned by the show's 50th anniversary (measured from 1972) included a tribute to Bob Barker with outtakes and flashbacks but no Bob. Rather, he did a *People* magazine interview. In his late 90s, he prefers to be remembered as he looked in his 80s and younger. Marcia Wallace, a *Match Game* panelist with Barker, recalled, "Bob was very keen on being well-groomed and well-coiffed. . . . He was also quite the ladies' man . . . I mean he winked and he flirted, rather outrageously."

Over the years sun worshipper Barker was regularly treated for skin cancers but also experienced head and knee injuries, severe back pain, an extreme allergic reaction that made him miss a taping, prostate surgery, and falls at home. In a Washington, DC, hotel room in 1999 he suffered a ministroke and found out he was on the verge of a major stroke. He underwent surgery to clear the partially blocked left carotid artery that was obstructing blood flow to his brain. He was in DC to speak about the Captive Elephant Act that banned the use of elephants in circuses.

A former personal assistant said, "Bob is quite protective on the topic of elephants ... almost like [he has] exclusive rights. I'm glad he cares but I'm not the only one who feared to cross him. . . . It's his way or the highway."

The 35th season of *Price Is Right* and Barker's 50th year in show business was in 2007. No surprise when he announced the time was right to retire, although subsequent rumors (see chapter 24) suggest he may have been pressured to leave and thereby avoid publicity damaging to the show.

Barker returned as a guest more than once, making nice with new host Drew Carey. (A February 2009 appearance to promote Barker's autobiography had to be postponed due to his replacement's pneumonia.) Bob told *TMZ* that Drew "does the show differently than I did . . . I tried to make the show real exciting. He just plays the games."

Many would say Drew Carey brings more sincere joy to the games. Drew said the retiring Bob Barker advised him to not try and copy him, but to make *The Price Is Right* his own. Insofar as any new host can—for, the game and playing basically remain the same—Carey did. Since 2007 he's hosted a show that was a solid hit with Bill Cullen, with Barker, and himself. Despite *Price*'s self-sustaining nature, whether a future host could do anywhere as well is doubtful.

Interestingly, though Drew is 35 years younger than Barker, he started hosting *Price* at 49 compared with Bob's 48. Besides their differing and sometimes opposing generations, the two men vary considerably. Carey's persona is not only more youthful and spontaneous but sensitive and accessible. TV critic David Sheehan felt, "He's more suitable for the job and to the times . . . minus the dark or at least dubious baggage of his predecessor."

"He has such a contrasting vibe," stated a crew member who also worked under the Barker regime. "Overnight the workplace became more casual, fewer eggshells to worry about. . . . When Drew smiles it's from inside, it fills his face. Bob's smile was more, shall we say, practiced."

Carey gratefully remarked, "I started hosting a number one show thanks to [Bob Barker]."

But the modest, self-effacing Drew had more to offer than many game show hosts who moved directly to hosting from radio or announcing, with occasional acting or writing experience. Born in Cleveland in 1958 (his father died of brain cancer when he was eight), Carey did a six-year stint in the Marines and then began writing jokes for a morning radio show. To solidify his craft he checked out a library book, *How to Write Comedy*, and studied it intensely. In Cleveland he emceed and did stand-up before traveling the comedy circuit.

He soon realized writing comedy for television and possibly creating a sitcom, preferably one he could star in, would be more lucrative, lasting, and satisfying than the circuit grind. The dream sustained Drew during hard times. When he was too broke to buy food, he donated blood to get the money. He plugged away, eventually appeared on *Star Search* in 1987, moved to Los Angeles, and got his big break appearing on *The Tonight Show* in 1991. Likeable, with an everyman touch and a wide smile beneath the omnipresent black glasses, the rising star appeared on various comedy specials and won a Cable Ace Award for *Drew Carey, Human Cartoon*.

The upbeat, enthusiastic image wasn't phony but wasn't the entire picture. Drew began experiencing depression upon the loss of his father. During childhood he experienced sexual abuse, which he revealed in his 1997 book *Dirty Jokes and Beer*. At times lacking self-esteem, he chose to drop out of college. He ultimately learned to overcome recurring feelings of worthlessness and anger that had led to two suicide attempts.

Carey climbed a professional rung in 1994 when he was cast as John Caponera's sidekick on the NBC sitcom *The Good Life*. Drew's persona and physical type—more specifically, Hollywood's casting habits—would likely have locked him into comedic sidekick roles had he not been a writer, ambitious, and hard-working. He topped the ladder in 1995 when he created, wrote, and starred in *The Drew Carey Show*. The hit series ran until 2004.

Additionally, in 1998 he became cohost and executive producer of the comedy improv show *Whose Line Is It Anyway?*, based on a popular UK series.

Despite his seeming openness and willingness to share feelings that Bob Barker wouldn't have admitted to, Drew is basically private and in some ways an enigma. Unlike Barker he's pro–women's rights. Where Barker used the excuse of a medically induced 14-pound weight gain to fire one female model, Carey was responsible for keeping one model on during her visible pregnancy. He favors a harmonious and more equitable working atmosphere than Barker did.

"Drew roots for the contestants. To him they're individuals," remarked an anonymous staffer. "Behind the scenes he can be excitable . . . but he's the star, with a lot on his plate. But still he's reasonable, and he'll listen to you."

Price Is Right's almost 80 games include favorites like Dice Game, Cliff Hangers, and Punch-a-Bunch. The most popular is Plinko, inspired by Japan's Pachinko and introduced in 1983. Using round Plinko chips and a board of pegs, it provides a chance to win $50,000. An unforgettable episode for Carey occurred during his second season of hosting and involved a female college student who probably couldn't believe her luck. "She dropped her first three chips right down in the $10,000 spot. People were on their feet, jumping up and down and cheering.

"She dropped the fourth chip, the floor director comes over, stops the chip, and leans into me, and he goes, 'The game is fixed.'"

Drew's mind filled with thoughts like "I'm going to jail." (Nobody went to jail over the 1958 fixing scandals.) "I'm losing my job." "There's gonna be a scandal."

It was an innocent mistake. Before the new season, an ad for *The Price Is Right* video game was shot using the Plinko board fixed with a fishing line to create a winner for the camera. Surprisingly, nobody since had seen to it that the line was removed before the show's new season.

Off-camera the college student was given $30,000 in Plinko winnings, public scandal was averted, and presumably somebody got a well-deserved bawling out.

Like Bob Barker, Carey has never fathered a child, though he mentored Connor, the son of his first fiancée, Nicole Jaracz. It was during that five-year relationship (starting in 2007) that Carey, who reached a maximum weight of 262 pounds, decided to healthfully reduce—settling at around 187 pounds—after finding to his dismay he was "not fit enough to play with" Nicole's young son (Drew had previously "dabbled" in pro wrestling).

The twosome split amicably and remained friends. Carey has had two public relationships with women.

In 2018 he became engaged to marriage and family therapist Amie Harwick, author of *The New Sex Bible for Women*. The engagement was broken off the same year. Again, it was amicable. Again, the reason or reasons remained private. Tragically, in 2020 Harwick was strangled and then thrown from the third-story balcony of her Hollywood Hills apartment by her former boyfriend.

Drew expressed himself lucky to have known a love as great as that he shared with Amie. He also publicly forgave the culprit, who had an abusive childhood. The statement drew mixed reactions because the man's childhood could not justify his behavior. Harwick, who'd broken off the abusive relationship, had taken out two restraining orders against him, as had at least one prior girlfriend.

Carey's still-single state at 65 has drawn comment, which he seems to accept with good humor. In an introduction to a 2009 collection of Friars Club jokes and one-liners he recalled being "roasted on national television" amid barbs about "how many men I've had sex with . . . my little dick, and how fat I am." He remembered it as "one of the greatest nights in my life."

According to HollywoodMask.com, "It is not known if Drew Carey is gay or not, since he has never explicitly mentioned it."

Carey's eponymous sitcom touched on gay themes and humor and included a character named Steve, the protagonist's elder brother, a heterosexual cross-dresser. Drew has long joked about his sex life (e.g., "My idea of an orgy was using more than one magazine"). Kidding aside, in *Dirty Jokes and Beer* he declared, "I let myself do whatever I want, with whomever I want. . . . I'm talking about living a life without caring if people like the way you have your fun." He cheerfully admitted he had his nipples pierced.

At one point Drew shaved off the trademark crew-cut he acquired while in the Marines. He jested that with a shaved head and pierced nipples "I looked incredibly gay," and then added, "Just because a guy has a shaved head, pierced nipples, and doesn't have sex with women doesn't make him gay. It just makes him down on his luck."

His book's photo section included a fetching photo of Drew in drag in college and four asseverations: "But I swear I'm not gay," "I told ya I'm not gay!" "I'm not gay, honest," plus "I'm not gay. Really." Carey was comfortable repeatedly bringing up the subject (would he be less or more comfortable now, 26 years later?).

Said one book reviewer, "Me thinks the comic doth protest too much."

Gay TCM movie host and writer Robert Osborne pointed out, "During her widely popular TV talk show Rosie O'Donnell went on and on about her kids (adopted) and her supposed crush on Tom Cruise (of all people), but after her show ended she felt free to come out and be honest.... TV is the widest medium but the most confining. No celebrity is irreplaceable, any individual can be canceled."

Carey has admitted to "welcoming and enjoying all things 'gay' save for any actual sex acts." So take it from Drew: He's not gay. Really. And maybe it's really true.

There are few taboos Carey won't tackle. One isn't politics. A former Republican, he became a Libertarian and in the wake of Trump's refusal to accept the voting results of the American people and of the Electoral College he called him "the worst president we ever had," whom he hopes "ends up in jail." He endorsed Joe Biden in 2020 and donated to his election campaign.

And then there's religion. Drew, who attended Presbyterian Sunday school and a Pentecostal junior high school, is a Buddhist and has a home shrine. He's joked about the seeming contradiction between hosting *Price Is Right* and Buddhism's de-emphasis of materialism and worldly status.

Among Drew's pastimes and interests is photography, which he's "passionate" about, and soccer—he bought a stake in the Seattle Sounders. He has donated generously to public libraries. And he's a passionate Cleveland booster. His character on his eponymous TV series worked and played in Carey's "favorite city in the world."

A friend of more than two decades revealed, "I don't know for a fact that he earns $12.5 million for [*The Price Is Right*, annually]. I've heard that amount mentioned at different times but I've never asked.

"I can only say he's one guy in this town [Hollywood] who enjoys his money and isn't soured like so many older VIPs. . . . My opinion is, whatever Drew endured . . . what he transcended, it's made him more appreciative of where he's at. His thing is, he's a survivor and he lives in the moment."

And the pricing continues.

21

Romance and Marriage: Newlyweds and Love Connections

"JERRY AND I WERE TWO OF THE SIX HEAVILY MATRIMONIED PREMIERE celebrities on *Tattletales* in 1974," quipped Anne Meara, half of the comedy team Stiller & Meara (parents of Ben Stiller). "We were glad for the exposure, don't knock it, but I was nervous. Were we helping initiate another flop?

"Still, the host was a lot cuter than Joe Garagiola. I think he [Bert Convy] and the new title made a big difference that it became a winner."

Meara referred to the fact that Mark Goodson and Bill Todman's *Tattletales* was a reboot of their 1969 *He Said, She Said*, hosted by former ballplayer Garagiola. It ran one season. "There was a sitcom I think called *He and She* with I think Paula Prentiss and Dick Benjamin, who were married. Maybe people confused the shows. *He and She* laid an awful big egg."

Where "he said, she said" were simple and bland words, "tattletales" implied spilling the marital beans. Mark Goodson reportedly decreed that the title should be one word, not two, to sound more like an accusation. The show had a difficult birth. In 1966 it was a pilot, *It Had to Be You* (a popular song's title), hosted by Johnny Carson sidekick Ed McMahon. In 1969, it became the syndicated *He Said, She Said*, and in 1973 Gene Rayburn hosted a new pilot, *Celebrity Match Mates*, for CBS.

In 1974 *Tattletales* bowed on CBS daytime with Bert Convy as emcee because Rayburn was by then hosting *Match Game*'s successful revival. The reboot highlighted three celebrity married couples, each playing on behalf of a color-coded third of the studio audience. Separately, husbands and wives tried to guess their other half's response to a given question.

The show mostly lacked the risqué element of *The Newlywed Game* or *The Match Game*, but its unique draw was satisfying viewer curiosity about what a given celebrity's wife or husband was like. Sometimes both partners were celebrities. Occasionally a celebrity didn't appear with a legal mate but with an opposite-sex date (or "date") or costar. Among them Jay Leno, Michael J. Fox, and Meg Ryan, who was costarring on *As the World Turns*. She guested with her romantic interest from that soap.

Tattletales ran from 1974 to 1978 and 1982–1984. A 2022 HBO Max reboot featured celebrity couples playing for charity. Its name was changed to the more suggestive *About Last Night*. The chef Ayesha Curry and NBA player Stephen Curry were its married hosts.

Paul Alter, *Tattletales*' producer-director, observed that despite the medium's fondness for game shows built around romance and marriage, surprisingly few become lasting hits like *Tattletales*, *The Newlywed Game*, and *The Love Connection* or to a lesser extent *Singled Out*. "The public makes hits of formats that are clever but real. They can usually tell when a program is manufactured for ratings . . . when it's exploitive or insincere.

"I believe the big hits are often the simpler shows."

As to why shows like *Gamble on Love; Love Story; Wedding Party; The Love Experts; Perfect Match; Love Me, Love Me Not; Second Honeymoon; Sweethearts; Straight to the Heart; All About the Opposite Sex; Studs; A Perfect Score;* and *Swaps* turned out turkeys, more, anon.

Game show producer Chuck Barris once compared himself to actor-director Orson Welles by semi-joking that he started big and worked his way down. His first two hits were easily the biggest of his career: *The Dating Game* and *The Newlywed Game*. The latter debuted in 1966 (for more on *Dating Game*, see chapter 17) and helped to buoy ABC, the third-place network; it also prevented its sale to billionaire Howard Hughes (again, see chapter 17).

There was no *Newlywed* pilot because the demonstration for ABC executives went so well that it jumped to series, skipping that usual step. Abetting the demonstration was guest celeb and funnyman Dom DeLuise, whose every response drew laughter. When the wives were asked to

()

share their nicknames for their husbands one said "Numbnuts," which sent the execs into gales of laughter.

The day *The Newlywed Game* debuted, July 11, it got a lucky break because Secretary of State Robert McNamara gave a televised update on the Vietnam war that aired on CBS and NBC but not ABC. Thus, the brand-new show had virtually no competition, including the popular *Password*.

Newlywed started in daytime and added nighttime and went through several revivals. The host most associated with it is Bob Eubanks, who still hosted it late in the 1990s. After 2000, the Game Show Network presented a new version.

The format was simple, with four newlywed couples answering questions—husbands and wives separately—to gauge, when they reunited, how well they did and didn't know each other. The results ranged from amusing to funny to hilarious, and it was all too easy for disagreements to reveal more than a couple intended. Often a contradicting or bickering pair seemed to forget they were on national TV.

Chuck Barris staffer Jaime Klein explained that couples "would argue even though Bob Eubanks was staring at them. . . . They weren't 'people on TV' anymore. They were a real couple and you were seeing the inner nature of a real marriage. That is spellbinding to watch."

In time, the questions became increasingly risqué and complaints about the show's unsuitability for children mounted. ABC forbade Eubanks to say "sex" or "making love." He said "making whoopee" instead. Yet there were questions and answers like: "Husband number 3, what's your favorite part of the *Newlywed Game* set?" Husband number 3: "Wife number 2."

And "Ladies, what will your husband say is the one thing he absolutely forbids you to put on his wiener?" One responded: "Ben-Gay."

By 1977 viewer pressure resulted in a parental warning in some cities at the start of the show when it aired in early evening. "You know, when we look back," said Canadian talk and game host Alan Thicke, "game shows supply us with social markers about where society was at . . . how different things were then from what they were before and how different they would be later.

"I remember from grown-ups' comments that *Bride and Groom* was controversial, even sacrilegious to some viewers."

Bride and Groom, which did produce newlyweds, was for all intents and purposes a reality series that ran from 1951 to 1954 and 1957–1958 on CBS and then NBC. Hosted by Robert Paige (likely best known for *Son of Dracula*, 1943) and Frank Parker (born Frank Ciccio), it was based on a popular radio series. Couples planning to be married could apply to appear on the show.

If accepted, they had a song sung to them, then were married on live TV, and given wedding gifts for participating. In 1957 an article claimed that couples married on *Bride and Groom* divorced less frequently than the national average. The series was apparently ripped off by Los Angeles's KLAC-TV, whose *Wedding Bells* was adjudged too similar to *Bride and Groom*, whose producers were awarded $800,000, today's equivalent of a multimillion-dollar settlement.

"I had a teacher," concluded Thicke, "whose sister in Wisconsin believed 'getting married in plain public' and getting free merchandise was sacrilegious and sinful." (She'd have loved *The Newlywed Game*.)

The Love Connection aired from 1983 to 1994 and confirmed Paul Alter's thesis that simpler relationship shows are more popular than complex or quirky ones. The syndicated series, hosted by Chuck Woolery, was basically a video-dating show. After supplying personal data, contestants watched three opposite-sex videos from which they chose one for a date. The studio audience also chose a date for the contestant, who had the option of choosing that one.

After the date, the two returned to the show and told what happened. Could it be much simpler?

Singled Out, via MTV, was also a dating show. It ran from 1995 to 1998 and made a celebrity of cohost Jenny McCarthy, a *Playboy* centerfold who quit the series in 1997 to do *The Jenny McCarthy Show* on MTV and then *Jenny* on NBC later that year. She was replaced on *Singled Out* by Carmen Electra. The male host from 1995 to 1998 was Chris Hardwick.

Not as long-lived as *The Love Connection*, *Singled Out* was definitely more complex. For starters, it had 100 MTV-generation guys and dolls competing to win one of two dates. The prize individual, backside to the opposite-sex 50, got to eliminate most everyone during various rounds.

For instance, she could be rid of would-be dates who didn't fit her height or hair length or wardrobe preferences. However, as the rejects paraded past Miss Picky on their way out of the studio, she had the option of handing one a Golden Ticket, which put him back in the running.

She then questioned the remaining contestants and could ask them to perform a stunt. The Winner's Circle comprised three finalists, with more questions. If there was a tie on the basis of matching responses, the two opponents answered a numerical question and the one that came closest won.

The second half of the (tiring or tiresome?) show was a guy who got to eliminate most of the gals.

Livening up the show during one 1998 episode was Adam "Batman" West, who acted as cohost and did a skit where he had to rescue Hardwick and Electra. Fun for viewers but possibly a bit sad for the star of one of the mid-1960s' most popular TV shows. Now, turkey time:

- *Gamble on Love* aired in prime time on the DuMont network from July 16, 1954, to August 13, 1954. Its amatory theme permitted employing a rare "hostess," Denise Darcel. Four years earlier she'd costarred in the epic *Tarzan and the Slave Girl*. Inane was often the name of the game in early TV. This show presented three couples "married, about to be married, or just plain in love." (Or faking, to get on TV or to pass, as all gay people had to do then.) One half of a couple got to spin a wheel of fortune—whee!—the other got to answer questions for prizes.

  For the show's final week Darcel was unexplainedly replaced by cigar-chomping comedian Ernie Kovacs.

- Once upon a time there was a 1955 CBS game show called *Love Story*, hosted by Jack Smith (*the* Jack Smith). Aimed at housewives in the daytime, it focused on retaining their attention and consumer loyalty (it was a Procter & Gamble production) by having "two people in love" tell their story. Host Smith sang them a song and the pair got to answer questions for cash and prizes. It lasted almost half a year.

- *Wedding Party* (it premiered on April Fool's Day) was a 1968 three-month daytime show on ABC hosted by Alan Hamel, later best known as actress-turned-endless-author Suzanne Somers's husband-manager. Its contestants were young engaged couples who got to tell how they met and what kept them together. The show resembled *Tattletales* and *The Newlywed Game*, except *Wedding Party* sought to match prizes, not answers. Half a couple was sent backstage while the other half chose one prize from each of three sets of three prizes. The other half returned and tried to guess which prizes the future spouse selected. A correct match allowed the couple to keep the prize. Three out of three matches and a couple won a honeymoon trip.

 Wedding Party demonstrated that audiences usually prefer the naughty aspects of "fun and games" (as in *The Newlywed Game*) to actual fun and games.

- *The Love Experts* was a presumptuous title. This syndicated 1978 one-season entry didn't sound like a game show and barely was. Hosted by the likeable Bill Cullen, it featured a panel of four celebrities offering advice to unfamous contestants about love and romance (and divorce, just in case?). What made it a game show was the prize won at program's end by the contestant the quartet decided had the most unusual or interesting love problem.

 "Experts" included David Letterman, Jamie Lee Curtis, and much-married actor Peter Lawford.

- Rather surprising that *Perfect Match* (1986) lasted only one season, as it resembled *The Newlywed Game*—to the extent that had the latter been a Mark Goodson-Bill Todman Production, the company would likely have sued Lorimar, the entity behind *Perfect Match*. Contestants on the syndicated show hosted by Bob Goen were three (not four) married couples, not necessarily newlyweds. How well did they know each other? (Sound familiar?)

 Each couple got a $200 bankroll that the husband, specifically, got to bet part of on his confidence in how his wife would respond to three questions. Example: "You're in the middle of a romantic encounter, the doorbell rings and it's your mother-in-law. What would you do?"

The show concluded with a "love note" read to the spouse but with blanks in it (Holy *Match Game!*) for the other to fill in. The first completed note was worth $100, but the second was worth $200. The couple with the most money won and got an extra $1,000. If a couple matched on every question they earned a $5,000 bonus.

- *Love Me, Love Me Not.* In keeping with its title, the bonus round of this one-season 1986 cable TV show was played on a giant eight-petal daisy. The host was Ross Shafer and cohost and announcer was Marilyn Smith. The contestants were three men and two women. The goal was for one woman to "catch" more men than the other. (Inane hadn't died out.) Each guy made a statement, and then each gal guessed if it was true or false. If he deceived her, he got $100; if she guessed right, she got a better chance at him. So, he wins, he gets money; she wins, she gets a man.

   The runner-up could console herself with Gloria Steinem's dictum that a woman without a man is like a fish without a bicycle.

- *Second Honeymoon*, a Wink Martindale Production (no cracks) aired on cable TV in 1987 for one season. Some critics labeled it "moronic," "embarrassing," "tacky and stunted," or "engrossingly gross." Its three player families were a dad, mom, and two or three of their progeny. It was halfway to a kids' show in that the children tried guessing their parents' responses to Wink's questions from among multiple-choice answers. A sample question was "What would your mom do if the phone rang at 4 a.m. and a sexy female asked for your dad?"

   Reviewer Sigrid Peterson observed, "Multiple choice replies denote the inarticulateness of juvenile contestants who foreground a show that doesn't aim high—or even junior high." The game's object was to win one pair of parents a second honeymoon. Sweet.

- Oddly enough, *Sweethearts* was hosted by gay actor-director Charles Nelson Reilly, best known as a *Match Game* regular. This daily syndicated 1988 "comedy show" lasted a whole season. Its format was three celebrities (Betty White was a debut guest) questioning three couples in an effort to learn which was telling the truth about how they met. It probably played better than it sounds. For each celebrity fooled, a couple got $500, and if they fooled all three, a second-honeymoon trip.

• *Straight to the Heart* (syndicated, 1989, less than six months) wasn't necessarily about the heart. Former Miss America and *I've Got a Secret* panelist Bess Myerson noted, "When TV says 'heart' it usually means somewhere lower than the chest." *Straight to the Heart* tried to make couples out of six strangers: three men and three women. Each man was asked, for example, his best "romantic move" on a date? The women were then read the men's answers— host was Michael Burger, and hostess/announcer Barbara Lee Alexander—and each chose the answer she liked best.

 Then the women were asked and the men chose. The woman and man who chose each other most often won, then played a bonus round for a possible trip. The runners-up got a night on the town.

• *All About the Opposite Sex* (syndicated, 1990) was hosted by David Sparks. Its silly and ambitious title belied the complexity of this show whose goal was proving which gender knew more about the other (wow). The players were seven studio contestants, with 25 audience members of each sex voting on certain questions. Answers were multiple-choice (three possible answers), but the rules and steps were rather complex, though final round questions had only two possible answers. The show didn't last two months.

 Psychologist Betty Berzon maintained, "Male-dominated media prefer to exaggerate differences. . . . 'Entertainment' has repeatedly returned to the theme that women are inscrutable opposites to men, who are held up as the stable and stabilizing norm. . . . When they say 'opposite sex' there's always an agenda."

• *Studs* didn't sound very romantic and included questions like "Who is most likely to make love [read: have sex] on the beach?" Syndicated, hosted by Mark DeCarlo, it lasted from 1991 to 1993. Two men tried matching answers with three women they'd both dated. First, the women answered questions about the men and the dates. The men tried matching the answers with the woman who said it. Each time he did he got a "heart." Winning men got hearts, a winning woman might get a man. Familiar?

Part two had the women selecting which man best matched a question like the on-the-beach example. The men then guessed whether the question was about him or his rival. He got a "heart" for a correct guess. Finally, each man chose which woman he'd like to date again. If she also selected him and if he was the contestant with the most hearts, they won the date. Hooray.

- Ironically, *The Perfect Match* was the title of a 1994 ESPN sports-themed game show, while *A Perfect Score* was a 1992 late-night CBS program not dissimilar to *The Dating Game*. Host Jeff Marder presided while three close friends of a player tried to find the player an ideal date (whom she or he couldn't see, separated by a partition). Questions could be routine or saucy, like "What's the most dangerous location you ever made love in?" After the three candidates were interviewed the three cohorts chose one for their friend.

  The new twosome were introduced, then sent out on a date, and returned the following week to tell how it went. *A Perfect Score* lasted half a year.

- Finally, *Swaps* (1995, syndicated, hosted by Scott St. John) presented three unmarried couples who'd broken up. A fresh concept but too complex (six rounds) and too gimmicky (revolving chairs and large soft hammers to "hit" the opposite sex with, etc.). The sextet tried to match answers and then decided if they wanted a date with their ex or with a new face. Correct guesses translated to cash and cash totals plus the luck of who picked whom decided the winning couple that got to go on a date. The end.

  "Romantic game shows are decreasingly popular," vouched media psychology professor Stuart Fischoff in 2012. "They're no longer exciting enough to capture a wide audience or a younger one. . . . Romance isn't dead, but titillation is today's operative word for televised success."

Private Lives

Few game show hosts have married only once. One wife offered, "It's a competitive field, with ambitious men. A very male field . . . so there's more ego-clash [between hosts] than between actors and actresses."

Betty White, married to *Password* host Allen Ludden, affirmed in 1993, "Game shows aren't immune to the ageism of show business. Networks and production companies typically prefer to 'go younger' . . . [they're] all too ready to replace a proven host with a younger face that may not be around next year."

The focus on youth which cost Gene Rayburn the chance to host a new edition of *The Match Game* after it was discovered he was older than he looked—in a looksist business, yet—also affects hosts' wives. "The aging performer," explained psychologist Dr. Joyce Brothers, "doesn't notice himself aging quite as much as he does his wife's aging. In his attempt at a younger image one of his first thoughts may be [getting] a younger wife. She can give him the illusion that he's hardly aged."

Several hosts have gotten one (or more), the age difference between hubby and the second wife being substantially more than between him and his first wife.

Ray Combs, a host of *Family Feud* who died by suicide at age 40, felt, "It [hosting] often isn't easy for you or your family . . . worrying over ratings, program changes, and possible host changes." Combs had just one wife but six children.

Unlike actors, a game show host almost never weds a famous woman. One reason is the struggle to become a successful game show host and then remain one. A nationally known wife could pose a psychological threat. Gene Rayburn once half-joked, "Even if you're the most successful host on television, does that make you a real star?"

In the pecking order of status-conscious Hollywood, TV game show hosts don't rate highly. A cousin of comedian Gary Morton was quoted after his marriage to Lucille Ball, "Thank goodness Gary was a genuine entertainer, doing stand-up, not standing in front of some game show podium . . . reading off of little cards." The inference was that a big star wouldn't look twice at a game show host.

Bert Convy, temporarily a Broadway star before transitioning to hosting, believed, "Successful stage or screen actors sometimes have better marriages [because] they're busy, heavily involved in or out of town doing a movie or play. . . . The hours for hosting a game show aren't many. It's like you work for a weekend, taping several shows back to back, then you get the whole week off—the opposite of a normal guy.

"If your wife doesn't have a job or outside interests, you're around a lot to get in her hair. . . . You're not out toiling away and doing something all-consuming and highly anticipated."

Many current male game show hosts have wives with careers. Few did in the past. *Concentration* host Jack Narz's third wife Dolores was a TWA stewardess for 48 years. "The times that Jack wanted to work but didn't get offered work were rough on him. He eventually didn't want to do any more hosting or telethons, which made it easier on both of us. . . . For me, my job was a lifesaver. I loved it and it made me more rounded and satisfied as a person and wife.

"It meant the time we did spend together was more special."

For TV's first few decades, game show hosts seldom got interviewed—after all, there were movie stars. . . . Art Fleming, original host of *Jeopardy!*, noted, "We're not the most sparkling personalities. I guess journalists figure our lives couldn't be very exciting or we don't have much to say. Hosts do tend to ask questions, not answer them." Host interviews became more frequent if not common during the 1980s with the spread of celebrity journalism.

Like many gay men who were once married (to a woman), no matter how briefly, *Family Feud* host Louie Anderson deflected questions about his private life with that one long ago and largely immaterial bio-factoid. "I like to talk about my work, not me . . . my work is me. I'd rather people watch it than put me on the spot."

Openly gay *Weakest Link* host Jane Lynch says, "Ask me most anything. No problem. But my everyday life when I'm not working isn't very remarkable. It's the work that's interesting.

"I've learned that it's more important to be interested than interesting."

22

Monster Egos: *Family Feud* Then and Now

"I NEVER TRIED TO PLEASE EVERYONE, UNLIKE SOME FOOLISHLY AMBI-tious entertainers," said former *Family Feud* host Richard Dawson. Not that he wasn't ambitious. His relish at presiding over two teams of five family members belied the fact that for years he'd sought his own national show and, since 1973, "apprenticed" as the most prominent celebrity panelist on *The Match Game*.

By the time of *Family Feud*, the Englishman, in his mid-40s, was a showbiz veteran of two continents and had been on his own and making a living since 14.

Glib and intelligent, Dawson exuded confidence and command as a host but also on *Match Game* where some viewers felt he was too com-petitive with host Gene Rayburn, whom he occasionally challenged or engaged in one-on-one conversation, sometimes addressing the studio audience directly and doing imitations of Groucho Marx, Stan Laurel, Paul Lynde, Brando as the Godfather, and so on.

Mark Goodson took note of Dawson's *Match Game* popularity and the volume of his fan mail. He wished to exploit it but hesitated to build a show around such an un-host-like personality. The man wasn't necessarily polite, could be moody, and occasionally answered back. If something or someone struck him as inane or dumb, he just might say so.

Richard's manager repeatedly encouraged Goodson to spotlight his client. The tycoon explained, "He is an instinctively good player.

That did not necessarily mean he would be a good host. They are very different skills."

Game show executive and director Ira Skutch revealed that Richard had been tried out but "because of the previous failures Mark had given up on Richard as an emcee. But I insisted that he be given a chance." Finally a show was created for him, however, the pilot displeased Goodson. "I thought it was just awful." ABC's Fred Silverman, known for disliking most game shows, felt otherwise: "I think it is the best game show ever."

Much of the success of the noisy, debatably garish yet smooth 1976 show owed to the iconoclastic, take-charge—and he certainly would— Richard Dawson.

Family Feud's format involved contestants guessing what a surveyed group of 100 people had said. The premise derived specifically from *Match Game*'s Audience Match round in which the winner had to match one of the three most frequent answers given by a group of 100 people. But the carefully planned new show was more than contestants guessing what other people had replied (e.g., Name a famous George, from the first episode). The concept of two families competing yielded the theme of a "feud," as in the Hatfields versus the McCoys, ergo the "Okie" show opening with two families portrait-posed as if for old-fashioned country photos, plus the fleet fiddle music reminiscent of *The Beverly Hillbillies*.

After Dawson delivered a question, the first contestant to buzz in and match an answer on the then-slatted board won the right to continue playing or pass a difficult question to the opposing family. An incorrect answer was a "strike." Three strikes and the competing family could claim the whole payoff by matching one of the board's answers. The winning family played the Fast Money bonus round involving two contestants.

Dawson's upbeat banter with family members kept the show lively, as did his spontaneity. He wasn't afraid to gently mock a contestant. When one man delivered a bizarre response, the host asked whether he was "on narcotics." A moronic answer from another player prompted Dawson to advise watching less television and "read some books."

Richard soon acquired a personal trademark: kissing female contestants on the lips. Though he told *People* magazine that the adjective best describing him was "smarmy," the fact that he was dapper, debonair, and English made his kisses less shocking. "My mother always said you can't ever hate anyone you're on kissing terms with." As publicity about "the kissing bandit" spread, more viewers tuned in.

Nonetheless there was angry mail, even hate mail. Predictably, the letter writers were exceptions. Eventually Mark Goodson went on camera to ask viewers to vote for or against kissing. The result was 14,600 for and 704 against.

Nor did Dawson shy away from controversy. He often made derogatory jokes about disgraced former president Richard Nixon. After one sponsor asked him to desist, on air Richard told the sponsor to take his business elsewhere. When ABC decided not to air the remarks, Dawson threatened to quit. Goodson backed his host and warned ABC about interfering with freedom of speech. The remarks aired.

The controversy, the familial format, and the fresh host's unpredictability soon took *Family Feud* to number one in the daytime TV ratings. In 1977 ABC added a weekly syndicated prime-time edition with double the amount of prize money.

A handful of *All-Star Family Feud* nighttime specials were shown in 1978. They were inspired by daytime specials that had featured the casts of ABC soap operas playing for charity. Since the daytime specials boosted the soaps' ratings, the network ordered prime-time specials featuring the casts of ABC nighttime programs. The nighttime shows' ratings likewise improved.

Meanwhile, the successful daytime and nighttime host was contractually still—since 1973—a panelist on *The Match Game*. Once his own 1976 show became a hit, his relationship to *Match Game* and his colleagues began to change. "My take," offered panelist and former *Laugh-In* costar Arte Johnson, "is Richard didn't have anything more to prove. He got what he wanted and now he was none too happy sitting down in daytime with the rest of us."

Regular panelist Brett Somers, as voluble and aggressive as Dawson, got the coldest shoulder, especially because she insisted on calling him Dickie, which he disliked. Panelist Marcia Wallace explained, "He was rarely rude but he became withdrawn and uncooperative. He stopped chumming around with the bunch . . . and became overly concerned with his dignity. . . . He saw himself as the star of *Match Game*."

Dawson's discontent intensified in 1978 when *Match Game* introduced the Star Wheel whose spin gave an even chance to all six panelists to be selected for the head-to-head final match. As "the smart Englishman" Richard was used to nearly always being chosen. "He felt intruded upon," said Gene Rayburn.

One of the last straws occurred during a 1978 episode's end when a *Match Game* audience member requested that the glum-looking Richard Dawson smile. He refused, stalling with words. He told the host, who always closed the show, "Say 'goodbye,' Gene."

The smiling Gene answered, "I'm not going until you smile."

"All right." Dawson turned to the audience and declared, "We'll see you tomorrow on *Match Game*."

Rayburn moved behind Dawson and jokingly tried to manipulate Richard's mouth into a smile. The audience viewed the shenanigans as par for the course, but Ira Skutch allowed that "the staff was disturbed.

"[Richard] was contributing so little and seemed so unhappy that we offered to release him from his *Match Game* contract. He accepted at once. At the end of the [final] taping session he left the studio without so much as a goodbye to anyone, even his fellow performers of five years' standing."

Skutch, who'd stood up for Dawson before *Family Feud*, added, "Several weeks after he left *Match Game* I was told that even though I never went there he had insisted that I be barred from the set of *Family Feud*."

With his panelist days behind him, the host, who was also an actor, took the opportunity to appear on shows like *Love Boat* and *Fantasy Island*. ABC's success with the *All-Star Family Feud* prime-time specials was such that in 1979–1980, it also aired *Family Feud* nighttime specials starring the casts of CBS and NBC shows. The specials included *The Waltons*, *Three's Company*, *The Love Boat*, *The Jeffersons*, *Eight Is Enough*, *The Dukes of Hazzard*, *Dallas*, and *Benson*.

During its heyday, *Family Feud* was unbeatable. When it shifted in April 1977 to 11:30 a.m.—a risky move—it outperformed the second

30 minutes of *The Price Is Right*. In January 1979, the show's syndicated version added a second night a week. In June 1980, ABC moved the daytime edition to 12:00 p.m., where it ruled the ratings roost for almost four years. In September 1980 *Family Feud*, the top-rated syndicated prime-time game show, expanded to five nights a week.

The workaholic Dawson often guest-hosted *The Tonight Show*. When Johnny Carson considered retiring in 1979, Dawson's name was high on the list of likely replacements. Then Carson changed his mind.

Such success enabled Richard Dawson's behind-the-scenes ego to expand. In 1984 *TV Guide* reported that he lost his temper about items like broken microphones and burnt-out light bulbs and often ran the program several minutes beyond its allotted time to perform jokes and anecdotes that had to be cut from the tape each week. The article, in an issue with several game show hosts on its cover, also revealed that Dawson refused to be on the cover unless he were solo.

"We all heard Richard's ego had accelerated," said producer Bob Stewart. "He apparently no longer wanted to share attention or authority." Dawson had clashed frequently with the show's chief authority figure, producer Howard Felsher. They got along the first four or five years. "Then he began to become a big star," said Felsher. "That's when he became difficult and we stopped getting along. He was the boss. It was his show."

In 1983 Dawson had Felsher barred from the set. Mark Goodson made Felsher executive producer so he could retain a measure of control over *Family Feud* without being present on set. The new producer was Richard's daughter-in-law Cathy. Why was such behavior tolerated?

Ira Skutch noted, "High ratings are ephemeral [so] there's a deep fear of change, a reluctance to tamper with success. As a result, everyone catered to Richard and treated him with kid gloves. . . . As *Feud* became a bigger and bigger hit, Richard became infected with the virus [of] belief that he alone was responsible for its success."

Veteran character actress Mary Wickes, a *Match Game* panelist, put it succinctly. "I think Mr. Goodson created a monster!" Mark Goodson, increasingly disenchanted with Dawson's pettiness and demands, made it known that after *Family Feud*, the host would work for him again only after his death.

The host's reputation tarnished but not the show's golden run until the newly syndicated *Wheel of Fortune* (1983) began beating it in the ratings. In 1984 the syndicated *Family Feud* was canceled. The following year ABC's daytime program was canceled. It boasted one of the most teary, emotional goodbyes in TV history. Viewers and critics debated whether Richard Dawson's final speech was from the heart or for the camera. He may have guessed that future work would be hard to find, owing to his self-made reputation.

So in 1985, after 20 years, the Englishman born Colin Emm in 1932 was out of work. At 14, Colin had run away from home, lied about his age, and become a merchant seaman. During three years at sea he earned an impressive $5,000 (equivalent) boxing. He next worked as a waiter at an Isle of Wight resort before touring for two years with a repertory acting company. Tired of being part of an ensemble, he contacted a British talent agency and said he was a famous Canadian comedian seeking work while visiting England. Billy Bennett, a 90-year-old comedian, took Dawson under his wing and helped him sharpen his comedic skills.

Working his way up to leading London nightclubs and theaters during the 1950s, Richard met his first wife while costarring in her live variety act, *The Diana Dors Show*. At the time, Dors (née Diana Fluck) was advertised as "Britain's answer to Marilyn Monroe." She'd tried Hollywood in vain. After the death of her husband-manager, she and Richard wed in 1959 and had two sons.

They worked in the UK and US and settled in Beverly Hills. As Hollywood had a superfluity of blondes, Diana often returned to England for extended periods to work. Richard became cohost of a local radio talk show but didn't find steady employment until 1965 when he joined the cast of TV's *Hogan's Heroes*. He played English prisoner-of-war Peter Newkirk for six years.

The marriage disintegrated though the pair remained friends. Dawson raised their boys in the US. The divorce reportedly devastated him, as did Diana's death in 1984 at age 52 from ovarian cancer. In 1969 Dawson took over hosting an LA game show, *Lucky Pair*, reminiscent of *Concentration*. Like *Hogan's Heroes* it was canceled in 1971, at which time he got hired for *Rowan & Martin's Laugh-In* for two years. In 1972–1973, he was a frequent panelist on the rebooted *I've Got a Secret*.

In 1973 he landed two jobs: as the next-door neighbor on *The New Dick Van Dyke Show* and a regular panelist on the revived *Match Game '73*. The first show didn't last long. Dawson lasted five increasingly bumpy years on *The Match Game*.

True to his word, Mark Goodson did not rehire Richard Dawson when *Family Feud* returned in 1988. He selected successful stand-up comic Ray Combs, a former Midwestern furniture salesman. Dawson remained mostly unemployed, if wealthy. His one coup was the big-screen role of a vicious game show host in *The Running Man* (1987), set during a 2019 dictatorship. Arnold Schwarzenegger's pacifist character is forced to participate in *The Running Man*, a game show whose "contestants" are prey for hunters instructed to capture and kill them. The game, zealously overseen by Richard's character, is viewed by its audience on an oversized monitor.

Some wags labeled Dawson's role typecasting. Real-life hosting proved elusive. In 1988 he did a pilot that hoped to resurrect *You Bet Your Life*, the old Groucho Marx hit. It went nowhere, partly due to NBC's misgivings about Richard's future misbehavior. (It returned briefly in 1992 with Bill Cosby.) In 1989 Dawson auditioned to host the Donald-affiliated *Trump Card* but that short-lived show was instead hosted, with its namesake's approval, by former football player Jimmy Cefalo.

Reluctantly resigning himself to retirement, in 1990 Richard had a daughter with a former *Family Feud* contestant, Gretchen Johnson, whom he wed in 1991, his second and final marriage.

Meantime, in 1988 Ray Combs (1956–1996) signed a seven-year contract with Mark Goodson Productions—Bill Todman died in 1979—to host the new daytime *Family Feud* plus one in syndication. The attractive, energetic host, who was also 24 years younger, kept his considerable ambition under control. In 1992 CBS retitled the daytime version *Family Feud Challenge*, and it was now 60 minutes. The syndicated version remained 30 minutes and was now called *The New Family Feud*.

The slightly revised format proved hardy and the host was well-liked. But after ratings dipped in 1992–1993, the daytime version was canceled. Combs continued hosting the syndicated show but Jonathan Goodson succeeded his late father and approached Richard Dawson about hosting the remaining program. Richard immediately said yes but with provisos. One was that his son Gary be made producer, replacing Howard Felsher, who'd returned during Ray Combs's tenure. So Combs was fired and Dawson took charge again in 1994. Ratings improved but not enough, and *Family Feud* ended with the 1994–1995 season.

One reason for audience disinterest was the 62-year-old host's heft. During his nine-year retirement he'd gained so much weight that to secure his return he had to promise to lose 50 pounds. Howard Felsher disclosed in 2006 that "He didn't lose half a pound [but] the stations had already bought the show based on his being there and that was that."

Match Game panelist Ron Palillo of *Welcome Back, Kotter* recalled, "I knew Richard as elegant, proud of his appearance. Now he looked bloated . . . and he wasn't sassy anymore." Dawson softened his reactions to contestants who were not quick-witted and ceased on-air kissing after informing his little girl he wouldn't kiss anybody but her mommy.

After *Family Feud*, Dawson occasionally appeared on Game Show Network interviews and specials. Late in 1995 he and Ray Combs, together for the first time, shared memories of hosting *Family Feud*. In 2000 Dawson hosted the TV special *World's Funniest Game Shows*.

Richard left *Match Game* (1973–1978) minus any farewell to his colleagues. Ray Combs left *Family Feud* (1988–1994) in like manner. The difference was he'd been fired and felt humiliated (see chapter 23). Like Dawson after *Family Feud*, Ray found it hard to get quality work but not for the same reason. The firing left a stigma, as did his subsequent announcing for the World Wrestling Federation, a failed pilot for his own talk show, and the bankruptcy of two comedy clubs Combs invested in.

A car accident resulting in intermittent back pain, a marriage heading for divorce, financial obligations (six children . . .), nonpayment of back taxes, a large mortgage, and Combs's Ohio home going into foreclosure preceded a 1996 suicide attempt in which he banged his head against the walls and single-handedly demolished much of his house in Glendale, California.

His estranged wife told police Ray had been hospitalized for attempted suicide the previous week. Combs denied it but was taken to a local hospital and placed under a 72-hour psychiatric observation hold. The next morning it was found he'd hung himself in the closet using hospital bedsheets. (Richard Dawson died of esophageal cancer exactly 16 years later.)

Four years after its latest cancellation, *Family Feud* reappeared and hasn't gone away. Its subsequent hosts: Louie Anderson (1999–2002), Richard Karn (2002–2006), John O'Hurley (2006–2010), and Steve Harvey (since 2010).

Anderson, a rounded comedian and writer who often employed obesity to make comedy (as in his 1995 cartoon series *Life with Louie*), was a surprise choice for emcee. He invited Richard Dawson to return for the premiere and deliver his "blessing" but "awesome Dawson," as former fans called him, declined. Louie drew some complaints about his voice—alternately described as "nasal," "whiny," "gravelly"—his infamous "butt scratch," and occasional bumbling that required repeating a question during the show's Fast Money round. *MadTV* sketches mocked him and pointed up his increasing boredom as host.

When *Family Feud* let him go in 2002, there was speculation it was over having been blackmailed (he paid between $75,000 and $100,000) about his sexuality. The blackmailer later demanded $250,000, at which point the actor's attorney contacted the FBI. However, the payments were in 1997–1998. (The perpetrator was sentenced to 21 months in jail.)

During and after *Family Feud*, Anderson wasn't done with game shows. In 2000 he was a panelist on the latest *To Tell the Truth*, which was hosted by John O'Hurley. The next year he won $31,000 on *Weakest Link* and in 2017 competed in *Celebrity Family Feud*, hosted by Steve Harvey. In 2018 he was a regular panelist on *Funny You Should Ask*.

Comedy and acting remained his staples. From 2003 to 2012, Louie did a Las Vegas act titled *Larger Than Life*, in 2012 a stand-up TV special, and in 2016–2019 costarred on the FX comedy series *Baskets* as Christine

Basket, a cross-gender role for which he won an Emmy Award. Anderson died of cancer at age 68 in 2022.

Replacement Richard Karn was best known as Al Borland on the long-running 1990s sitcom *Home Improvement*. More of a comic actor than a comedian, Karn was said sometimes to push too hard to get his hosting humor across. But he was enthusiastic—it didn't wane with time—and had a sizeable fan base. In 2008 Karn replaced former *Dallas* star Patrick Duffy as host of the GSN's short-lived *Bingo America*. He was also on GSN Radio.

Where Dawson, Combs, Anderson, and Karn all came out of comedy, John O'Hurley—clean-shaven, trim, and silver-haired—was more stereotypically a game show host and, thus, an offbeat choice to emcee *Family Feud*. A self-taught pianist and composer, in 2000–2002 he'd hosted a *To Tell the Truth* reboot after becoming a familiar TV face on *Seinfeld* as Elaine's boss J. Peterman. Each Thanksgiving since 2002 he's hosted Purina's National Dog Show. Besides comedic roles, he'd appeared on soap operas, did voiceover work, and in 2004 hosted the limited-run game show *The Great American Spelling Bee*.

O'Hurley chose to depart a program he believed was no longer a "family" show, later claiming that every other *Family Feud* Q and A wound up being a "penis joke" (come again?).

That left the door open in 2010 for comedian, actor, and talk host Steve Harvey, who brought *Family Feud* to new highs (or lows) of raunchiness. Like Richard Dawson, Harvey didn't hesitate to call out a contestant's dumb answer. A stand-up comic (he quit in 2012) who slept in his 1976 Ford during gigs that didn't include a local hotel, he later moved up to a Rolls-Royce. Besides hosting daytime *Family Feud* and prime-time *Celebrity Family Feud*, Harvey helped initiate *Family Feud Africa* (for South African TV) in 2020.

Harvey grew up poor and overcame severe stuttering and earned money as a boxer, as did Dawson. He became an autoworker, mail carrier, insurance salesman, and carpet cleaner. With time, Steve racked up one showbiz credit after another, but like Dawson, he became increasingly controversial and egotistical. In 2017 on his eponymous talk show he laughed at the idea that "a black woman or a white woman" would want to date "an Asian man," gratuitously adding, "I don't even like Chinese food."

Eddie Huang, who wrote *Fresh off the Boat*, criticized the hypocrisy of the African American who "perpetuates the emasculation" of East Asian men. Others cited Harvey's assumption that all Asians are non-white, and still others added that he's verbally proven himself far from pro-feminist or pro-gay. Though Harvey was forced to apologize about meaning no "malice or disrespect whatsoever" about his "Asian" comments he also stated, "I ain't been laughin' that much over the past few days. They're kinda beatin' me up on the internet right now for no reason. But you know, that's life, ain't it?" No, it ain't.

When Harvey was threatened with public release of early racist tapes in which he allegedly urged blacks to "spit on whites" and "attack elderly white women," the multimedia star was less emphatic about the tapes' content than the attempt to diminish his company, Steve Harvey Global. On his website the workaholic host calls himself "America's Favorite Entertainer." This is not necessarily true with his employees. A memo to *Steve Harvey Show* staffers read in part: "Do not open my dressing room door. IF YOU OPEN MY DOOR, EXPECT TO BE REMOVED.

"My security team will stop everyone from standing at my door who have [sic] the intent to see or speak to me." He explained, "It is for the good of my personal life and enjoyment."

Regarding his personal enjoyment it was observed that the host "is the kind of guy who orders Krug champagne for himself and Cook's for everyone else." And so it seems that *Family Feud*'s first and latest hosts are basically brothers under the skin.

23

Four Lives Cut Short

"Nohow can you guess you're going to become a game show host," declared Bert Convy. "The entertainment business should really be called exit-ainment, because most people who enter it have to exit. Not enough jobs and not enough success to go around."

Good-looking Convy assumed he would succeed in acting. He did, but not on his desired stardom level. "The UCLA dean told 500 of us, 'If you are very, very lucky one of you will make his living in this business . . . *one!*' I remember walking out, feeling sorry for the other four-hundred-and-ninety-nine."

When handsome Peter Tomarken was urged to consider emceeing he reacted, "Why would I want to be a game show host?"

These four hosts couldn't guess that despite considerable success their futures held fewer years than they would have wished.

Jack Barry (1918–1984) was born Jack Barasch on Long Island to a Jewish family. As a teen, he headed a jazz band but graduated from the Wharton School of Finance and Commerce in 1939. His father's handkerchief business didn't hold his interest. Rather, people's comments on his fine speaking voice led Jack into radio. In 1946 while announcing *The Uncle Don Carney Show*, a WOR kiddie program, Barry met audio engineer Dan Enright. They became friends and then partnered in Barry & Enright Productions.

Uncle Don inspired them to create *Juvenile Jury* in which five children, ages 3 to 12, had to come up with solutions to everyday problems submitted by listeners. The show bowed on WOR in 1947 and, five weeks later, made it to television, where it had an eight-year run on NBC. Barry became a game show host in 1955 with *The Big Surprise* (not via Barry-Enright). The following year he was dismissed because he was deemed too dull and replaced by future *60 Minutes* fixture Mike Wallace (who was *not* dull?).

Half a century later, *Tic Tac Dough* producer Howard Felsher told radio deejay David Baber his favorite host was Jack Barry, "a very easy man to get along with. He had no temperament. As a talent he was one of the better ones."

Barry-Enright developed two big-money game shows, *Tic Tac Dough* and *Twenty-One*, that debuted in 1956 and were hosted by Barry. In 1958 the men devised the long-running *Concentration* and Barry hosted *Dotto*, which didn't survive the 1958 rigged-shows scandal. Soon after hosting his final *Tic Tac Dough* episode in October 1958, Jack Barry became persona non grata on national TV. Barry-Enright was dissolved, and in 1959 Jack and his wife divorced (he remarried in 1960).

Jack became an executive in a small chemical firm he part-owned before moving to Los Angeles in 1962 after a jobless year. He worked for an LA TV station packaging and hosting local game shows, including *You Don't Say!* But when the latter went national, hosting duties were given to Tom Kennedy. When the station sold to new owners in 1964, they fired Barry, who was still tainted by the 1958 scandal. He got work as a consultant for certain game shows—without receiving credit. When Jack created an ABC game show, *Everybody's Talking*, he was given a royalty but no public credit. His alcohol intake increased.

Dan Enright, who'd moved to Canada, invited Jack to host game and children's shows he was producing there. Jack didn't move but became a frequent airplane commuter. His schedule was such that in 1968 his wife threatened divorce. Instead, he borrowed money from her father to commence purchase of a Southern California radio station. After the Federal Communications Commission approved his operator's license, he was, at 50, "clean" and employable under his own name.

In 1969 Jack Barry resumed hosting on national television and in 1971 resumed producing on national TV with a pilot for *The Joker's Wild*, which debuted in 1972 with Jack hosting. Barry-Enright was reconfigured and thrived. But although Barry's bitterness was dissipated and his drinking curtailed, he suffered from high blood pressure. He dieted (losing 40 pounds by 1979), swam 50 laps daily, and jogged.

In 1983, the year he turned 65, Barry ceased hosting *The Joker's Wild* full-time, in favor of part-time substitute Jim Peck. In 1984 after visiting their daughter in Europe, Jack (who also had three sons) and his wife stopped off in Manhattan en route to LA. On the morning of May 2, 1984, while jogging in Central Park, Jack had a massive heart attack. Taken to Lenox Hill Hospital, he was pronounced dead on arrival, at age 66.

Bert Convy (1933–1991) was born in St. Louis and moved at seven to southern California with his mother after his parents' divorce. A first baseman in high school, after graduation he was a minor league player for a few years but saw no long-term future in baseball. He enrolled at UCLA and became interested in acting and rock 'n roll. He joined the Cheers, whose record hits included "Black Denim Trousers" and "I Need Your Loving."

Acting offered more opportunities and a longer-term future. Convy debuted on TV in a *77 Sunset Strip* guest spot in 1958 and then appeared on several programs. In 1959 he costarred in the first of numerous pilots that never went to series and briefly had a regular role on the daytime soap *Love of Life*, also small roles in a few movies. Since it didn't seem he was headed for fame on big- or little-screen, in 1962 Bert, his wife, and daughter (first of three children) moved to New York City.

On Broadway he achieved some success in musicals, including *Fiddler on the Roof* and a lead in *Cabaret* (whose film version was entirely recast). In between stage work, he broke into game shows in 1967 as a guest on NBC's *Snap Judgment*, hosted by *The Tonight Show*'s Ed McMahon. Early in the 1970s, he was a panelist on the revived *What's My Line?* and in 1972 moved back to Los Angeles to focus on TV.

His focus was on acting and not game shows. Convy appeared on *Love, American Style* and *The Mary Tyler Moore Show* and costarred in the short-lived *The Snoop Sisters*. He also did more failed pilots. Out of desperation, he auditioned to host *Tattletales*, a new 1974 CBS game show featuring three celebs (each playing for one-third of the studio audience) "tattling" on their spouses. Bert asked executive producer Ira Skutch, who favored him for the job, whether it would "ruin my career as an actor and that people would no longer think of me as an actor but only an emcee?"

Skutch felt hosting would enhance Bert and let the public see him in "a different role." Bert got the job, but it did type him and all but obliterated big-time acting opportunities. However, *Tattletales* was a ratings hit, airing right after *Match Game*, daytime's number one game show, and lasted through 1978 plus two seasons starting in 1982. While playing a minor part in the movie *The Cannonball Run* (1981) Convy bonded with star Burt Reynolds, and in 1986 they formed Burt and Bert Productions. Meanwhile, in 1984 Convy hosted *Super Password* until 1989.

Burt and Bert's *Win, Lose or Draw* bowed in 1987. Convy hosted the syndicated prime-time edition for two of its three years. To his chagrin, he was fired and replaced for the 1989–1990 season by the younger Bob Weller.

So he took Peter Marshall's intended hosting job on a forthcoming Burt & Bert production titled *3rd Degree*. Marshall filed a million-dollar-plus lawsuit for fraud and breach of contract in Los Angeles Superior Court against Burt & Bert. Convy did host the show, which lasted one season. He was then due to host ABC's revived *Match Game* in 1990. But that April, while visiting his hospitalized mother following her stroke, he collapsed, was tested, and found to have a brain tumor.

Radiation treatment, chemotherapy, and two operations failed to eradicate all the cancer, and the new *Match Game* was instead hosted by Ross Shafer. In 1991 Convy divorced his longtime wife and weeks later married a 25-year-old. His final three months of the five-month marriage were passed at home. He died on July 15, 1991, at age 57.

Like Convy, **Peter Tomarken** (1942–2006) was a handsomer-than-average emcee who experienced a varied career en route to, in his case, *Press*

Your Luck. He's a good example of the hits and especially misses involved in the often temporary careers of game show hosts. Born in Olean, New York, his family moved in 1950 to Los Angeles. Peter's first job, at age 12, was winding watches and polishing diamonds at his father's jewelry store. While Peter was a teen, his father killed himself, leaving his wife to look after three sons.

A would-be writer, Peter enrolled at UCLA and during college got married (like Convy, he would have three children). With his degree in English the couple transferred to Manhattan where he became a clothing editor for *Women's Wear Daily*, later working for *House and Home* magazine. Tomarken believed he was stagnating and moved back to LA and into advertising, founding his own company.

An expansive personality, he'd long wished to perform and entered commercials as a producer-director before acting in them. Next came guest shots on TV programs, then TV movies, and then a regular role on a series that lasted three months. To make a living he still produced and acted in ads but was dissatisfied. His agent suggested hosting a game show. "Why would I want to be a game show host?"

Because besides the visibility (which did go hand in glove with pigeonholing) he could work four days a month and earn in the six figures. Peter okayed going out on game show auditions. His first hire was a pilot, *Rodeo Drive*, that didn't go anywhere. Nor did *Duel in the Daytime*, with its medieval theme. But *Hit Man* did, via NBC in 1983. However, its time slot opposite *The Price Is Right* put it at a disadvantage, and the show was canceled on April Fool's Day, 1983.

Shortly after, Peter signed to host the big-money game show *Press Your Luck*, an instant hit distinguished by its flashing-squares big board and the animated Whammys that automatically bankrupted a player (four of them, and the contestant was out). Although the lights traveling across the squares that hid prizes and Whammys seemed random, they weren't. They moved according to five patterns. CBS hadn't felt the need for extra patterns, which would have required upgrading the computers that controlled them.

(In 1984 a contestant who carefully studied the light patterns used his knowledge to win a record jackpot. See chapter 8 sidebar.)

In 1985 *Press Your Luck*'s doom was sealed when CBS determined it couldn't afford to pay what Mark Goodson wanted to renew its contract for airing *The Price Is Right*. Tomarken explained, "Basically Goodson said they wanted our time slot [10:30 a.m.] since we were such a juggernaut." So *Press Your Luck* was moved to 4 p.m. (its time slot was taken by Goodson's *Card Sharks*), which meant that by 1986 *Press Your Luck* had fallen to number 25 out of 26 daytime programs. It was canceled that September. That autumn Tomarken auditioned to host a new NBC show, *Wordplay*.

"I was asked to behave like Pat Sajak . . . to minimize my style. I agreed to it and it was a mistake. The show tested well but I tested poorly. I was not hired to do it."

In 1987 Peter hosted ABC's *Bargain Hunters*, which aired for less than two months. "The show tested poorly and I tested through the roof. . . . My personality is what I am and I'm not suited for some shows."

Wipeout, also in 1987, lasted one season and was followed by two pilots. The second was *Monopoly*, based on the classic board game. It was beset with problems and Tomarken clashed with the production company's head, Merv Griffin. A people person, Peter was appalled to learn he wasn't allowed to speak to the little person disguised as Mr. Pennybags, the wee mustachioed man with the tall hat who was the board game's mascot.

Peter was told she was just an "entity," with a female voice that wasn't meant to be heard. He replied, "There's a human being in front of me constantly and I can't talk to it and [I have to] treat it as if it's an inanimate object? I thought the days of slavery were over."

Griffin eliminated the little person before securing a 12-week nighttime commitment from ABC in 1990. He also eliminated Tomarken as host, replacing him with a man who'd been a contestant on *Jeopardy!* and the *Monopoly* pilot. A few unproductive pilots later, Peter threw in the towel. Game shows were less popular than during the 1980s, temporarily giving way to talk shows.

Tomarken turned to producing and directing on TV, and in 1991, his 29-year-marriage ended. In 1994, he joined the new Game Show Network's (GSN) production team and hosted two interactive shows for the network. They didn't last long, so he left GSN and hosted infomercials. In 2000 he hosted *Paranoia* for the new Fox Family Channel. It didn't last one month. Reruns of *Press Your Luck* on the GSN in 2001 and the success of *Who Wants To Be a Millionaire?* inspired GSN to come up with *Whammy: The All-New Press Your Luck*, for which Peter had to audition.

Not only did the job go to a newcomer, but the original host was also instructed to downplay his personality. "It was terribly hurtful and I think I was doomed before I did it." (A newer *Press Your Luck*, still running, debuted on ABC in 2019, hosted by *Hunger Games* actress Elizabeth Banks.)

Exiting entertainment, Peter Tomarken went into real estate, and then began his own mortgage brokerage, real estate firm, and contracting company—that's three firms—living in Los Angeles with his second wife. He enjoyed piloting his own plane and in 2005 began volunteering for Angel Flight West, a charity providing free air transport for medical patients. On March 13, 2006, he and his wife took off for San Diego to fetch a cancer patient to UCLA's medical center.

When Tomarken's 1973 Beechcraft A36 experienced engine trouble, he attempted to turn it toward Santa Monica's airport. But some 200 yards from the Santa Monica Pier, the plane dove into the Pacific and Peter, 63, and his 41-year-old wife Kathleen were both killed.

Ray Combs (1956–1996) was determined to become a big comedy star and did very well in comedy, but his major recognition was as a game show host. Several sources reported that unfortunately he looked down on that genre.

A Midwestern Mormon, Combs was a furniture salesman who essayed stand-up comedy before moving to Los Angeles where he became a warm-up comic for audiences at tapings of sitcoms like *The Golden Girls* (on which he later guested). In 1988 he signed a seven-year contract to host a new daytime edition of *Family Feud* and one in syndication. In 1992, CBS retitled the daytime version *Family Feud Challenge*, which was now 60 minutes. The syndicated version remained 30 minutes and was now called *The New Family Feud*.

Ratings dropped during the 1992–1993 season and the daytime version was canceled. Combs continued hosting the syndicated show until he was fired and replaced with original *Family Feud* host Richard Dawson. Ratings improved, but the show was canceled after the 1994–1995 season.

Combs's final hosting appearance aired in May 1994. One contestant's lousy performance prompted him to state on air, "I think it's a damn fine way to go out. Thought I was a loser until you walked up here—you made me feel like a man!" As the show's end credits rolled, Ray walked off the set to his dressing room. He left the building without any farewells and drove home.

Combs then struggled professionally. He was a guest ring announcer for the World Wrestling Federation, shot a pilot for an eponymous TV talk show that didn't materialize, and two comedy clubs he invested in went under. A 1994 spinal-disc injury from a car accident resulted in frequent pain, and the next year wife Debbie (they had six children) left him. They reconciled and then refiled for divorce.

On June 1, 1996, police were summoned to Combs's Glendale, California, home. He'd already single-handedly destroyed much of it and banged his head against the walls. He claimed his injuries were from falling down in his Jacuzzi. When his estranged wife got there she told police Ray had been hospitalized the previous week after attempting suicide. He was now transported to a hospital and put under a 72-hour psychiatric observation hold.

However, on June 2 at about 10 a.m., hospital staff found Ray Combs, age 40, had hung himself in the closet using bedsheets.

As a widow Debbie discovered that despite earning a million dollars a year during his salad days, Ray owed $100,000 in back taxes, $150,000 in loans and credit cards, and had a $470,000 mortgage. Apart from the failed comedy clubs, his Ohio home had already gone into foreclosure.

24

Scandals, Bleeps, and Bloopers

OF COURSE THE BIGGEST GAME SHOW SCANDAL WAS THE REVELATION late in the 1950s that several game shows were fixed. "What everyone thought was genuine entertainment based on really smart contestants or luck," said historian Martin Greif, "proved to be an admixture of greed, big business, conniving, bigotry, and fooling a righteously betrayed public." Game shows and their ratings went into the dog house for a while.

One future game show host (of the *Pyramid* series) lucky to avoid scandal was Dick Clark, best known as host of ABC's teen-oriented music showcase *American Bandstand*. In 1960, the House Committee on Legislative Oversight investigated Clark regarding the "payola" scandal that involved kickbacks and ownership stakes in the music business. Clark had financial stakes in several of the acts featured on *American Bandstand* and in their record labels—in fact, in 33 music companies.

Thus, if an appearance on *Bandstand* upped record sales, that singer and their label weren't the only ones who profited. Clark became rich early and quickly. He later groused that he'd been targeted because of his fast rise, but he was saved from scandal and its possible consequences because ABC forced him to sell off his investments in the myriad record labels.

It was later said that the youthful-looking Clark's reputation as a notable tightwad (despite his success as a TV producer) was due to his having been shorn of future profits—or profiteering—by his rightfully concerned network.

An incident some partisans wished had been a scandal had to do with President Harry Truman. The news-themed game show *It's News to Me* aired on CBS prime time from 1951 to 1953. One evening a dollar bill autographed by the president was displayed on the air. Several upset viewers phoned in. The panicked network, which supported the McCarthy era's political blacklisting, officially acknowledged that it was a federal offense—for the POTUS or anyone else—to "deface" US currency. (Ho-hum. . . . Wait until Nixon and Trump.)

Some potential scandals are swept under the rug by multimillion-dollar payouts, as with Michael Jackson (a *Dating Game* contestant in his teens). Another game show VIP fortunate to evade scandal was the longtime host and eventual executive producer of *The Price Is Right*. An online article titled "The Untold Truth of Bob Barker" described him as "a vengeful workplace tyrant." The first crack in the friendly façade occurred in 1994 when Dian Parkinson sued Barker for sexual harassment. From 1975 to 1993, she was one of Barker's Beauties, as the show's models were called. Dian claimed her boss coerced her into an ongoing sexual relationship from the late 1980s to the early 1990s whose alternative was losing her job.

Parkinson wasn't the last woman to challenge the widower whose wife died in 1981. The article noted, "Multiple women who've crossed Bob Barker lost their jobs. Some even lost their homes. That's a high price, and it doesn't seem right."

The Associated Press reported the allegation that Barker sometimes used force to get Parkinson to perform oral sex on him every week for 3½ years. After leaving the show in 1993 she received $1,000 each month, apparently to keep quiet about what happened. One producer called it "severance pay." Barker claimed in *People* magazine that the sex had been consensual.

Holly Hallstrom, a model on *The Price Is Right* since 1977, sued Barker in 1995 for age, gender, and medical discrimination. Prescribed medication had caused her to gain 14 pounds, which she claimed was the excuse Bob Barker used to fire her but was a cover-up. She declared that he'd urged her to smear Dian Parkinson in prearranged interviews and when Holly refused she was fired in 1995. Dian eventually dropped her lawsuit for health reasons.

Hallstrom persisted despite high legal expenses that resulted in her living in her car. Besides refusing to discredit her fellow model, Holly said she declined lying about a fired director. Barker sued Hallstrom for slander in 1995 but later dropped his suit. Holly's wrongful termination suit against Barker and *The Price Is Right* was resolved in 2000 with a multimillion-dollar settlement.

On *Larry King Live* in 2002 Bob Barker claimed Hallstrom had been dismissed because of budget cuts. Holly Hallstrom wasn't invited onto King's show.

Model Janice Pennington had been on the show for 29 years. In 2000 she and model Kathleen Bradley were abruptly fired. Bradley believed it was payback because she'd contradicted Barker regarding Hallstrom's lawsuit. Also fired in 2000 were longtime director Paul Alter, executive assistant Sherrell Paris, and editorial consultant Sharon Friem.

Deborah Curling, an African American, had screened contestants for *The Price Is Right*. She claimed in her 2007 lawsuit that after Barker became the show's executive producer he "made it his life [sic] mission to destroy the livelihood of every person who contradicted him or did not do what Barker ordered him/her to do, whether it was legal or not."

After she testified in a wrongful-termination lawsuit on behalf of a former *Price Is Right* producer Curling said she landed on Barker's enemies list. She confirmed that Hallstrom was not fired due to supposed budget cuts. Curling detailed a hostile work environment and racial slurs directed against her. But lacking proof, the presiding judge threw out her case in 2009, which is the same year Barker vented his competitive anger at fellow animal activist Betty White. "Bob can hold a grudge for a long time and form it pretty quickly," observed one of the directors of *The Price Is Right*.

"His ego mushroomed with time, and making him exec [sic] producer worsened it and put more power in his hands."

Other game shows had introduced male models to enhance the merchandise, but Bob Barker resisted the inclusive trend and banned the boys. Not until 2012 (Barker retired in 2007 at 83) did *The Price Is Right* get a male model. For either gender it was an undemanding job, requiring good looks, an arm that outstretched expressively, and the ability to look elated by prizes for other people.

"Bob did not want handsome young guys around. He wanted pretty girls around him," volunteered a production assistant. "I think he saw himself as the 007 of game shows. . . . In some of the promotion photos from when his hair was still dark Bob's all dressed up like [James] Bond with three damsels beneath him. It really resembles a Bond promo."

Said an anonymous female staffer, "What disappointed me was how people mentioned his wife had been a strong woman who helped push him ahead, yet he looked down on women's rights.

"He was all out there for animal rights. Same here. But if the subject came up, he didn't have a kind word for *our* equal rights . . . he had some pretty nasty words, at least twice that I heard."

It's since been speculated that Bob Barker was ushered into retirement in 2007 to protect *The Price Is Right* from negative publicity that added charges of racism to the ongoing sexism.

In his zeal to create button-pushing game shows creator (and *Gong Show* host) Chuck Barris sometimes flirted with disaster. His big hits *The Dating Game* and *The Newlywed Game* were succeeded mostly by a string of disappointments. He became known to network executives for his kooky, usually rejected pitches (most of his shows were syndicated rather than network programs). To play a trick on the suits, Barris and his casually dressed staff devised the pitch for *Greed*, a fake game show. With a straight face he explained its concept: Contestants would be offered money to kick the crutches out from under an old disabled man or to kill a child's dog.

Most would refuse, and each subsequent contestant would be offered less money. The "winner" would be the contestant who did the deed for the least money.

"*Greed*," explained Chuck, "was a gag, but we never let on that we were kidding, and one buyer actually left promising to check with his boss to see if he'd like the show for syndication."

In time, it was suggested Barris try doing a "normal" show, so he bought the rights to a 1950s game show and, in 1973, syndicated *The New Treasure Hunt*, which was hosted by Geoff Edwards. Instead of treasure chests, it used big, gaudily wrapped boxes. Because Barris feared that a male contestant might become angry enough at Geoff's merciless teasing to punch the host, only female contestants were chosen. (Somehow that was legal.)

A contestant's *Treasure* box might conceal confetti, a jack-in-the-box, Kleenex, or something valuable in it or behind a portal. She got offered a particular sum of money to give back her unopened box. The process was milked for all it was worth and took an emotional toll on some contestants. A show highlight was when the revealed prize was a restored 1937 Rolls-Royce Phantom; the woman fainted.

The investigative TV program *60 Minutes* confronted Chuck Barris about his manipulating people for ratings and profit. Adamantly delighted that the contestant had fainted, he informed one newspaper, "Some of the contestants are absolutely incredible. There is a hatred in their eyes when they lose a $50 prize, and we darned near had to pull one housewife off of Geoff Edwards when she felt he hadn't given her enough help in locating a $25,000 cash prize!"

Barris made the show increasingly extreme. The break with Edwards came after four seasons, when Barris proposed displaying a shiny new car to an excited contestant, then informing her that her prize was a tiny, near-worthless trinket on the car's roof. Geoff exited the show, which ceased production. However, Barris brought it back in 1981 with Edwards hosting. It lasted a season.

Geoff's return was surprising. A friend named Sande Stewart explained, "There was a magazine article titled 'The Cruelest Quizmaster of All.' . . . [Edwards] shouldered the blame for carrying out Chuck Barris's bidding. *Treasure Hunt* came off as a mean show sometimes, and there were producers who wanted nothing to do with Geoff because of what he had done on that show."

Six months before Barris hired him in 1973, Edwards got his first network game show, *Hollywood's Talking*, created and produced by sometime host Jack Barry, who'd been boycotted for his part in the 1958 rigged quiz shows scandal. Edwards recalled, "He walked into my dressing room one day, maybe the second week we were taping, and he said, 'You know, you have a really annoying voice. Can you do something about that?' I said, 'Jack, I have a contract for 13 weeks. At the end of 13 weeks don't renew it. And don't ever come into my dressing room again.'"

The poorly rated CBS show lasted less than three months. "I never worked for Jack Barry again. I think Barry had a difficult time having anyone be an emcee and get any attention away from him."

When *The Price Is Right* returned in 1972 after an absence of seven years, its prime-time edition was hosted by TV pioneer Dennis James, who didn't get along with *The Price Is Right* producers Mark Goodson and Bill Todman. One reason was he sometimes dissed the show's prizes, albeit in jest. After he called a shiny new car "a hunk of junk," producer Frank Wayne screamed at him after the show.

Dennis's attempts at humor sometimes curdled. For instance once during the pricing game Cliff Hangers, featuring a motorized yodeler ascending an inclined ramp marked in dollar increments. For each dollar off an item's actual price, the climber moved up the ramp, closer to falling off the mountain and crashing. When that happened, James announced, "There goes Fritz!"

Fritz was the name of the presumed-dead husband of Janice Pennington, one of the show's models. Two years earlier he'd vanished during a mountain climbing expedition. When Janice heard what Dennis said, she departed the stage to spend the rest of the show in her dressing room crying. Eventually she found out the expedition had been a front for an espionage operation; Fritz was never found. Pennington wrote a book titled *Husband, Lover, Spy*—shades of Chuck Barris, whose memoir claimed he'd been a CIA assassin.

Barris's *The Gong Show* was at times unpredictably risqué. During one episode, celebrity judge Jaye P. Morgan flashed her breasts and then was fired. (When an audience member from *The Price Is Right* wearing a 1970s "tube top" heard "Come on down!" she excitedly ran, jumping up and down. Her top dropped and her breasts popped out. Of course in the two instances, all four offenders were visually bleeped.)

Sometimes an "offense" passed the censors by. Two teenage girls billing themselves as the Popsicle Twins appeared on the *Gong Show* stage, sat down, and proceeded to eat orange popsicles. Their fellatio imitations didn't occur to anyone in charge until the show had aired on the East Coast. It reportedly didn't make the West Coast.

One entire *Gong Show* episode comprised singers of varying awfulness singing the awfully popular 1974 song "Feelings," which became a global hit via Brazilian singer and supposed composer Morris Albert. In fact the melody belonged to a 1957 French song. Morris was successfully sued and the real composer's name reinstated.

Daytime game shows could get away with more than nighttime shows. The most vigilantly censored were programs airing during the evening "family hour." Syndicated game shows were typically more difficult, censorship-wise, for they could air on any of the three major networks. Some popular shows therefore yielded three separate versions, making censorship cuts that adhered to each network's specific standards. Due to competitiveness and corporate paranoia, affiliates of a given network were shown only the version tailored to that network (e.g., NBC affiliates didn't get to see the CBS affiliates' version).

Most no-no's did make it past the censors. *The Match Game* host Gene Rayburn meant to compliment a female contestant on her dimples but accidentally said aloud that she had nice nipples. To fill airtime at the end of *Let's Make a Deal*, host Monty Hall often proffered cash to audience members if they could produce certain items (e.g., a bottle of nail polish in a woman's purse). When he saw a young woman holding a baby bottle with a rubber nipple he innocently offered $100 if she could produce another nipple. (She didn't.)

Break the Bank was a 1976 daytime update of a popular 1950s Q and A show. When host Tom Kennedy asked, "You have just bent your epée. What are you doing?" male celebrity guest Jan Murray answered, "You should know, you were the one who straightened it for me last time." The show's coproducer Jack Barry disapproved but told one newspaper, "The networks believe that very risqué material is what makes it on daytime television."

Newlywed Game host Bob Eubanks asked one husband, "Is your favorite sport played with a big ball, a medium-sized ball, a small ball, or no ball at all?" Answer: "Two balls." The reply drew many viewer complaints. Because the network censor had ordered Eubanks not to say "sex," he employed "to make whoopee." He queried a contestant named Olga, "Where is the weirdest place that you . . . have ever gotten the urge to make whoopee?"

She replied, "In the ass."

For years Eubanks denied the incident, which was kept from airing in reruns. In the 1990s he got asked about it so often that he claimed he would pay $10,000 if someone could come up with a videotape of his Q and A with Olga. Videotape recorders were pretty rare when the interchange occurred in 1977. It finally returned to the airwaves in 2000 during a Game Show Network *Newlywed Game* marathon (also in a 2002 NBC special on game show bloopers).

Back in the day, background checks on contestants were far from thorough. A fugitive wanted in three states got onto *Super Password* in 1988 and won a record one-day jackpot of $58,600. He'd grown a beard, used a college professor's name, and fake-confided in the show's producers that he'd been posted to the North Pole by the CIA to intercept Soviet transmissions. The con man, who'd faked the death of his estranged wife to acquire $100,000 on an insurance policy, didn't get to keep his winnings and was sent to prison (see chapter 9).

Potentially fatal, a serial killer got onto *The Dating Game* as bachelor number 1. At one point the "bachelorette" coyly asked, "I'm serving *you* for dinner. What are you called and what do you look like?"

He answered, "I'm called the banana and I look good."

"Can you be a little more descriptive?"

"Peel me."

He won the date. The year was 1978, and bachelor number 1 was in the middle of five murders he committed in California between 1977 and 1979. The young woman, after a brief interaction, informed the contestant coordinator, "I can't go out with this guy. There's weird vibes that are coming off of him. He's very strange."

Showbiz identities can fluctuate early on. Handsome Sam J. Jones, who later starred as movie hero *Flash Gordon*, was a *Dating Game* contestant. When he posed nude in *Playgirl* magazine—which pretended it had only female subscribers—before he found fame, he was assigned a fake name even though his chest bore a tattooed "Sam."

Most contestants win or lose graciously (not much choice). But some refuse to lose. *Password* producer Bob Stewart recalled "pests who demand another chance, a rematch . . . pestering the offices dozens, even hundreds of times. . . . I've heard of excuses like they got the answer wrong because the host lowered his voice or another contestant coughed. Or one lady's hat had pressed down too hard on her brain. Or they misunderstood her because she had a Southern accent. Or . . . but that's part of the territory."

Likewise scammers proliferated. *Concentration* producer Norman Blumenthal, who wrote a book on how to get on game shows ("and win"), recollected a "sweet middle-aged woman" who sent the show "a bill for her bus fare [from Chicago], three days' charges at a hotel, and $15 a day for meals." It turned out she wasn't registered at the hotel. She lived in Manhattan, a bus ride away from the TV studio. "We also found out she had been a contestant on nine other game shows and had lied every time. I'm sure the fact that we caught up with her won't prevent her from trying again elsewhere."

Each team of contestants on the 1993 show *Family Secrets* comprised a mother, father, and child. The "Hansen family" was actually a man, his 10-year-old daughter, and his live-in girlfriend. The trio won some $6,000 in prizes. The girl's real mother found out and, furious at the deception, contacted NBC and Dave Bell Associates, the show's packagers. They yanked the episode before its airdate and substituted a rerun. However, the man's girlfriend became his wife on the same day, June 11, 1993, that *Family Secrets* was canceled.

The race for ratings can embarrass or even kill. A 1992 game show hosted by Bob Eubanks, *Infatuation*, was inspired by an episode of *Sally Jessy Raphael* that its coproducer watched. That talk show episode had people with secret crushes revealing them, on national TV, to the crush object. *Infatuation* featured contestants revealing their secret crushes to the crushee in hopes that it might be reciprocated. It usually was, more or less, due to audience pressure.

The show lasted a season and was predictably boy-girl. But in 1995 *The Jenny Jones Show* included a gay man, Scott Amedure, confessing his crush on a heterosexual. Three days later Scott was fatally shot by his crush. The man was released from prison in 2017.

Most anything on TV is closely scrutinized, perhaps especially game shows. Allen Ludden often opened *Password* looking into the camera and uttering, "Hi, Doll." Inevitably some people wondered who—or what—he was addressing. Wife Betty White? An old flame or a girlfriend? A life-sized inflatable doll in his bedroom? In fact "Doll" was his nickname for his mother-in-law. Betty, an only child, was close to her mother Tess. So was Allen, also an only child. Shame on those naughty minds!

File under Bigotry

Original *Wheel of Fortune* host Chuck Woolery has more than once declared he doesn't believe in civil rights, whether based on gender, race, or sexual orientation. He's also indulged in anti-Jewish "humor." In 2019 he caused an uproar with his comment, "Racism has nothing to do with race," blaming it on "the Progressive Left."

When Bob Eubanks appeared in Michael Moore's 1989 documentary *Roger and Me*, he proffered a joke that was anti-Jewish, homophobic, and misogynistic all at once. In 2012, hosting a stage parody of *The Newlywed Game*, Eubanks recorded another homophobic "joke" on tape.

Former weatherman Pat Sajak, who therefore should know better, has said he doesn't believe in climate change and announced, "Global warming apologists are unpatriotic racists." (Racists?) After COVID-19 hit, the antiscience *Wheel of Fortune* host inveighed against staying in place. He mocked the concept of coming out of the closet by "proclaiming" his heterosexuality, as if heterosexuals ever get fired and otherwise discriminated against for not being gay.

In recent years, his testiness and even rudeness toward certain contestants has made news, and in 2021, he allegedly imitated a contestant's speech impediment, specifically a lisp. Sajak has also stated, "It's plain and simple fact that the majority of those who vote don't like them," referring to Democrats.

"The older some of these men become," said journalist and literary agency owner Gil Gibson, "the more embittered and far-right . . . the less logical."

Some of African American Steve Harvey's antigay and other bigoted verbiage—belittling East Asian men, and so on—is touched on in chapter 22. Black comedian Kevin Hart, host of *Celebrity Game Face*, lost the coveted gig of hosting the Academy Awards ceremonies in 2019 due to his recurrent homophobia. One reason this author declined an offer to write a biography of *Jeopardy!* host Alex Trebek (apart from there likely not being enough interesting material for a whole book) was that three times before I appeared on the show, Trebek had made antigay comments on the air, which is three times too many.

Hollywood Reporter journalist Scott Timberg said, "It's surprising, the disconnect between so many game show hosts and reality. It may have to do with their coming from a time when they held a monopoly—all the hosts were white males. It's just as perplexing when the bigotry comes from minority members. . . . But no one ever said hosts are chosen for their sensitivity. Or their brains."

25

Who Doesn't Want to Be a Millionaire?

"YANKS HAVE LITTLE NOTION HOW MANY OF THEIR FAVES ARE OUR shows, retooled," reminded UK journalist Ken Ferguson. "Comedy, drama, shows old and new since *All in the Family, Sanford and Son, The Office, House of Cards, Shameless*, em [sic], varieties like *Dancing with the Stars, American Idol*—so-called—*Whose Line Is It Anyway?*, game shows like *Who Wants to Be a Millionaire?*. . ."

Stop right there. The US redo in August 1999 of the hit 1998 UK quiz show was a ratings phenomenon. ABC aired it 13 nights during a two-week period, and it became a national hit faster than any game show before or since. In neither country had insiders predicted the success of *Who Wants to Be a Millionaire?* It was considered rather grim—its lighting and music, the knowledge element, and its slower pace. Some felt the questions were too hard, and others that multiple choice dumbed it down.

Who Wants to Be a Millionaire? was distinctively memorable. If the questions were difficult, the format was simple enough to quickly become familiar. The player in the Hot Seat who answered the first question correctly won $100. The 15th question was worth a million dollars—more in Britain, a million pounds. Part of the audience appeal was finding out who would win the ultimate prize because few did. But five questions correctly answered guaranteed a player $1,000 and 10 correct answers guaranteed $32,000.

If a contestant read the next question and balked, there was the option to depart with the amount won on the last correct answer. To further aid players there were three lifelines. "I'd like to use a Lifeline" became a national catchphrase, more so the host's conclusive confirmation, "Is that your final answer?"

The choice of American host was offbeat. Regis Philbin was a sidekick and then a talk cohost. He was 68, and his two 1970s game shows were short-lived. His style was energetic, contrasting with the tempo of *Who Wants to Be a Millionaire?* Some reviewers maintained it didn't matter who hosted, the show was about the money and the suspense. Chris Tarrant, the UK host, explained, "It was only really in one of the pilots we started thinking, this is really tense! This is serious stuff . . . there was going to be this other element . . . this huge soap opera, which is why it works."

Part of the "soap opera" occurred when contestants used the Phone a Friend Lifeline, the call often placed to a relative. Another lifeline involved in-person spectators: Ask the Audience. The third was the 50/50 which eliminated two of the three incorrect answers. "I was usually curious myself," Philbin recalled. "I'd learn things along with the audience and contestant. . . . It was fun to see how far someone could go. . . . I sure didn't want to be in their place."

The audience, often 30 million-plus viewers per episode, brought *Who Wants to Be a Millionaire?* back for a two-week run in November 1999 and in January 2000 as a regular series, three nights a week. "I thought *three times*, this show is digging its own grave, or ABC is," said *Let's Make a Deal* director Joe Behar. "I was right and I was wrong. The network did overdo it, ratings fell away.

"But the decline was gradual, unlike so many shows. That show's concept and its human content is so good that it didn't die . . . it's alive and kicking in this and many other countries."

The show that was to have been titled *Cash Mountain* stepped down to daytime and syndication in 2002, the year ABC canceled it. The new, eventually record-setting host was Meredith Vieira (see chapter 19). After stepping down in 2013, she was followed by a string of hosts from Cedric the Entertainer on until 2019. A 2020 ABC prime-time reboot brought back the inherently popular show whose multiple-choice answers play a role in its watchability. "You watch *Jeopardy!* and either you know the answer or probably not," observed playwright and former *Beat the Clock* writer Neil Simon.

"With *Who Wants to Be a Millionaire?* you have four choices . . . even if you don't know, you might guess right. With other people it's more fun to watch this."

The reboot, hosted by Jimmy Kimmel, boasted all celebrities, and is played for charity. Almost certainly it's a matter of time until ordinary people are again allowed to go for the pot of gold.

As soon as *Who Wants to Be a Millionaire?* scored extra big, the networks and game show companies scrambled to put out their own ratings winners. The promise of bigger-than-ever rewards was the common lure. "Promise big, deliver minimally," said TV critic David Sheehan about 21st-century game show methodology because not many people won the much-touted jackpots. "Greed is again in fashion."

It was indeed, for the first time since the 1950s game show scandals. But as typically happens with imitators, most fell away quickly or before very long. *Who Wants to Be a Millionaire?*'s influence was evident in the proliferation of "Million" in game show titles. Like *The Million Dollar Word Game*, *The Million Dollar Money Drop*, *The Million Second Quiz*, and *Awake: The Million Dollar Game*, in which contestants had to stay awake 24 hours before submitting to various physical and mental challenges. Scoffed classic game panelist Orson Bean, "You've seen one Million Dollar game show, you've seen them all" (except for the silly and sadistic *Awake*).

Existing shows tried to jump their ratings with specials like *Million Dollar Password* in 2008, hosted by Regis Philbin, and *The Price Is Right Million Dollar Spectacular*, hosted by Bob Barker and later Drew Carey, even *Who Wants to Be a Super Millionaire?* The seven-figure come-on seldom made much difference. Francine Bergen was contestant coordinator on *The $10,000 Pyramid*, the 1970s show often credited with making five-figure prize payments routine.

She felt, "It's silly to think that offering more money would draw more viewers. . . . Nobody cares how much money people win on *Jeopardy!* . . . they watch to see how well the game is played. That's why *$10,000*

Pyramid worked. We developed a game that was fun and compelling to watch regardless how much money was offered. The money was just icing on the cake. It's the game that drew people in."

Wink Martindale agreed. "The money [was] more of a selling point for the networks than the viewers . . . that would get the executives' attention. . . . A game's popularity is built on the format and in a small part on the host. But mostly the format."

Betty White noted there would always be room for "brainier shows . . . word and knowledge shows, separate from out-and-out game shows," but that game shows often draw viewers who enjoy watching people "having fun. That's the essence of a game show, I think. Fun!"

One game show blogger opined, "The fun of *Who Wants to Be a Millionaire?* is watching someone else sweat. It's a heavy show. . . . On TV you want to see people behaving not like in daily life—they should be enjoying themselves or sort of suffering, but with money at the end."

One of the first shows out of the box inspired by *Who Wants to Be a Millionaire?* was the frankly titled *Greed* in November 1999 on Fox from Dick Clark Productions, hosted by Chuck Woolery. Its full title was *Greed: The Multimillion Dollar Challenge* (the *multi* was misleading because the top prize was two million dollars). Where many critics had praised *Who Wants to Be A Millionaire?*, most disdained *Greed* as a rip-off or mean-spirited. It did well in the ratings but not spectacularly enough for Fox.

In June 2000, Fox put on another contender, *It's Your Chance of a Lifetime* (a variant on *Who Wants to Be a Millionaire?* that included the chance to pay off one's whole credit card bill). The show aired five times in its first week, prior to settling down to once a week. But *It's Your Chance of a Lifetime* didn't interest viewers, and its dismal ratings led not only to its cancellation but also that of *Greed*.

Fox executives' unrealistic expectations were underscored by *Greed* creator Bob Boden. "We were under constant pressure to deliver big ratings. . . . But in all the years that have passed since, Fox has never performed better in that Friday night time slot than we did. We were the strongest show they ever had in that slot."

Another British adaptee was *Winning Lines*, which was hosted in the US by Dick Clark. A poor time slot and lukewarm backing by CBS, the network least fond of big-money quiz shows, doomed the fast-paced show that might have done well had it not toiled in the shadow of *Who Wants to Be a Millionaire?*

NBC was much more gung-ho, reviving the infamous *Twenty-One* in January 2000 after 42 years off the air. Its ad taunted its chief rival, "Who wants to be a millionaire . . . when you could win a *lot* of money?" The quiz show so angrily axed in 1958 had been out of sight and mind until Robert Redford's 1994 film *Quiz Show*. Precautions were taken to assure the resurrected *Twenty-One*'s honesty (e.g., question writers weren't allowed in the studio while contestants were there and questions were secreted in an attaché case handcuffed to the executive producer, who delivered them with a security guard in tow as he marched onto the stage).

Emceeing the new *Twenty-One* was talk host Maury Povich. Besides stressing its honesty, the show was overeager to give away money. Adam Nedeff critiqued that where *Who Wants to Be a Millionaire?* highlighted its contestants, *Twenty-One* highlighted its dollar amounts. A first-time contestant could win $100,000 during the first game. Too much money and too-easy questions, including total trivia. Said Nedeff, "The idea that a contestant could win $400,000 for knowing which Nickelodeon series starred Melissa Joan Hart probably seemed downright obscene to many viewers."

Question writer Aaron Solomon felt the first big winner's hollow triumph proved *Twenty-One*'s flawed structure, whereby a contestant could win a million with minimal effort. He observed that the taped facial expression of the winner on his fourth win, which brought him a million dollars, "is pretty interesting, because you got the sense that he was thinking, 'I didn't really earn this.'"

Some viewers complained about the ease of winning, and Povich commenced one episode by acknowledging the games had been too easy. So *Twenty-One* reduced its sums, with a first game paying $25,000 instead of $100,000 and seven games, not four, required for the seven-figure payout. But changing the rules annoyed some viewers, confused others, and made clear that NBC had greedily foisted a show on the public before it was ready.

Solomon derided the networks' "mad rush" to combat *Who Wants to Be a Millionaire?*, "NBC put us on the air without shooting a pilot first, [which] would have enabled us to discover these flaws . . . before [the public did]. And the prevailing theory that 'bigger jackpot equals bigger ratings' was immediately disproven."

Twenty-One was axed in May 2000.

Another show—another British import, including its host—that NBC expected to go over big-time was *The Weakest Link*, or *Weakest Link* in "the shortcut-loving USA," per Anne Robinson. NBC Entertainment chief Jeff Zucker enthused, "She's cold, she's ruthless, she's rude. She's everything that makes a great TV executive. There's nothing else like her on American TV."

Robinson coolly declared, "I'm not there to crush people beyond what they can take." (More on Robinson in chapter 19.)

The Weakest Link had a long run in Britain, where it wasn't overexposed—NBC did multiple broadcasts a week—nor saddled with silly gimmicks. Toward the end of *Weakest Link*'s run (April 2001 to August 2002), the imperious Anne Robinson was confronted with eight Elvis impersonators as the eight contestants.

The game's unique format had players voting off one contestant, the presumably weakest link, at the end of each round. Foolishly and often jealously, they would vote off a smarter link whom they feared would vote them off after the next round. That often led to a "duh-off" among the least smart players—the actual weakest links. *Weakest Link* never awarded a million dollars. To host Robinson's scorn, the most money awarded was $188,500.

Overexposure didn't help *Weakest Link* and, as with *Who Wants to Be a Millionaire?*, viewers sometimes didn't know when the show was airing thanks to unannounced and seemingly arbitrary schedule changes (if the show "underperformed" during a given time slot). Too, Robinson was not universally welcomed; in truth there had been nothing like her on US TV. A year after *Twenty-One*'s return in January 2000, NBC actually shot two pilots for the US version, *Weakest Link*. One hosted by the Englishwoman, and the other by Richard Hatch, the openly gay champion of *Survivor*'s first season. NBC chose the sourpuss for host.

"It was logical to pick the host who made the show such a hit, but in a quite different culture despite our common language," remarked Hollywood agent Ed Limato. "I feel Hatch wouldn't have alienated people to the extent she did. On the other hand, homophobia's not quite extinct."

Weakest Link, like *Who Wants to Be a Millionaire?*, transitioned to daytime in 2002, and was hosted by George Gray but only for one season. When NBC brought *Weakest Link* back to prime time in 2020, it picked a host almost no one but a disgruntled old game show host could dislike, openly gay actress Jane Lynch. Viewers and critics welcomed her, and the network didn't—and doesn't—overdo airings. Were lessons learned? The overkill that eventually downed imitators of *Who Wants to Be a Millionaire?* eventually brought down *Who Wants to Be a Millionaire?* itself. Many insiders, critics, and viewers felt it could have become a long-running prime-time staple like *Jeopardy!* But a disappointed ABC cut it loose in 2002. "Thank goodness for syndication," said fan Limato.

Classic game show host Tom Kennedy told *Today* that ABC had "trampled" *Who Wants to Be a Millionaire?*, and when Bob Boden, executive producer of *Greed*, was asked why every single big-money game show had vanished, he uttered the title of his late program. And so, close on half a century later, the reign of big-money game shows terminated for the second time, once again thanks to greed, though minus rigging this time. Progress, eh?

26

The 21 Worst

CHRONOLOGICALLY AND SEMI-OBJECTIVELY, THE 21 WORST TV GAME shows follow.

IT PAYS TO BE IGNORANT

This debatably comedic program was a spoof of brainy shows like *Professor Quiz*, *Dr. I.Q.*, and *The Quiz Kids*. It debuted on CBS nighttime in 1949 as a summer replacement series and then as a 1951 NBC nighttime summer replacement series.

The show was more about laughs than prizes (it didn't *pay* much). Questions were selected from a Dunce Cap and a celebrity panel gave inane answers or indulged in jokes and gags. Tom Howard hosted the radio and TV versions. One critic said the goal was "to make it impossible for a sensible answer to be heard."

A syndicated 1973–1974 version was coproduced by Monty Hall and hosted by Joe Flynn, best known as *McHale's Navy*'s fussbudget Captain Binghampton.

WHO'S WHOSE

Seemingly a mix of *What's My Line?* (1950) and *To Tell the Truth* (1956), this 1951 show was hosted by Phil Baker and announced by a party named Gunga. A celebrity panel of four tried to match a woman contestant with her husband (but not vice versa) from three possibilities. The program offered three sets of contestants and, in lieu of a mystery celebrity guest, a non-mystery celebrity (Dizzy Gillespie) whose wife was one of three women the panel got to question.

Sponsor General Foods canceled *Who's Whose* after one episode, replacing it with the events-oriented game show *It's News to Me*, whose summer 1954 version was emceed by Walter Cronkite. Phil Baker had been a host of radio's *Take It or Leave It*, the forerunner of TV's infamous *The $64,000 Question*.

GLAMOUR GIRL

This 1953 NBC show that lasted six months had four female contestants explaining why they wanted to be glamorous. (*Jeopardy!* it was not.) The glamour-hungriest winner was chosen by audience applause and treated to a 24-hour beauty makeover and then invited back onto the following show to display her new look—and glamour. This funfest had two 3-month hosts, Harry Babbit and Jack McCoy.

Obviously the golden age of TV wasn't all that golden.

DO YOU TRUST YOUR WIFE?

Influenced by the Groucho Marx hit *You Bet Your Life*, this 1956 quiz show focused on host-oriented interviews. The CBS prime-time offering was emceed by ventriloquist Edgar Bergen (father of Candice) and his three dummies. The "trust" part concerned the husband's confidence in his wife's smarts. Players were all married couples; the wife had to be there but required *his* permission to answer a question.

In 1957 a desperate ABC picked the program for its daily afternoon schedule. CBS and NBC commenced broadcasting at 7 a.m. and ABC not until 3 p.m. Bergen didn't care to do five shows a week, so ABC hired a young comedian with a list of failed shows on his resumé named Johnny Carson. The network changed the title to *Who Do You Trust?* because it desired (de$ired) more female input to the show. It ran until 1963.

Ed McMahon was an announcer. He and Johnny departed in 1962 for NBC's *The Tonight Show*, where Carson began his reign as king of late night. (*Trust*'s subsequent host was Woody Woodbury, no relation to Woody Woodpecker.)

CHANCE FOR ROMANCE

The coproducer of this 1958 ABC matchmaking product that endured less than two months was Irving Mansfield, later best known as husband-manager of novelist Jacqueline Susann. It featured audience participation and a panel of human relations "experts"—a sociologist, a marriage counselor (presumably not divorced), and a psychiatrist—who introduced three young men to three young women . . . a chance for romance!

The surprise was that the host was John Cameron Swayze, NBC's first nightly news anchor. He headlined the *Camel News Caravan* from 1948 to 1956. After anchoring the news, the dignified Swayze advertised Timex watches for several years.

YOU'RE IN THE PICTURE

You're in the Picture lasted one episode in 1961 on CBS prime time and was hosted by Jackie Gleason, whose nickname "the Great One" referred to his girth. It boasted a framed picture screen 7 feet high and 10 feet wide with porthole cutouts through which the four celebrity guests stuck their heads, literally putting themselves in the picture. Clever?

None of the celebs knew what the body illustration below their porthole was (e.g., a male's head topped a caricature of a bearded lady in a flowing evening gown). So the guests asked Gleason questions to shed light on who they depicted and what they were pictured doing. Simple? Or simple-minded?

Gleason pulled the plug, preventing a second episode. Instead, he used the airtime to fill a chair on an empty stage and apologize for the first show and then talked to the audience. Guest Jan Sterling, perhaps best known for the film *Ace in the Hole*, later remarked, "Jackie wasn't meant to be a host. He didn't have an ingratiating bone in his body."

LET'S PLAY POST OFFICE

This show is not what you think. This cutesy nine-month 1965 Merv Griffin Production hosted by Don Morrow featured fake letters "written" by famous people that were read to three players who tried to guess the supposed writer's identity. The contestants sat in post office stamp windows while each letter was revealed, a line at a time, on an envelope-shaped game board.

The letter's envelope's cancellation mark was a clue to the correct answer, as it showed the place and year the letter was "written." The game ended with a "zip round"—five short messages appeared on a screen, with players trying to name the "sender." Host Morrow later quipped, "What we had was a failure to communicate."

IT'S A TIE!: *DREAM GIRL OF '67* AND *DREAM GIRL USA*

Dream Girl of '67 was a daily beauty pageant! It consisted of five female contestants, ages 18 to 27 (one must draw the line somewhere), via producer Chuck Barris of *Gong Show* fame. It ran a year, starting in 1966 and had four separate hosts (Dick Stewart, Bob Barker, Wink Martindale, and Paul Peterson)—what does that tell you?

The "girls" were judged on poise, personality, and fashion consciousness, the latter via a daily fashion show. The celebrity judges were all males, single ones, and each daily winner returned on Friday to compete for "Dream Girl of the Week."

The weekly winners returned at season's end to compete for, you guessed it, "Dream Girl of '67"!

Two decades later, things hadn't really progressed. *Dream Girl USA* bowed in 1986 and also ran a year. The host was actor Ken Howard, former star of the prime-time series *The White Shadow*. The four "girls" were judged by four judges in four categories: beauty and style, figure and form (redundant?), talent, and personality. Every fifth week, an exciting semifinal with the prior winners led to a one-hour finale that crowned, what else, "Dream Girl of 1987"!

HOW'S YOUR MOTHER-IN-LAW?

Chuck Barris was the "brains" behind this 13-week wonder from 1967, hosted by Wink Martindale. Its three male comedy guest stars were "defense attorneys" speaking on behalf of the mothers-in-law (fathers-in-law were above reproach). The show's questions derived from information supplied by each woman's son-in-law (daughters-in-law need not apply).

Each celeb built a "case" to "defend" the mother-in-law he represented. The jury of five single men and five single women then chose which mother-in-law they'd wish to have for their very own. The winning mother-in-law reaped a grand prize of $100.

Awesome.

(The show's intended title was *Here Come the Mother-in-Laws!*, likely inspired by the then-popular Desi Arnaz-produced sitcom *The Mothers-in-Law*.)

LETTERS TO LAUGH-IN

Because *Rowan & Martin's Laugh-In* was a major prime-time hit, somebody figured this NBC daytime oddity was a good idea. It lasted three months in 1969. The host was *Laugh-In*'s on-air announcer Gary Owens. The show offered four celebrities, including one *Laugh-In* regular, telling jokes supplied by home viewers and judged by a "joke jury" of 10 members from the studio audience (TV juries often comprised 10 individuals rather than 12).

Prizes were awarded for the day's best joke and for the worst joke. The week's best joke won a Hawaiian vacation and the worst joke won a week in "beautiful downtown Burbank."

THE BETTER SEX

Lots of questions, no sex, lots of sexism, and no real point. At least this six-month ABC 1977 show was cohosted by Bill Anderson and Sarah Purcell (the country singer emceed *Fandango* in 1983, the first country music quiz show on the Nashville Network, and she went on to NBC's *Real People*). It was comprised of six men versus six women. A team member had to guess if an opposite team member had answered a question correctly or was bluffing. A wrong guess eliminated two team members.

When one team, presumably the lousier sex, had vanished, the surviving team played 30 opposite-sex members of the studio audience, using six questions (six: sounds like sex). If the team won, they divided $5,000. Otherwise, each remaining audience member split $500 with the rest.

Proof that not every Mark Goodson-Bill Todman Production was a winner.

THE CHEAP SHOW

This 1978 one-season syndicated series was hosted by comic actor Dick Martin of *Rowan & Martin's Laugh-In*. It featured two couples and two celebrities. The latter two were asked a question. One answered truthfully, one didn't, and the contestants had to guess which wasn't lying. The winners got a cheap prize, worth less than $16. The losers received a pie in the puss or a bucket of water, and so on (the show included two male Purveyors of Punishment).

After three rounds, the final winners got to guess which hole Oscar the Wonder Rodent would enter on the game board, affording them a chance for a pricier prize.

Bob Newhart and Truman Capote were big fans of the show, which routinely announced invited guests who were no-shows, such as Richard Nixon. (Nixon did appear on *Masquerade Party* in 1954 while vice president and *Your First Impression* in 1962 after losing the 1960 presidential race to John F. Kennedy.)

The *Philadelphia Journal*'s critic deemed *The Cheap Show* such a dud that he had a viewer write the review instead.

THE $1.98 BEAUTY SHOW

This syndicated 1978 Chuck Barris production actually ran two years and was hosted by flamboyant (did you guess he was gay?) comedian Rip Taylor. A spoof of beauty pageants, each episode showcased six female contestants from ages 18 to 80.

A celebrity panel rated them on beauty, swimsuits, and last but least, talent. The winner won the titular $1.98 and a none too impressive crown.

"It was more democratic than a regular pageant," said Taylor. "We had viable contenders and, you know, in-betweens, and ladies who were allergic to mirrors." One contestant was rising comic Sandra Bernhard.

The show's announcer, Dick Tufeld, had voiced the robot on TV's *Lost in Space* ("Danger, Will Robinson!").

THREE'S A CROWD

Another Chuck Barris taste-dropper, this elitist, sexist syndicated 1979 series lasted five months and was hosted by Jim Peck. Its aim: deciding who knows a man better, his wife or his secretary? (It didn't define "know.") Contestants were three husbands, three wives, and three secretaries. Competitors were wives versus secretaries. The wives had it tougher; to win, they had to match the answers of the husbands *and* the secretaries.

ABC had already declined Barris's proposed game show *The Divorcée* (bear in mind that TV was so conservative when *The Mary Tyler Moore Show* debuted that her character, no spring chicken, wasn't divorced but a single "career girl"). *Three's a Crowd* reportedly caused three real-life divorces and at least one firing.

DUELING FOR PLAYMATES

Two men didn't duel, but they competed to win a date with a *Playboy* Playmate. The 1983–1988 show was broadcast by *Playboy*'s cable channel and hosted by Lonnie Shorr.

It had four stages of competition. The first stage involved guessing how three Playmates would respond to given questions. The second stage, believe it or not, the guys entered a mud pit and had to put as many balls as they could on a ledge in a given amount of time. In the third stage, the fellows watched filmed profiles of each Playmate and then had to answer questions about what they'd viewed (or ogled). In the fourth stage, turnabout is fair play, so each man had to perform a striptease in front of a trio of Playmates who judged the dudes on "personality, body, movement, and sensuality." Winner: the he with the most points.

But what did the dated Playmate win?

LIARS

This syndicated 1995 show that lasted 2½ months had both a host, Fran Solomita, and a lie-detector expert, Joe Paolella. (Its music was via Trey Parker, later cocreator of *South Park*.) The host interviewed two people, one of whom accused the other of some transgression like "You slept with my girlfriend." A three-person "expert" panel (the first shows included presidential sibling Roger Clinton) voted whether the accused was guilty or not.

The finale found the accused taking a lie-detector test administered by the polygraph expert. Aha. Ho-hum.

FEAR FACTOR

Many rate this one tops in grossness. The 2001 NBC show hosted by Joe Rogan gave sensationalism a bad name. Its required stunts made those on *Truth or Consequences* look like child's play. They were disgusting—eating maggots, horse rectums, ad nauseum—or terrifying. Some were literally death-defying but got on the air anyway.

Fear Factor was canceled in 2006 but returned in 2011 for one season. Its ratings had declined each year.

It performed best among younger viewers "bred with less feeling and manners than their parents or grandparents," said critic Rex Reed. NBC dropped it for good after word leaked out that contestants had a choice between ingesting donkey urine or donkey semen. That filmed episode never aired.

An obviously desperate MTV revived the spectacle in 2017, which was hosted by Ludacris. It endured two seasons.

THE CHAMBER

Some rate this the worst ever. Only three of its six taped episodes aired, in January 2002, on Fox TV. Hosted by Rick Schwartz, it was Q and A with a difference: the two contestants, both genders, were strapped into a torture chamber where they suffered very hot and very cold temperatures, as well as simulated windstorms and earthquakes. "Sadism as entertainment . . . this could have been shot in the Colosseum," said TV critic David Sheehan.

The show's developer, Mike Darnell, was quoted, "I want to hear if [the contestants] are in pain or suffering." *The Chamber* was axed due to low ratings and controversy.

"Would ratings skyrocket if a contestant had an on-air heart attack?" wondered Sheehan.

"A long hard look needs to be taken at the irresponsible creators, producers, and network that would sink to this level," declared game and talk host Alan Thicke.

ANOTHER TIE!!—ARE YOU HOT? AND THE SWAN

Looksism typically embraces sexism. But ABC's *Are You Hot?* was equal-opportunity looksist. Women and men were judged as to their heat factor "on the sole criterion of their physical attractiveness" (no talent competition!) by a good-looking celebrity panel. The 2003 show, hosted by J. D. Roberto, lasted one season—that is, six episodes.

More extreme and more sexist—hosted by a woman, Amanda Byram, to reduce complaints—was Fox's 2004 *The Swan*. Women judged to be "ugly ducklings" were subjected to "extreme makeovers," sometimes involving cosmetic surgery. Reviews were uniformly negative, referring to the tired concept of a woman's worth being tied to her looks.

The show lasted 18 episodes (April to December) and got canceled less because of bad press and controversy than ratings that kept dropping—or drooping. It might have lasted longer if a fear factor or torture chamber had been involved (not that plastic surgery isn't "torture" to some people).

Index

Quigley, Bob, 9, 31
Quiz Kids (radio show), 6
The Quiz Kids Challenge (TV show), 6
Quiz Show (film), xvi, 59, *B*
quiz shows, 1–6, *16*, 57–63. *See also specific shows*

race, 168–69
Race, Clark, 153
radio. *See specific radio shows*
Radio Days (film), 136
Rafferty, Bill, 80
Randall, Tony, *D*
Rayburn, Gene: career of, 97–101; Carson and, *102*; on *Celebrity Match Mates*, 189; Dawson and, 201, 204; on *Dough Re Mi*, 9, 98; as guest, 108; Hall, M., and, 115; on *Match Game*, 32–33, 47, 87, 90–94, 157, *E*; reputation of, *198*; support from, 24–25
Rayburn, Lynne, 90, 97, 101
Reach for the Top (TV show), 141
Reagan, Michael, 77
Reagan, Ronald, 132
The Real Match Game *Story* (documentary), 91
The Rebel (TV show), 30, 130
Redford, Robert, xvi, 59, *B*
Reed, Rex, 248
Reed, Robert, 39
Reel to Reel (TV show), 162

Reel to Reel Picture Show (board game), 162
Reilly, Charles Nelson, 79, 88–89, 91–92, 98, 195
Reiner, Carl, *133*
Remember This Date (TV show), 136
Remote Control (TV show), 13
reruns, 30–31, 35, 47
Reubens, Paul, 128, 149
Revson, Charles, 58, *174*, *174–75*
Revson, Martin, *175*
Rey, Alejandro, 21
Reynolds, Burt, 70, 79, 132, 159, 162, 216
the Rhythm Rascals (band), *102*
The Richard Boone Show (TV show), 30
Richards, Mike, 86
Rickles, Don, 110
rigged shows. *See* cheating
Ritter, John, 126
Ritter, Tex, 126
Rivers, Joan, 163, 172
Road Show (radio show), 46
Robbins, Brian, 76
Roberto, J. D., 249
Robinson, Anne, 171–72, 238
Robinson, Dale Roy, 111
Robinson, Edward G., 128
Rock Concert (TV show), 10
Rodeo Drive (TV show), 217
Rodriguez, Paul, 155
Roemheld, Ann, 47–49
Roemheld, Jack, 47

About the Author

Boze Hadleigh is the author of 29 books, most of them Hollywood-themed. The *Los Angeles Times* labeled him "a pop culture phenomenon." He has a master's in journalism, speaks five languages, has visited more than 60 countries, and won on *Jeopardy!* His books without Hollywood themes include *492 Great Things about Being Italian*, *Broadway Babylon*, *Life's a Pooch*, and *Holy Cow!*